The Climber's Guide to North America

The Climber's Guide to North America

Volume III

East Coast Rock Climbs

by

John Harlin, III

illustrations by Adele Hammond

CHOCKSTONE PRESS

Denver, Colorado
1986

Published by
Chockstone Press
526 Franklin Street
Denver, Colorado 80218

Printed in the United States of America

Cover photo by Adele Hammond

LIBRARY OF CONGRESS CATALOGING-IN-PUBLICATION DATA

Harlin, John, 1956-
   East Coast rock climbs.

   (The Climber's guide to North America ; v. 3)
   Bibliography: p.
   Includes index.
   1. Rock climbing—United States—Atlantic Coast—
Guide-books. 2. Atlantic Coast (U.S.)—Description
and travel—Guide-books. I. Title. II. Series:
Harlin, John, 1956-   . Climber's guide to North
America ; v. 3.
GV199.42.A83H37 1986   917.4   86-17096
ISBN 0-934641-00-5

ISBN 0-934641-00-5 (East Coast Rock Climbs)
ISBN 0-9609452-5-3 (Climber's Guide to North America – full series)

ACKNOWLEDGEMENTS

A number of people have helped to make this book possible. The list below is of those who have made the most significant contributions. If I have inadvertently forgotten someone, my most sincere apologies are hereby extended.

The following people have made an extra effort to help me with this book. The hours and sometimes days that they have put in have made this a far better book than it would have been without their help. Were I not so lazy, I would give them all the individualized acknowledgements they deserve.

Mike Artz, Louis Babin, Bruce Burgin, Jeffery Butterfield, Ad Carter, Russ Clune, Rick Cobb, Bruce Cox, Jim Detterline, Benoit Dubé, James Eakin, Todd Eastman, Mike Fischesser, Tim Fisher, John Forest Gregory, Adele Hammond, Marilyn Harlin, Alain and Jean Hénault, David Hessler, Tom Howard, Arno Ilgner, Eric Janoscrat, Thomas Kelley, Matt Lavender, S. Peter Lewis, John Markwell, Don Mellor, Mark Meschinelli, Ken Nichols, Stuart Pregnall, Hunt Prothro, Rob Robinson, Jon Regelbrugge, Al Rubin, Sam Streibert, Rick Thompson, Laura and Guy Waterman, and Perry Williams.

These people have also helped in various ways to make this a better book.

Henry Barber, Bob Bates, Bruce Beard, Gerard Bourbonnais, Chris Caldwell, Johanne Croteau, Lyle Dean, Robyn Erbesfield, Dan Frankl, Cheryl Hammond, Lynn Hill, Bob Hopkins, Dan Koch, Chris Lea, Marcel Lehoux, Jim McCarthy, George Mettler, Casey Newman, David Rosenstein, Craig Sabina, Thom Scheuer, Olaf Sööt, Todd Swain, Ed Webster, J. Williamson, and Dick Williams.

The following maps have been adapted with only minor changes (and complete permission) from those drawn by others:
Chattanooga and Whitesides by Arno Ilgner and the New River Gorge by Richard V. Thompson II.

Near Sand Beach

ENVIRONMENTAL IMPACT

While this guide may reduce the environmental impact on certain popular climbing areas, it will cause increased strain on others. To alleviate this stress, climbers are strongly urged to respect the individual character of each area that they visit.

Many people can be absorbed into a wilderness and still maintain a quality experience if one basic rule is followed: minimize your impact. Shouting, including belay signals, should be reduced or eliminated. Camping, if out of designated sites, should be kept as discreet as possible; above all, nothing should be left behind that leaves any indication that you have been there.

Littering is unthinkable in the outdoors. This includes not just scattered garbage, but also unburied excrement, new fire-rings, and dishes washed in lakes and streams.

People who are disrespectful of the environment should be tactfully educated about the consequences of their actions. In addition, we should pick up after those who defile our communal space. This demonstration of love for the environment is the best educational eye-opener. It also means that we don't have to endure that particular piece of litter more than once.

TABLE OF CONTENTS

INTRODUCTION

Fort Wetherill, RI   photo: Adele Hammond

THE CLIMBER'S GUIDE TO NORTH AMERICA

For many years, the imagination of most climbers could be caught by only a few famous cliffs and mountains. But as the sport grew in popularity, climbers began searching out unheralded areas – places where they could explore new territory and leave behind some of the increasing crowds. Soon, they discovered that North America holds a great diversity of climbing areas, each unique in its climbing experience.

This series of guides was conceived to provide an efficient sampling of many different North American climbing areas. Based primarily on photographs, the books also offer selected route descriptions, access maps, and background information for each covered area. *The Climber's Guide to North America* will allow travelling climbers to experience for themselves the special character of these places through several days of excellent climbing.

AREA SELECTION

The areas for this volume were chosen with the following criteria: the climbing must be accessible by moderate hiking from a car-camping basecamp, and it must be interesting enough to make it worth a special trip. In addition, the popularity and quality of the area has generally gained it national or international attention.

Because some people deeply resent the popularization of their favorite haunts – fearing that publicity will spoil the original environment and atmosphere – climbers are urged to respect the individual character of the place they are visiting. It is especially important to minimize one's impact on the environment.

The many areas not included in this book will remain a bit mysterious and wild. Eventually, some of these may be opened to the public through guidebooks or magazine articles, but it is not for this book to do so prematurely.

SELECTION OF ROUTES

A sufficient number of routes have been included to provide a good sampling of the climbing in each area. Depending on the size of the area, this will vary from several days' to a couple of weeks' worth of climbing. Routes are included in the most popular difficulty range: from 5.6 to 5.13.

While the routes included are intended to represent the better routes at an area, not all will be considered "classic." Sometimes, especially in the lower grades, lesser routes were included in the book in order to provide climbing at a particular level. Some classic routes may not be included because of layout considerations.

HOW TO USE THIS BOOK

Each chapter has the same format. Photographs and route information follow a written description of each area, including the nature of the climbing and environment. Below is a more detailed explanation of how to interpret each chapter.

HIGHLIGHTS This is a one paragraph overview of the characteristics of the area.

CLIMBING This section comments on the different cliffs, the type of rock, the nature of climbing (whether it be face, crack, slab, free, or aid), the approach hikes, and descents.

ENVIRONMENT The natural and social environment described in this paragraph gives a feeling for the area. The climbing experience can, of course, vary from wilderness, to that of a crowded climber's gymnasium. This section will also mention some alternate attractions that the area offers, including hikes, scenery, and river rafting.

CLIMBING HISTORY A brief overview of the local climbing history is presented in this section. Individual names have been omitted, however, because in such a brief treatment it is difficult to properly recognize those people who have contributed to the development of an area. The important names can often, though not always, be garnered from the first ascent list. Local guidebooks will sometimes help considerably in providing a more in-depth historical overview.

CAMPING A description of the availability and nature of camping (legal), showering, and laundry facilities is covered here. Free illegal or discretionary camping can often be found, but such information cannot be put in this book. Because prices are likely to increase through the years, treat any specific dollar figures as approximations. Adjectives usually are given in place of actual dollar figures. These are: inexpensive (less than $5), moderate ($5-$9), and expensive (more than $9). Up to six people are typically allowed per site, in one or sometimes two vehicles. As mentioned in *A NOTE ON SAFETY,* lake and stream water can rarely be trusted for drinking. To protect the water, toilets should be used where available, or excrement should be buried not less than 100 feet from any stream or lake. A biodegradable soap should also be used.

SEASONS AND WEATHER This is a general chart of the seasonal weather and likelihood of finding good climbing days. Temperatures are given by ten degree intervals with a plus (+) or minus (−) sign designating that temperatures are frequently found either above or below this range. Thus, 70's indicates that temperatures are typically somewhere between seventy and eighty degrees Fahrenheit. 70's+ indicates that the temperature frequently reaches into the eighties. 70's− indicates that often the temperature never reaches seventy degrees. The column "High" is for the typical highest daytime temperature, while "Low" is for the typical overnight lowest temperature. "Likelihood of Precipitation" gives a clue to whether the visitor will encounter rain or snow that will inhibit climbing.

"Frequency of Climbable Days" is a summation of the temperature and precipitation data and some of the "Comments" listed below the chart. It is the best indicator of whether moderate climbers will be able to enjoy themselves during a visit. If an area indicates "low-medium" frequency of climbable days, then a short visit might typically be rained out or the temperatures might be too high or low. A longer visit would probably yield at least a few days to climb in.Of course, zealots will find climbing possible even on hot or wet days.

These charts, based as they are on weather average data, are as variable as any weather.

RESTRICTIONS AND WARNINGS Some of the listings here, such as whether one may encounter rattlesnakes, or thieves, are for the reader's personal benefit. More important is such advice as "go slowly through the residential area" because this information is necessary for maintaining access privileges for the entire climbing community. PLEASE READ AND HEED THIS SECTION!

GUIDEBOOKS This section lists the local guidebooks and how to obtain them. A climber on an extended visit may require information for additional routes beyond those provided in this book. In addition, a local guidebook can be invaluable for more information on the area's history and geology.

GUIDE SERVICES AND EQUIPMENT STORES Local equipment stores can be a good source of updated information. The locally based guide services are listed for those in need of either instruction or a well qualified partner.

EMERGENCY SERVICES The nearest hospital and the appropriate contact for rescues are described here. In many cases, the county sheriff is in charge of coordinating rescues (except in National Parks where the rangers are responsible). Because telephone numbers can change, simply call the operator (dial "0") to make the connection. Rescues should be called only in case of dire emergencies. Not only does this save the climber and the taxpayer a great deal of money, but self-rescue does not generate the ill-will towards the climbing community that often is the result of public rescues. A European-style climber's rescue insurance policy is not yet available in North America.

GETTING THERE This section describes the public transportation available to the climbing area.

ROUTE DESCRIPTIONS
Most of the route descriptions in this book follow a series of dots placed directly onto photographs. Difficulty, fixed protection, and belay notations are written next to the route lines. As noted repeatedly in this introduction, this is only a guide. The lines on the photographs are approximate in their placement and route finding skills are a necessity.

On many longer climbs and on cliffs where trees block views of the routes, supplementary drawings – "topos" – are also included. The following drawing explains the symbolism used.Suggested protection is only given when it differs from the standard rack most climbers usually carry with them. In the case of free climbs, assume that the listed protection is in addition to a clean (no pitons) rack with one nut from each of the standard size increments from one quarter inch to two and one-half inches.

Unless they are listed in the guidebook, or needed in emergency situations, PITONS OR BOLTS SHOULD NEVER BE PLACED ON ESTABLISHED NORTH AMERICAN ROUTES!

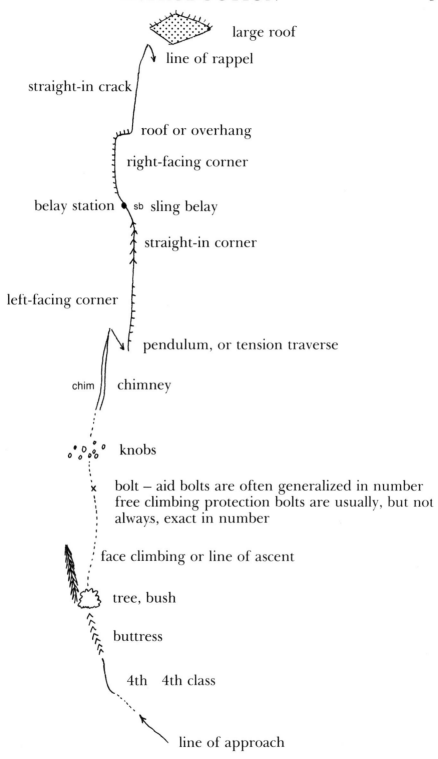

large roof

line of rappel

straight-in crack

roof or overhang

right-facing corner

belay station sb sling belay

straight-in corner

left-facing corner

pendulum, or tension traverse

chim chimney

knobs

bolt – aid bolts are often generalized in number
free climbing protection bolts are usually, but not
always, exact in number

face climbing or line of ascent

tree, bush

buttress

4th 4th class

line of approach

fp	fixed piton
lb	lieback
sb	sling belay
ow	offwidth
chim	chimney
thin	thin crack
165'	165 feet
KB	knifeblade piton
LA	Lost Arrow piton

Key to the Maps

freeway	▬▬▬▬
paved road	———
unpaved road	– – – – –
trail	·············
camping	Δ
area location or summit	★
mile	mi.

RATINGS

North American climbers use a combination of four rating systems for assessing the difficulty of climbs. The first is a rough classification that distinguishes between the various stages from trail hiking to aid climbing. The next system breaks the technical free climbing category down into much more specific ratings. This Decimal System (widely referred to as the Yosemite Decimal System – YDS – but actually developed at Tahquitz) is the mainstay of rock climbing route ratings. These free ratings refer to the hardest individual moves on a particular section of rock. Sometimes an overall route rating will be raised somewhat if the climbing is extremely continuous, but this practice is not universal. Rarely does a lack of protection affect the free rating of a climb; instead, protection considerations are mentioned more as a footnote to the grade. Aid climbing is also differentiated into various degrees of difficulty; seriousness is a part of the rating.

Many routes are additionally given a roman numeral grade to indicate their length. Thus, an example of an overall route rating might be VI 5.10 A3. Individual pitches might be labelled 5.6, 4th, or A2. An explanation of each category follows.

CLASS DESCRIPTION

1	Trail hiking
2	Rough hiking, frequent use of hands for balance
3rd	Rock scrambling using hands, sometimes with enough exposure that inexperienced climbers will prefer to use a rope
4th	Technically more difficult and sufficiently exposed that most climbers use a rope and belay for safety
5th	Free climbing sufficiently difficult to require the use of a rope and placement of protection for safety
6th	Artificial (aid) climbing where hardware is used not simply for protection, but also for hand and footholds

5th class climbing is subdivided by the use of a decimal point. Thus routes are rated 5.0, 5.1, . . . 5.11, 5.12. Currently the most difficult American climbs are in the 5.13 category, but the numbers will continue to march upwards. Many routes receive further subgradings in the form of letters (a, b, c, or d) or + and − signs. In this book, only + and − signs are used; almost all routes 5.10 and above are subgraded in this way. Note that gradings will usually vary somewhat between areas and sometimes within an area. Always be prepared for a route to be harder or easier than its rating in this book indicates. The following is an approximate comparison of the most popular rating systems used throughout the world.

Decimal	UIAA	English Numerical	Australian	French
5.0	III		4	
5.1	III +		5	
5.2	IV −	3a	6	
5.3		3b	7	
5.4	IV +	3c	8,9	
5.5	V −	4a	10,11	
5.6	V	4b	12,13	4c
5.7	V +	4c	14,15	5a
5.8	VI −	5a	16	5b
5.9	VI		17	5c
5.10a / 5.10b (−)	VI +	5b	18	6a
	VII −		19	
5.10c / 5.10d (+)	VII	5c	20	6b
	VII +		21	
5.11a / 5.11b (−)		6a	22	6c
	VIII −		23	
5.11c / 5.11d (+)	VIII	6b	24	7a
	VIII +		25	
5.12a / 5.12b (−)	IX −	6c	26	7b
	IX		27	
5.12c / 5.12d (+)	IX +	7a	28	7c
			29	
5.13	X	7b		

The aid ratings reflect the security of using the latest available technology. The same route climbed with the pitons of the 1960's instead of the modern aid climbing rack would require entirely different ratings. Frequently, difficult modern routes could not be done without the technology of camming nuts, bashies and hooks.

A1   Easy placements, completely secure.

A2   More difficult placements, less secure.

A3   Even more difficult placements that will usually only hold a short fall.

A4   Each placement will hold body weight but would not sustain a fall.

A5   A series of A4 placements long enough to risk at least a 50 foot fall should one fail.

C1, C2, . . . are used as an aid rating prefix, where known, to indicate the aid rating when the route can be done completely clean – i.e., with no hammer blows.

Roman numerals, intended as a grading of overall difficulty, were designed to reflect many factors about a route, including commitment, difficulty, and length. In current usage, they primarily reflect length in terms of time invested into a climb. Grades I through IV are usually self-evident and have not been used in this book.

I   About an hour of climbing, usually one or two pitches.
II   Less than a half day of climbing.
III   A half day of climbing.
IV   A full day of climbing.
V   Typically, one overnight is spent on the wall. Since many traditional two-day aid routes are free climbed in a day, this grade on a free climb usually means one very long day.
VI   At least two nights are usually spent on the climb.

WARNING ON ROUTE LINES, SYMBOLS, AND FIXED PROTECTION

The format taken for most of the route descriptions in this book – route lines superimposed on photographs – is helpful only if one keeps in mind the inherent imprecision of route information. In this book, the placement of route lines or protection/belay symbols is not exact. The notations are subject to interpretation, and route finding skills are just as important as ever. The symbols and route lines are guides only.

There are bound to be ways to improve the accuracy of the route line drawings or topos in this book. While any guidebook takes away some of the adventure in climbing, it is not the intent of this guide to mislead. As a user of this guide, your suggestions for better descriptions would be invaluable. A photocopy of a photo with corrections to the route line is ideal. Likewise, feedback concerning the routes selected for this book is appreciated. Suggestions for better routes are welcomed. All route information, corrections and suggestions should be sent to Chockstone Press, 526 Franklin Street, Denver, CO 80218.

As further warning, be aware that fixed pitons and bolts labelled in this guide might have been removed or supplemented. Fixed anchors should always be carefully inspected. They may be weak due to weathering, poor initial placement, or any number of reasons. That they are listed in this book does not imply that they are trustworthy or even exist! Where not considered necessary for route finding, known fixed pitons or bolts have often been left out of the route description.

Pitons should not be trusted without testing, preferably with a hammer. Since few climbers free climb with a hammer, fixed pitons are rarely tested and can easily be unsafe.

Bolts should be checked with a strong jerk on the hanger (using a carabiner) and inspected for cracks. They should *never* be tested with a hammer, as this can severely weaken them! Because defective or poorly placed bolts are a possibility anywhere, no bolt can be fully trusted.

A NOTE ON SAFETY

Those using *The Climber's Guide to North America* as a guidebook are assumed to be competent and experienced climbers. It is not the intent of this book to educate anyone in *how* to climb, but simply to provide suggestions as to where to climb and what it will be like.

It must be noted, however, that many of the places covered by these books are relatively remote. Assistance from fellow climbers, rescues, or hospital facilities may be difficult to obtain quickly. This is a serious consideration that should be taken into account when deciding just how far to "hang it out" on a particular climb.

Water sanitation can be a problem in some areas. Beware that few streams and lakes can be completely trusted to be safe from contamination – no matter how far away from "civilization." The bacteria Giardia is a common infectious agent and can produce extreme intestinal illness that can completely ruin a climbing vacation. It is best to thoroughly boil and/or treat with purification tablets all stream and lake water.

To avoid further water contamination, all human waste should be *buried* not less than 100 feet away from the nearest open water.

Theft can be a definite problem in some areas, particularly those with large numbers of people. As a general rule, keep all valuables, including climbing equipment, locked out of sight in a car. Ropes and equipment fixed on routes, or stashed at the base of cliffs, may not be safe.

IF YOU DON'T HAVE A CAR

Public transportation in North America is not nearly as extensive as it is in Europe. Nevertheless, one can certainly reach many of the best climbing areas on the continent without a car. If the climber is willing to hitch-hike, there is almost no place that cannot be reached. Though trains bypass almost everything interesting to climbers, buses connect the major cities with many small communities and some popular recreation sites. From the major airports, it is usually necessary to take a connecting bus to the bus station located downtown.

If you don't have a car, turn to the text under *GETTING THERE* for the area you are interested in visiting.

Another option is to rent a car. The major car rental companies found at airports are fairly expensive. The same rental agencies located downtown often offer considerably lower rates. Much cheaper, though riskier, alternatives are the small local companies that rent used cars – sometimes *very* used. By getting together a small group of climbers one of these cars can be rented for very little money and will provide a great deal of mobility. Likewise, even climbers with limited resources can usually afford to buy a suitable used car by pooling their funds. An important fringe benefit to having a car is that the trunk provides a storage place for gear.

If travelling alone or with one other person, consider first visiting one of the more popular areas. There is a good possibility of meeting a climber with a car who can be persuaded to visit new places.

AMERICAN ROCK CLIMBING STYLE AND ETHICS

Traditionally, there has been a difference in free climbing attitudes between Europe and America. These stem in large part from the fact that Europeans have emphasized getting up big mountains fast (crag climbing was often considered practice for the real stuff). Popular American cliffs are low in objective dangers, thus Americans have emphasized the style of the ascent. Now, many Europeans are also concentrating on pure rock climbing and have adopted many similar standards of style. Nevertheless, a short discussion on American attitudes may help visitors from different climbing cultures.

In the United States, the ideal free ascent is a route climbed unpreviewed, unroped, barefoot, and without chalk. Any compromise of this style is just that: a compromise. To provide a greater margin of safety and comfort, few climbers follow such strict guidelines in their climbing style. Many climbers use chalk, most use shoes, and almost everyone uses a rope and protection. They strive simply to climb a route with the minimum number of falls or reliances on equipment, knowing that the further that their style deviates from the ideal, the less the accomplishment of their ascent.

There are many ways of compromising good climbing style, from merely falling, to resting on protection, yo-yoing (making upward progress by lowering to rest, or exchanging leaders), previewing the route by rappel, or pre-placing protection. "Improving" hand or footholds by altering the rock is unthinkable.

Some Europeans consider it good style to practice a route by resting on aid with the intent of finally re-leading the route with no weighting of protection. Most Americans would rather complete the route in one push using their best possible style, even if it means taking falls and lowering to a rest position. Many people prefer to retreat from a short route than to ever rest on aid.

Damaging the rock is the biggest transgression in American rock climbing. Because of their damaging impact on the rock, the use of pitons is discouraged on all free climbs and wherever avoidable on aid routes. On first ascents, any necessary pitons are usually left fixed. The use of bolts on established routes is even more deeply scorned. On the free climbs described in this book, both pitons and bolts should be thought of only as emergency tools.

Chalk is disapproved of by many climbers – both because it is an aid and because it is visually obnoxious on some rock types. It also leaves a "white-dotted line" that shows where to go and where all the hand-holds are. Nevertheless, the stuff works wonderfully in securing grip and is used by most climbers.

Discussions on ethics and style are taken quite seriously by many people. Generally these discussions center on first ascents, because a route that is put up in poor style can take away the thrill and credit for a first ascent by someone who would later do the route in a more accepted style.

Many Americans will be seen bending the "rules" of good style, but when all is said and done, most climbing peers condemn only those who 1) damage the rock, 2) misrepresent their particular climbing style, or 3) grossly deny other climbers a first ascent in better style.

SUPPLEMENTARY INFORMATION

Road Atlas to North America A number of road atlases are available from bookstores and gas stations. A particularly good one is put out by Quaker State and published by Gousha/Chek-Chart, P.O. Box 6227, San Jose, CA 95150. These atlases do little that good individual state maps do not do, but they make visiting several states a bit more convenient.

FREE Campgrounds U.S.A. edited by Mary VanMeer, 1983, published by The East Woods Press, Fast & McMillan Publishers, Inc., 429 East Boulevard, Charlotte, NC 28203, $9.95. This book lists an incredible number of free campgrounds and can make travelling from one climbing area to another much less expensive. Also, sometimes free alternatives can be found to the more convenient campgrounds listed in *The Climber's Guide to North America*.

Let's Go: USA annual, published by St. Martin's Press, 175 Fifth Avenue, New York, NY 10010, $8.95. This is only one of many books on travelling in the US that could prove valuable to climbers with interests beyond the rocks. These books usually focus on cities and major recreation areas (e.g. National Parks) and cover historical overviews, interesting sights, hotels, restaurants, transportation. *Let's Go: USA* is written by the Harvard Student's Agencies, and focuses on budget travel for students. By listing Youth Hostels, campgrounds, and budget hotels, it is probably more interesting to climbers than most of the other books available.

American Youth Hostel Handbook 1332 I St. NW, Washington D.C. 20005, free with membership. Youth hostels are rarely available next to climbing areas, but they can often be relatively cheap and interesting places to stay while travelling or visiting cities (where camping is often not worth the hassle).

Climbing Magazine PO Box E, Aspen, CO 81612. Each issue lists climbing equipment stores that distribute the magazine. This can be a way of locating stores in cities between those listed in the *Climber's Guide to North America*.

Advanced Rockcraft by Royal Robbins, 1971, La Siesta Press, Box 406, Glendale, CA 91209, $3.95. Though not recent enough for the latest technology, this book gives an excellent introduction to big wall techniques.

Shawangunk Rock Climbing by Richard DuMais, 1985, Chockstone Press, 526 Franklin Street, Denver, CO 80218, $27.50. This is a large format book that displays in spectacular full color photos the climbing in this most popular of eastern climbing areas.

Climbing in North America by Chris Jones, 1976, published for the American Alpine Club by the University of California Press, and available from the American Alpine Club, 113 East 90th Street, New York, NY 10028. Hardback: $19.95, paperback: $9.95, plus $1.25 postage. This is the most comprehensive history to climbing in North America available in print.

Rock and Ice PO Box 3595, Boulder, CO 80307. As with *Climbing,* this magazine provides articles on the contemporary climbing scene.

Detailed books on the climbing histories of the Northeast and Southeast are being written by Guy and Laura Waterman and Mike Fischesser, respectively.

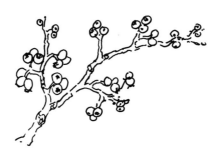

EAST COAST ROCK CLIMBS

A youth moved to the East Coast after growing up in Switzerland and Washington State; despite his mountaineering background, years passed before he became aware of climbing possibilities in New England. Sure, little chunks of rock might occasionally be seen peeking out above the treetops, but the thought of climbing these things barely crossed his mind. Certainly, no one could take these scruffy crags seriously.

That naive attitude paralleled the thinking of early Eastern mountaineers who travelled to the Alps and Canada to climb, without thought of what could be done at home. It is also the attitude of non-climbers who assume that massive walls and snowy heights are needed for the "glory of conquest." The attitude could not be further off base.

In fact, East Coast crags have not only been as seriously developed as any in the country, but their cliffs have a climbing history that extends virtually to the origins of the sport of roped rock climbing in North America. The wealth and diversity of crags is also staggering; it seems the closer one looks, the more one finds. Naturally, many of these cliffs are short, some so short that had they been out West, they would have been ignored for many years while the bigger, more dramatic walls were tackled. But there are also tall cliffs, several in the neighborhood of 1,000 feet high and many more between 200 and 500 feet high. Many of those that are 200 feet or shorter make up for their lack of vertical height with their extensiveness, sometimes spanning horizontal miles without interruption and offering superb one to three pitch routes the entire length. The East Coast is certainly nothing to scoff at – not if one's passion is the act of climbing, rather than attaining altitude.

These widely varying cliffs lie scattered through the most diverse cultural environments north of Mexico. Nearly 1,300 miles separate the Dixie-accented southernmost chapter of this book, Chattanooga, from the French-speaking northernmost chapter, Charlevoix. There are, however, characteristics that the fifteen areas (and two-dozen additional areas in the final chapter) have in common.

Within this great expanse, a remarkable similarity of geography and climate exist. The Appalachian Mountains extend from northern Alabama to Maine. Never are these mountains the jagged, steeply rising peaks one typically associates with the term mountain; instead, they could be considered overgrown hills – they are, in fact, the ancient, thoroughly eroded remnants of what was once a major range. Mount Mitchell, in North Carolina, is the Appalachian's highest peak, at 6,684 feet, while the highest summit in New England is 6,288 foot Mount Washington. Though the highest peaks rise above timberline, the majority of the range features rolling hills, wide river valleys and broad plateaus. Most climbers visiting the East will not consider themselves in a mountain range. The inevitable exceptions in this book are New Hampshire's Cannon Cliff and Maine's Katahdin, where timberline is nearby, and nasty, quickly changing weather can bring freezing conditions in the middle of the summer.

A look at any weather chart reveals another common denominator of the East Coast: moisture. Both rainfall and humidity are remarkably high compared to Western areas. Rainfall occurs throughout the year in relatively uniform doses. Thus the "Likelihood of Precipitation" chart for a chapter might read "medium" or "medium-high" for every season. And nearly every "Comment" on the weather will mention high summer humidity as limiting the climbing. These conditions may have a dampening effect on a climbing trip; however, unless luck is truly against the travelling climber, most days will be sufficiently rain-free for climbing (summer humidity is more inevitable). Rain does not usually come in the continuous drizzle typical of the Pacific Northwest, nor usually in the short, violent downbursts of the Rockies in summer, but instead it varies within these extremes, depending on the frontal system.

This common humidity and elevation results in a uniformly dense vegetation. Broadleaf deciduous trees dominate the entire East Coast, with occasional islands of evergreens (usually pine trees), depending on local soil conditions. Much of Charlevoix is sufficiently north to violate this rule, being covered instead with taiga spruce forests. Except where farms and grazing land have been painstakingly carved out and maintained, the entire East Coast is dense with forest – right to the base of nearly every cliff. Because of the dominance of deciduous trees, much of the region errupts in fireworks of color when the foliage turns in the fall.

The best climbing season for nearly all Eastern areas is autumn. This is true not just because of the dazzling colors, but also because it rains somewhat less frequently than at other seasons. Best of all, up and down the East Coast one may find low humidity and crisp, refreshing air in the fall. At other seasons, the climate varies with the latitude. Surprisingly, even the northernmost areas are very hot in July and early August, and the southernmost ones can be very cold in January.

One last common thread to note to Western visitors: the population density. In a full day's driving from Boston to Washington, D.C., one barely escapes one major city before entering another. Even inland, and even well away from what might be considered metropolitan areas, one will find people and their houses nearly everywhere. Cliffs in Connecticut lift directly out of suburbs, and while Connecticut is an extreme example, few cliffs on the East Coast are out of view from a town, a church steeple, or a heavily-travelled road. If none of these are seen, then a well-used hiking trail is usually found leading people into the wilderness. Some climbing areas seem quite remote, but more often the feeling is pastoral.

The West Coast has Yosemite, the Rockies have Eldorado Canyon . . . and the East Coast has the Shawangunks. This is the great climbing triad from the perspective of Westerners and Europeans, but the Gunks aren't quite as pre-eminent for Eastern climbers as are the Western areas for their residents. Instead, North Conway's cliffs draw many New England residents, while Seneca Rocks draws most Southerners. Population distribution certainly coincides nicely with the locations of these major crag systems. Of these three major Eastern areas, the Gunks is most serendipitously placed. It is both next to the major U.S. metropolitan complex – New York City and environs – and it has the greatest concentration of high quality rock on the entire East Coast. Other areas have more extensive or higher cliffs (never the two together), but none offer more climbing potential. Included in that assessment is the unprecedentedly high quality of the routes at the Gunks – at nearly every grade of difficulty. What more could one want from an area within two hours of a large city? Fewer climbers, perhaps.

Both the Shawangunks and Seneca Rocks are quartzite, while North Conway is granite. As one tours Eastern climbing areas, one will find approximately an equal distribution of sedimentary and intrusive rock types, with intrusive granites dominating in the more rugged mountains of the Northeast and the Carolinas. In the following descriptions, as well as in individual chapter descriptions, the geology is viewed from the perspective of a climber interested in relative comparisons of rock qualities that affect climbing; a geologist might easily be offended by occasional imprecisions and more frequent generalizations.

The sedimentary rock of the East is sometimes compact sandstone, while more often it has been metamorphosed into quartzite or something similar. The Gunks cliffs are a quartzite-conglomerate that is horizontally layered. Four-hundred miles south, Seneca Rocks is also quartzite, this time with its layering tilted on end, resulting in thin, slivery crags. Two-hundred miles further south, we find quartzite reappearing at Moore's Wall. As at the Gunks, its layering has remained horizontal, though the crag lacks the sharp-edged cleaness of its northern cousin. Each of these areas is reknowned for its vertical face climbing on cliffs that average about 200 feet in height. Due west of Moore's Wall, we again find metamorphosed sandstone, at the Linville Gorge. The walls here are somewhat higher – reaching nearly 500 feet in places – but not quite as steep, on the whole. The holds also tend to be less angular, and are often notoriously downsloping. The characteristics of the mica-schist at Carderock and Great Falls are reminiscent of Linville Gorge, though the height is under 70 feet.

Unmetamorphosed, but still extremely solid, are the sandstone beds of the New River Gorge and the Chattanooga region (the latter is often refered to as "the Sandstone Belt" because of the vast number of cliffs in a region covering several states). The climbs at these two areas, both south of the Mason-Dixon line but separated by 600 miles, are remark-ably similar. At each, the sandstone bed averages about 100 feet in thickness and is split by numerous cracks that are clean, deep and

straight. Also, at each area the rock is sufficiently solid that face climbing can also be good. The number of face routes lags behind the number of crack routes simply because the climbing history of these crags is so young. Both areas also have impressive overhangs, though the Chattanooga region has them in unprecedented size and density. Many of Chattanooga's roofs are split by cracks, providing possibly the finest big roof climbing on the Continent. (Roofs at the Shawangunks are at least as prevalent, but tend to be smaller and are only infrequently split by cracks. However, at the Gunks one often finds these short roofs stacked immediately on top of each other, resulting in overhanging staircases.) The diversity of climbing near Chattanooga is also somewhat greater than that at the New River, because Yellow Creek Falls offers 200 foot cliffs whose rock is almost continuously overhanging, with a few horizontal roofs thrown in for good measure.

Intrusive granitic rock is as widely scattered as, and even more diverse than, the sedimentary beds. Its best known faces show up in New Hampshire – aptly named "the Granite State," even by those unconnected with climbing. North Conway's rock is impeccably solid and not at all rough, yet features a myriad of small edges that supplement its cracks. Its cliffs are varied in angle, some faces rising perpendicularly for 450 feet; others are tilted more gently and provide superb friction for 800 feet of climbing. Nearby Cannon Cliff is New England's most massive crag, rising about 1,000 feet in a subalpine setting. Its granite is somewhat coarser and more angular than North Conway's, and crack climbing is the norm because Cannon's angle is usually too great for pure friction climbing.

Excepting the small granite crags of Mount Desert Island – which average 50 feet but can reach 200 feet – the other Northeastern chapters in this book feature rock that feels like granite, but doesn't technically qualify as such. Anorthosite is predominant in the Adirondacks; it fractures into cracks and face holds much like granite, but is somewhat rougher. Also in the Adirondacks, granitic gneiss is found at Pok-O-Moonshine; it is even more granite-like. Besides Pok-O's 400 foot face (the best known in the region), the Adirondacks hold numerous other faces between 150 and 700 feet in height. The tallest is the low-angled Chapel Pond Slab. Pok-O and the other cliffs tend to be vertical.

The most extensive and least developed granite (rather, granite-like) crags in the East are in Quebec. Again, anorthosite commonly adds its frictional characteristics to the superb qualities a climber associates with granite. Quebec's cliffs vary from the highly developed 50 to 250 foot crags of Val David, near Montreal, to the large walls in the hinterlands of Charlevoix. Charlevoix's size and diversity is legendary; in fact many of the cliffs there have only rarely been touched. A sample of the wide choices in climbing options include easy friction/face routes on Mont de l'Ours and vertical 1,000 foot aid routes rising out of a fiord at Cap Trinité.

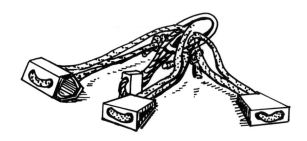

Skipping from Francophone "New France" (as Quebec was once known), past puritan New England, over the heterogeneous mid-Atlantic, and arriving, once again, in the warm bosom of Dixieland, we find large granite domes little known to the world's climbing community. Stone Mountain's 600 foot South Face offers fearsome friction routes (and tame ones as well) that are sun-heated even in the depths of winter. The Looking Glass is a peculiar lens of rock, with odd pockets known as "eyebrows" covering sections of its nearly 500 foot face. These can add a unique flavor to the climbing, while the frequent cracks offer fewer surprises. Nearby is the massive flank of Whitesides, whose 700 foot central section drops so steeply that cavers use it for rappelling practice – 400 feet of the descent is free in space. Both free and aid routes tackle the rough-textured rock that is almost devoid of cracks.

Climbers making a grand tour of the East Coast will find cultural dimensions to their trip that are diverse and interesting enough to easily rival the quality of the climbing. One would have to be truly single-minded to avoid Manhatten or Quebec City, to name but two of the fascinating towns. But even if one took every city by-pass on the interstates, the cultural differences will meet one at the crags: from the "how y'all doin'?" of Tennessee to the "comment ça-va?" of Quebec. The stock brokers and art dealers one is likely to meet on a belay ledge at the Shawangunks contrast to the river-guides of the New River Gorge. Bloodsucking blackflies are the curse of the Northeast in the late spring, while venomous copperhead snakes must be sidestepped in the South (fortunately, the snakes are much less common than the blackflies; conversely and unfortunately, the blackflies can seem far more deadly than the snakes).

The youth who moved to the East Coast thinking he had left climbing behind was naive indeed. As the cold spell of winter is broken and the laurels bloom near his neighboring crags, he realizes that the time for writing books has drawn to a close. The time to climb has come.

A BRIEF HISTORY OF ROCK CLIMBING
ON THE EAST COAST

By the time Europeans arrived in the New World, the Appalachian Mountains, which once would have rivalled today's Himalayas, were but stumps of their former selves. When the highest peak in the Northeast, Mount Washington, was spotted from shipboard in 1524, it measured but 6,288 feet. Still, it reaches well above timberline and in winter has some of the most severe weather on Earth. Thus, when Darby Field climbed it in 1642, he most certainly became one of the earliest non-Indian mountaineers north of Mexico's volcanoes.

Another early event in North American climbing came in 1876, when the Appalachian Mountain Club was founded. Though other similar clubs preceeded it, the AMC has become the oldest such organization still in existence in North America. At the time of its founding, the AMC was not involved in ascending rocks *per se*, but was active in ascending the "peaks" of the northeast (always attainable by rugged hikes). In the resort community of Mount Desert Island, land owners of the late 1800's took their scrambling seriously, often entertaining themselves by choosing difficult paths up their backyard cliffs. In one unfortunate instance, a route was serious enough that the owner's bride-to-be fell to her death. She may well be North America's first death in recreational rock climbing.

The litany of East Coast firsts was interrupted by Albert Ellingwood. When he returned to America in 1914 from a multi-year visit to England – where he learned to use ropes in rock climbing – his home state was Colorado. There, he introduced rope handling techniques and made the first known conscious use of a belay in North America. Ellingwood was only two years ahead of John Case, however, who in 1916 brought belayed climbing to his home in the Adirondacks. Where Ellingwood picked up his knowledge from the crags of England, Case's learning took place in the Alps.

John Case was not the first Northeasterner to climb in the Alps. The AMC was composed mostly of the college-educated elite, for whom trips to Europe were a standard rite-of-passage into adulthood. With Europe's mushrooming fascination with climbing, it is only natural that young Americans of means would hire an Alpine guide to lead them into the mountains. Back in North America, some of these AMC climbers would venture to the mountains of the Canadian Rockies and elsewhere out West, where first ascents could be had. Among the dedicated, there came to be an increasing competition for prized summits in the heavily glaciated Canadian Rockies – the North American peaks with the greatest resemblance to the Alps. Most AMC climbers, however, were happier visiting the sophisticated and romantic European Alps than hassling with the untamed West.

Around the turn-of-the-century, some of the AMC climbers who frequented the peaks of Canada and Europe were already bouldering in

the Boston area (the AMC was founded in Boston) and on Mount Desert Island. But not until the 1920's did the notion sink in of taking New England's rock crags a bit more seriously. In the mid-20's a small band of climbers from the AMC and the newly formed Harvard Mountaineering Club made regular visits to most of the local crags, including Quincy Quarries and Crow Hill, and in 1926 they investigated the Mount Washington area, home to the largest cliffs in New England. A rock route was climbed in the ravines of Mount Washington in 1927, but major developments by these Boston climbers waited until the following year. (Independent of these Boston climbers and without as much impact on the climbing scene at-large, Willard Helburn began leading the first New England multi-pitch rock climbs on Mt. Katahdin, Maine in 1919.)

The year 1928 saw the initiation of the first explosion in activity on Eastern crags. The thousand foot face of Cannon – the largest cliff in the Northeast – was the first major climb attempted. A six person team, led by Robert Underhill, tackled it via a broken section of the cliff. Still, they were stymied on the first attempt by a blank section. Returning later in the year, they tensioned across the difficult section using a wooden stake as an anchor. That same year Underhill, with his future wife Miriam O'Brian and her brother Lincoln, among others, pioneered routes on Whitehorse's slabs and completed the **Northeast Ridge of the Pinnacle** on Mount Washington. During the next five years, they climbed on most of New England's major cliffs and ferreted out many lesser cliffs as well.

When Underhill climbed Cannon, he declared his route (now known as **Old Cannon**) to be the only possible route on the cliff. This sort of statement has been common throughout the history of climbing, but rarely is it proved silly as quickly as it was in this case. The very next year, two Ivy League climbers who had been doing high-standard guideless ascents in the Alps, Bradley Gilman and his cousin Hassler Whitney, climbed the impressive arête that now bears their names. Not only was this 5.7 climb (possibly 5.6 at the time) as technically hard as anything climbed to date in New England, it was also long and bold; Whitney and Gilman used no protection other than their belays.

The end of the 1920's and the beginning of the 1930's – just when the Great Depression crashed its way into America but before its insidious effects were omnipresent – must rank as the most pivotal period of North American climbing history, and Eastern climbers had a great deal to do with its significance. Robert Underhill took over the editorship of the AMC's magazine *Appalachia* and immediately focused its attention on the newly developing art of crag climbing. His attention to the crags and his articles on rope work intrigued the editor of California's *Sierra Club Bulletin*. By invitation, Underhill published an article in that journal, "On the Use and Management of the Rope in Rock Work," followed by a visit to California in 1931 during which he participated in the first ascent of the East Face of Mount Whitney. Even prior to that Underhill, with Boston banker Kenneth Henderson, had pioneered new routes on their annual visits to the Tetons – where they demonstrated clearly advanced techniques.

In Connecticut, a group of climbers was active in the Hartford area and at Yale University. Eminent among these climbers was Bill House. House was not only very active on the home crags, he also travelled widely, climbing in the Himalaya, Canada, and the Western U.S. House's partner on the first ascents of Mount Waddington (British Columbia), and of the Devils Tower (Wyoming) however, eclipsed him and all other climbers of the period in travels, climbs, and reputation.

Fritz Wiessner stands out as the legendary North American climber until the tidal wave of legends that emerged in the 1950's and 60's. While Americans were learning something of climbing on their vacations in Europe, Wiessner grew up in Germany near Dresden – the scene of the highest contemporary rock climbing standards, standards which he helped to set and which were not equalled elsewhere in the world for generations to come. Wiessner also established major routes in the Eastern Alps before emigrating to the United States in 1929. In North America, he found routes so ripe for the plucking that his hardest routes of the 1930's, 5.8, simultaneously did not match in difficulty those climbs he had made in Europe and were considered nearly impossible by his American climbing partners. Some of Wiessner's hard routes in Connecticut and elsewhere went unrepeated for more than a decade.

Instead of pushing his personal standards (he was already beyond any American standards), Wiessner concentrated on travel and exploration of new cliffs. Rare is the Northeastern area that did not feel his touch in its early, sometimes earliest, stages of development; many Western cliffs were first climbed by Wiessner as well. Of all the prominent and obscure crags Wiessner is credited with opening, one dominates the others: the Shawangunks.

Despite the presence of an upper class resort, with carriage roads that run along the base of a vast collection of cliffs, and despite being located just 70 miles north of New York City, the Shawangunks were somehow never discovered by climbers until Fritz Wiessner spied them in the distance while climbing at Breakneck Ridge thirty miles away – in 1935! The weekend after spotting the escarpment, he drove up to check out his discovery and thereby ushered in the most significant climbing area on the East Coast. In 1938, another European climber moved to New York as well. Expatriates Hans Kraus from Austria and Fritz Wiessner from Germany became the driving forces of Gunks climbing until the 1950's.

The 30's saw the origins of the sport of rock climbing in Quebec as well. Eastern Canadian climbers had always been entirely focused on their country's spectacular Rockies, the only easily accessible peaks in North America that rival those of the Alps. It took another expatriate, this time from Switzerland, to demonstrate the joys of crag climbing near home. John Brett, with his wife and son, opened the cliffs of Val David as early as 1930, but it was not untill the late 30's that he and others, including members of the McGill Outing Club, started putting up a few more routes. Wiessner paid his first visit to Val David in 1943, coinciding with Brett's founding of the Montreal Section of the Alpine Club of Canada and the first surge in local rock climbing.

Though most climbers have considered East Coast synonymous with Northeast, a great number of fine climbers have emerged from the Southeast as well. Strong awareness of the climbing potential down South was still decades away when Washington D.C. residents began exploring the small crags around the Capital City. Their discoveries of the climbing potential of Carderock and Great Falls, within an hour of downtown, must have greatly excited them. Despite the small size of the cliffs – 70 feet at the outside limit and usually half that height – much of the initial climbing begun in the 1920's was on the lead. It didn't take very long, however, for the contemporary preference for toproping to dominate. One 5.9 was toproped as early as 1936, becoming possibly the most difficult technical route in the country. However, this climb was an exception, and the toprope style makes it unfair to compare this standard to, say, Wiessner's poorly protected 5.8's in Connecticut and the Shawangunks.

Washington, D.C. climbers did not limit themselves to their city limits. They soon began making the half-day drive to Seneca Rocks in West

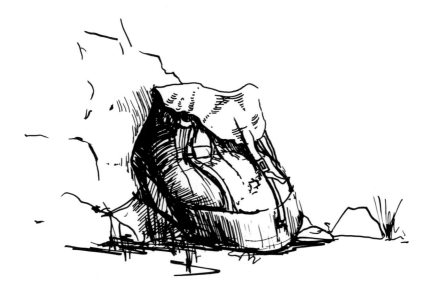

Virginia, where roped climbing made its debut in the mid-1930's. Still, the distance and the small number of climbers kept activity here very slow compared to the Northeast, while elsewhere in the South the rocks still lay untouched.

The World War II years were significant in North American climbing. Despite the expanding numbers of Quebec rock climbers during the 1940's, most of the few Eastern U.S. climbers who still managed to get out during the depths of the Depression stopped climbing almost entirely during the war years. Some of these formerly active climbers, however, joined the mountain troops of the Army, thus contributing to the development of equipment that would revolutionize the sport of climbing.

Above all else, these Army climbers initiated the use of nylon ropes in climbing. Nylon ropes were already being used in manufacturing, and when the Army tested them with climbing in mind, they were found to be ten times stronger than contemporary hemp and manila ropes. Much of this testing occured at Seneca Rocks, where angle pitons were also being developed – reportedly, 75,000 pitons were driven into Seneca's sandstone. Aluminum carabiners were another welcome development by Army engineers.

After the War, climbers had safer ropes – onto which one could feel relatively comfortable taking a long fall – pitons that were much more durable and prevalent than the soft-steel pins so far available from Europe, and less cumbersome racks due to lighter and stronger carabiners. Seneca Rocks, and probably other areas as well, were also left with new converts to rock climbing, as Army recruits kept up with the sport recreationally.

The immediate post-War years found widely differing amounts of activity around the Northeast. Where New Hampshire cliffs had played such a leading role in the early stages of North American rock climbing, they fell into relative disuse until the mid-1950's. The only significant new route was established in 1945 on Cannon Cliff by Washington, D.C. climbers Herb and Jan Conn, who knew nothing of established routes and proceeded to put up a 5.8 climb that has become one of the most popular on the cliff (it is currently climbed in the form of many variations to the original line which are collectively called **Moby Grape**). The only area in the U.S. which maintained significant activity was the Shawangunks, where Kraus and Wiessner continued to dominate. These two climbers had a split in philosophy, however, with Kraus opting to use aid in tackling some of the overhangs at the Gunks, while Wiessner refused to allow his partners to use any aid at all. Kraus teamed up with Bonnie Prudden during the 40's, the two making the first aid ascents of many routes that have now become classic hard free climbs. Ken Prestrud and Lucien Warner were also active through the early 1950's.

Where before the War, East Coast climbers had been forging the standards of technical climbing in America, after the War, West Coast climbers – specifically those at Tahquitz and Yosemite – became the standard setters. Royal Robbins' Tahquitz climb, the **Open Book,** established 5.9 in 1952, six years before the grade reached a lead-climb back East. But an exchange of climbers and ideas akin to what happened in the late 20's and early 30's was not to take place until later in the decade. As the 1950's progressed, the numbers of climbers at Eastern areas gradually increased. In Connecticut, the pre-war climbers had completely quit climbing in the state, and the new generation was in effect beginning anew, with no knowledge of past events.

Elsewhere, many new climbers were also coming into the sport, though usually with some help from those who had been active before. A prime example of this trend was Jim McCarthy, an undergraduate at Princeton (in neighboring New Jersey), who came to the Shawangunks in 1951 and proceeded to work his way up the grades on the established routes. His skill being readily apparent, he soon teamed up with Hans Kraus (Wiessner had by now moved to Vermont) for the hardest climbs, then continued on into unforged territory. Soon another serious young climber appeared, Art Gran, and the rivalry between the two continued to press the standards ever higher. Still, it was not until 1958 that they broke the 5.9 barrier. The Gunks' style of climbing was also different from the approach taken at Tahquitz. In the Gunks, new routes – especially once they exceeded 5.9 in difficulty – were usually a connected series of boulder problems, with the route being pieced together from protection placement to protection placement, and only rarely connected on sight. To a large extent, this was due to the forbidding aspect of Gunks roofs and faces, compared with the more straight-forward crack and slab climbs out West.

Judging by the number of climbers and their relatively high standards, the Shawangunks became the primary focal point of Eastern climbing during the 1950's, the position it would continue to hold to this writing. Besides McCarthy, Gran and a growing number of good Gunks climbers, however, there was another dominant figure in Eastern climbing, this person centered in Montreal and making forays into the Adirondacks and New Hampshire. John Turner was an Englishman living in Canada to avoid induction into the British military. He brought with him the high standards of climbing currently prevalent in England, as well as the British approach to protection: natural runners where you could get them in, next to nothing where you couldn't. Pitons were to be avoided; slung machine-nuts had yet to be discovered. In an era where wider angle pitons were virtually unknown outside of Yosemite, Turner's favored crack climbs could be only barely protected by blade pitons, even if he chose to use them.

Turner proceeded to single-handedly develop the Adirondack's Pok-O-Moonshine cliff and to put hard routes up in New Hampshire, including, in 1958, his severest testpiece, the 5.9 + off-width **Repentence,** on Cathedral. One piton was stepped on for aid, but this was not at the crux. The climb went unrepeated for over ten years. Turner inspired a number of Canadians, who accompanied him on many of his Pok-O trips and actively developed the cliffs of Val David. Among the notables were Claude Lavallée and Bernard Poisson. When Turner returned to England in 1962, much of his inspiration left with him and the Canadians remained behind the standards of the day.

(Standards, in this essay, imply measures of difficulty; climbing, of course, offers much more than simply a quest for difficulty. While the aesthetic and relaxed approaches to the sport may well be of more significance to most of us than the upward marching decimals, these personal aspects are timeless and are not the subject of this history.)

In the South, things were just beginning to heat up during the 1950's. Members of Washington, D.C.'s Potomac Appalachian Trail Club and the Pittsburg Explorer's Club made frequent excursions to Seneca Rocks, occasionally doing 5.8 routes. Still, activity during this decade came nowhere near the levels occuring up North. North Carolina and Tennessee rock had yet to be explored by climbers.

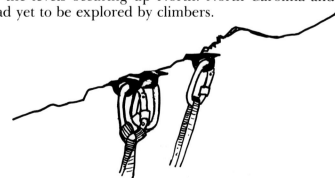

The Shawangunk phenomenon was far greater than the action on its cliffs alone. On the ground, a radical social evolution was taking place among climbers, with multiple factions splitting into separate approaches to climbing and socializing. The distinct factions could, in fact, be easily distinguished one-from-another by their clothing and hair styles. The antics of this period deserve volumes, not just paragraphs of text. To oversimplify, the scene to date had been dominated by AMC club members. Kraus and McCarthy distanced themselves somewhat from the conservative mentality of the "Appies," as AMC members would come to be known. Other groups of college climbers, mainly from MIT, also kept themselves apart from the Appies. But their distancing was nothing compared with the war that was to erupt between the establishment Appies and a new group, the "Vulgarians."

The magazine *The Vulgarian Digest* wasn't published until 1970 and played no role in the movement itself; however, its early cover photos captured the spirit of the group: roof climbing in the nude, a topless woman climber, and an orgy. That was the mature, tasteful side of the Vulgarians. The other side included raucous parties that led to the closing of campgrounds, urinating on Appies, and overturning cars. The Vulgarians were reacting to what they considered stifling rules that were being imposed on them by the establishment, in this case the AMC. The AMC was indeed going overboard in its own right, using fears of increased liability insurance and a possible closure of the Shawangunks cliffs as an excuse to exert control over Gunks climbers. They initiated a certification system for officially sanctioning both leaders and seconds and they patrolled the cliffs, ordering non-sanctioned climbers off of routes. The system was later abandoned as uninforceable and highly unpopular.

Despite all this commotion, certainly the most exciting event of the 1950's occured at the decade's end: the breakdown of parochialism in the major climbing centers around the continent. The best travelled climbers had already been meeting in the Tetons, which was the melting pot of North American climbing during this period. News of a place called Yosemite filtered through to Easterners, and in 1959, a car-load of Vulgarians headed out to the Rockies and California. Likewise, Westerners heard of Eastern developments and were equally curious, arriving around the same time. Shawangunks climbers found their skills were often not up to Yosemite's relentless cracks, but likewise Yosemite climbers often had trouble with the Gunks' strenuous and awesome roofs. The early 1960's saw the initiation of a wide dissemination of climbing ideas that had not taken place since the late 1920's. Now, of course, many more people were involved with a sport which had evolved to far higher levels. The fascination with travel and with keeping up with developments around the country became an ever increasing part of the climbing lifestyle through the coming decades.

In 1961, 5.10 arrived in the Gunks and Yosemite simultaneously. Jim McCarthy was still the leading Gunks climber, having personally broken every major barrier since 5.7 (the first 5.10 was **Retribution**). The following year he freed, at 5.10, a route put up by Californian Yvon Chouinard, who made regular tours of the Northeast during the next few years while selling his popular pitons.

A fascination with Yosemite's "big-walls" was permeating the nation during the early 60's, and climbers became interested in using New Hampshire's granite as wall training by doing hard "nailing." They also found their own "wall" in the imposing central portion of Cannon's 1,000 foot face: the Big Wall Section. As one of the leading big wall climbers of the early 60's, Chouinard's talents were highly coveted and in 1965 he joined with Shawangunk climbers Art Gran and Dick Williams to climb the **VMC** route (Vulgarian Mountain Club) on Cannon. Hard free climbing still hadn't arrived in North Conway; not until 1969 did **Repentence** receive its second ascent, while a 5.10 route wasn't established until 1971, ten years after the grade was entrenched at the Gunks. Clearly, New Hampshire had lost its former glory in the history of Eastern rock climbing.

The numbers of rock climbers active in the East continued to increase steadily. In the 1960's, things finally reached the inevitable point at the Gunks where "unknowns" could be spotted on the former testpieces. But the leading activists, as ever, were well aquainted with each other. Rich Goldstone and Kevin Bein joined McCarthy, pushing standards on big roofs and on hard 5.10. Dick Williams, author of the 1972 and 1980 guidebooks to the Gunks, not only introduced a dynamic gymnast's approach to climbing, but systematically devoured new routes at the hardest contemporary levels.

John Stannard, however, set the community on its ear when he freed the spectacular roof on **Foops** in 1970, thus ushering in the 5.11 grade. Though the climb was initially given a 5.10 rating, it still had a galvanizing effect on local climbers because the line was so outrageously improbable. It set people to rethinking just what, in fact, *was* possible. Stannard went on to climb **Persistent** the next year, reputedly spending 160 days to piece together the single 5.11 pitch. Stannard's driving interest in climbing was aid elimination, and in one year he systematically eliminated all aid from 33 of the 38 aid routes listed in Williams' 1972 guide.

Stannard was also influencial in popularizing the use of clean climbing – utilizing Chouinard's newly developed nuts. Clean climbing caught on quickly, in part because the invention of nuts timed nicely with the advent of the environmental movement. Stannard's leadership in this movement extended beyond the rocks themselves. He could often be found building trails and making efforts to preserve the beauty of the land surrounding the cliffs.

With the arrival of the 70's, the current leaders had to make room for a group of young climbers active at pushing hard routes. First among these was Boston area resident, Henry Barber. "Hot Henry," as he quickly became known, tore into Northeastern rock with a vengence, bringing 5.11 to New Hampshire's Cathedral Ledge in 1972, repeating **Foops** and putting up new 5.11's at the Gunks, and setting Yosemite ablaze in 1973 with the first ascent of **Butterballs** (5.11) and a 2½ hour solo of the **Steck-Salathé.** He followed this *tour-de-force* by travelling to dozens of less-known areas around the country, establishing the hardest routes there and stimulating the locals. Barber then went on to shake up the Australians and to check out the climbing in both Eastern and Western Europe, as well as Africa. Hot Henry was burning.

Barber's style was characterized by speed and boldness; he lacked the patience or desire for the 5.12 climbs that started coming in 1973. Not until the mid-80's were 5.12's done without enormous amounts of time; until then, attempts often spanned days of gradually moving protection higher, with numerous falls taken before eventual success was attained. Among the first of the Gunks 5.12's was John Bragg's ascent of **Kansas City,** while in 1974 Steve Wunsch climbed **Super Crack,** already at the upper limits of 5.12.

The pace at other Northeastern areas may not have kept up with that at the Gunks, but as the 70's progressed, so did activity everywhere. A guide service moved into North Conway, bringing with it resident climbers like Jim Dunn, formerly of Colorado. He did much to establish **The Prow** on Cathedral, an impressive climb with several pitches of 5.11+, whose reputation soon drew more Western climbers, eager to do early repeat ascents. Earlier, Joe Cote had written guidebooks to the North Conway area and climbed its cliffs more passionately than anyone else. Paul Ross moved in from England, bringing with him a tremendous appetite for climbing and some inovative approaches – tremendous girdle traverses of all the major cliffs being among his noteworthy contributions.

Dunn and Barber, among others, visited the Adirondacks, leaving 5.11 in their wake. But these "big names" did not have the Dacks to themselves, as a growing band of locals frequently plied the cliffs. Most of this admittedly small group of climbers lived near Plattsburg and climbed almost exclusively on Pok-O-Moonshine; their leader was Geoff Smith.

Barber also brought 5.10 to Connecticut in the early 1970's, and Sam Streibert and others soon continued the trend. Streibert was the primary moving force in Connecticut climbing through the mid-70's; the last part of the decade saw the emergence and eventual domination of the local climbing scene by Ken Nichols, whose single-minded devotion to Connecticut's climbing resulted in his participation in the first ascents of over a thousand new routes on the state's small cliffs.

The 70's, then, marked an explosion in the popularity of climbing. The aftershocks tumbled the psychological barriers that had surrounded hard climbing. Certain people stand out as leaders, but just behind them the masses were discovering that they, too, could climb hard. Barber had to move quickly to climb the ripe plums around the country, because the hordes were soon hot on his speeding heels. While 5.12 maintained its aura of near impregnability until the mid-80's, 5.10 and 5.11 quickly entered the public domain.

Just as the Vulgarian revolution of the 1950's was not out of context with changing attitudes outside the climbing world, so the popularity that climbing gained in the 1970's was also not an isolated event. The great outdoor movement reached its acme in the 70's, following growing interest during the 1960's and national attention from such media events as the first annual Earth Day in 1969.

The national scope of this movement extended south of the Mason-Dixon Line, finally bringing North Carolina and other Southern states into the climbing world. Of course, not all Southerners waited for the movement to reach its peak before discovering climbing; it's just that the 70's are when climbers could be found everywhere, when the sport began to have some of the popular appeal it already had up North (climbing in the South has never fully caught up in popularity).

Carderock and Great Falls, being on the outskirts of cosmopolitan Washington, D.C. never lacked for climbers, while Seneca Rocks was an anomaly in the South. Seneca's superb cliffs, within convenient reach of the Capital City, assured its popularity. During the late 1950's and throughout the 60's, 5.8 and 5.9 climbing was commonplace among a small band of serious climbers, with Matt Hale being most active. The 1970's at Seneca ushered in a new crowd and even more intense activity, with Gunks activist Stannard being one of the leaders. 5.10 arrived at the beginning of the decade, while 5.11 didn't officially come 'till the decade's end, though notoriously stiff local gradings probably obscure the prominence of routes that were freed earlier in the decade and would have been called 5.11 at other areas.

Seneca, then, dominated the South even more than the Gunks dominated the North. What was happening elsewhere in the South? Climbing had in fact begun, albeit very, very slowly, as the 1950's changed into the 60's. Two groups were independently responsible for getting things started.

In the northern part of North Carolina, George DeWolf watched a Walt Disney movie, "Two for the Mountain," which stimulated him to check out the book *Mountaineering: Freedom of the Hills* from a library. After teaching a few friends the ropes, in 1959 he began climbing at Hanging Rock State Park (including Moore's Wall), and by the early 60's his friends were joined by a small group at the nearby campus of the University of North Carolina. The climbers called themselves "The Carabiners" and soon initiated regular visits to Stone Mountain. Only the easiest lines were climbed by this self-taught group.

Simultaneously and quite independently, a few climbers were getting started in southern North Carolina. Steve Longenecker and Bob Gillespie were instructors at a camp near Hendersonville, which in turn was not far from Looking Glass and the Devil's Courthouse. Gillespie had just learned to climb on a vacation in the Tetons, and he and Longenecker taught the camp kids to rappel from trees. The two instructors then sampled the granite at their nearby cliffs – beginning in 1964 – and with Bob Watts in 1966 established what still remains the area classic, the 5.8 **Nose** route on Looking Glass. That route marked the end of a very short era of new routes at the Glass, as nothing else was put up until the end of the 60's. The climbing at the Linville Gorge was developed when the North Carolina Outward Bound School established its camp there in 1967.

Meanwhile, climbing in Tennessee and other Southern area seems to have occured on a widely scattered and extremely limited basis during the 1960's. Basically, the sport hadn't yet arrived, despite the vast girth of the Sandstone Belt.

So it remained until the 1970's for the outdoor boom to prompt momentum for climbing in North Carolina and elsewhere in the South. During this period, moderate level climbing gained in popularity, while a few individuals took to climbing with a passion that quickly made up for their late arrival into the game. Most of these climbers gained their stimulation through trips to the North and West, sampling Seneca, the Gunks and Boulder, and even venturing to Yosemite. Among the leaders were Bob Rotert, Rich Gottlieb, Tom McMillan and Jeep Gaskin. The group, and Rotert in particular, established a bold style of climbing that led to some very serious routes on the Looking Glass, Whitesides and Stone Mountain. Rotert travelled considerably, and was responsible for the first free ascent of the initial seven pitches of Cannon Cliff's **Labyrinth Wall** (5.11) in 1981. Though the first North Carolina 5.11's were established on the Looking Glass in 1975 during a whirlwind visit by Henry Barber, locals were soon producing their own routes of that grade, especially on Moore's Wall.

Out of the North Carolina scene came Rob Robinson, who at the beginning of the 1980's brought skills and strength gained on Moore's overhangs to the sandstone crags around his home city of Chattanooga, Tennessee. A few climbers preceeded Robinson, with Shannon Stegg and others bringing hard free climbing to Yellow Creek Falls in Alabama, and a few, including Gene Smith and Forrest Gardner, continued to be active at establishing hard routes. But it was Robinson who single-mindedly and almost single-handedly developed the sandstone cliffs near Chattanooga. Not until the mid-1980's did the climbing in the Sandstone Belt begin attracting more frequent visitors from the North. Lacking local competition, most of the motivation for Robinson's push into 5.12 in the mid-80's and 5.13 in 1986 came from within, though his strong desire to see Chattanooga recognized for its true potential plays a large role as well.

The 5.13 grade first arrived on the East Coast, of course, in the Shawangunks. It was 1983 (half a decade after 5.13 was climbed in the cracks of California) when a group effort freed **Vandals.** The group – Jeff Gruenberg, Hugh Herr, Lynn Hill and Russ Clune – was only part of the current cream of the Gunkies. Naturally, more were not represented, examples being Rich Romano and Russ Raffa. So many climbers

were now active at the Gunks that by the 80's it was no longer possible to pick out a single leader or dominant climber – even that role was now filled by a pool of immensely talented and dedicated people. The ranks of climbers at every other level had swollen radically as well: one climber claims to have counted 500 cars parked near the cliffs on a fall weekend in 1985 (this figure has been contested by the Mohonk Preserve – which manages the Gunks; they feel 350 is more likely).

An April trip to the Gunks became a regular rite-of-spring for many of the leading free climbers from the still frozen Northland of Quebec. Some of these climbers had by the early 80's broken away from the stiffling bureaucracy and lack of appreciation for hard free climbing that characterized most of Quebec's mountain clubs. With that break, they also launched themselves into the realm of truly difficult climbing, suddenly opening tremendous new or newly freed lines on their home cliffs. Hard 5.10's and soon 5.11's were established – starting in the late 1970's – by Gérard Bourbonnais and Guy Laselle, among others, while beginning in 1984, Thomas Ryan was instrumental in the quick appearance of numerous 5.12's in the Montreal area (mostly at Val David). These were only the most outstanding figures in a group of serious free climbers that totalled less than a dozen. This small band – all friends – who could climb 5.10 or harder, stand like an island in a sea of climbers whose conservative approach to the sport is dictated by their reigning club, the "Federation Québecoise de la Montagne." Especially lonely was Alain Hénault, whose outpost in Charlevoix removed him from all serious free climbers except the occasional visitor.

New Hampshire, while never regaining its once pre-eminent role in Eastern climbing, maintained its forward momentum through the 1970's. Jim Dunn and Ed Webster, both transplanted from Colorado Springs, were the leading figures in the last half of that decade. Webster, in particular, searched out new routes with a passion that bordered on mania. While activity slowed somewhat in the early 80's, that was followed by increased visits by Gunks activists, including Lynn Hill and Hugh Herr, which rekindled the top-level action. Numerous 5.12's had been established by the mid-80's, including Herr's outrageously dangerous 5.12 + : **Stage Fright.** While transplanted guides had dominated the climbing since the mid-70's, by the mid-80's the first truly local talent emerged: high-school student Jim Surette. Other climbers making waves included Neil Cannon and John Bouchard, while Conway resident Henry Barber quietly renewed some of his old passion for climbing while avoiding the limelight of his heyday.

Not mentioned so far in this history is the New River Gorge in West Virginia, whose extensive and magnificent sandstone cliffs were not even discovered by climbers until 1975 and not seriously developed until the 1980's. That Eastern climbers let such an extensive area lay dormant for so long is reminiscent of the late discovery of the Shawangunks in 1935.

These are but two examples of how the East Coast continues to surprise climbers – surprises that come despite a tremendous population density and an extensive climbing history. More revelations are in store for Northern climbers who cross the Mason-Dixon line for the first time. The era of travelling to explore new climbing options is not about to end.

Chris Jones' book, *Climbing in North America,* offers the only comprehensive history of climbing on the continent. Because this facinating book presents history by tracing the flow of events instead of simply reciting the facts, it provides very entertaining reading, at home or by fire-light. Everyone interested in the historical development of climbing on this continent is urged to read the book. Published in 1976 for the American Alpine Club, 113 East 90th Street, New York NY 10028, hardback $19.95, paperback $9.95, plus $1.25 postage.

Several other recommended books will be found in the bibliography. These books, the climbing magazines and the guidebooks listed in each chapter form the source material for this essay.

John Harlin photographing Rob Robinson on Golden Locks

photo: Eric Janoscrat

The Tennessee Wall

CHATTANOOGA YELLOW CREEK

HIGHLIGHTS

The city of Chattanooga, Tennessee, is the buckle of the "sandstone belt": its environs hold such a vast quantity of crags that any climber visiting the inland South is bound to center his activities here. Beds of horizontally stratified sandstone, 80 to 130 feet high, crown the green forested hills that surround the city. Sunset Rock, at the top of Lookout Mountain, overlooks town and is one of the more popular climbing cliffs in the mid-South. The Tennessee Wall, just a few miles out of town, was only recently discovered by climbers and has possibly the greatest concentration of routes in the region; its 100 foot high cliff extends unbroken for over two miles. Yellow Creek Falls is 70 miles south, in Alabama, and has probably the tallest cliffs in the sandstone belt: 200 vertical feet of radically overhanging rock. Near Yellow Creek Falls, Sand Rock sprouts an exciting collection of 50 foot boulders. Though these four crags are but a sampling of the vast potential of this little known region, their routes alone could keep a climber busy for many years. With its fine landscape, mild winters, and superb climbing – specializing in steep cracks and roofs – the sandstone belt will likely see a growing number of visiting climbers.

CLIMBING

From downtown Chattanooga, one can spy bands of sandstone on every neighboring hill. In these miles of exposed rock must lie hundreds, if not thousands, of potential routes. It may be decades before they are climbed, however, because these cliffs are outclassed by many others that are unseen from this vantage.

Whatever their location, sandstone cliffs in the Chattanooga region have several things in common. Most noticeable from afar is the uniformity of their size: all are less than 150 feet high, with 80 to 120 feet being most common at the frequented cliffs. From up close, one notices the steepness: all are close to vertical, and vertical down south doesn't just mean steep, it means 90 degrees. For every route that doesn't quite reach 90 degrees, there is one that exceeds it and another that is broken by a horizontal roof. These roofs might protrude three feet, or they might extend thirty feet, with the climbing between roofs being, once again, vertical. Wandering along the base of the cliffs, one notices the profusion of cracks that shoot upwards through the horizontal sedimentary bedding. Sometimes the cracks are discontinuous, but often as not a single fracture can be followed bottom to top. The cracks are usually deep and straight in; they provide excellent jamming, even when splitting a horizontal roof. Though the vast majority of routes follow these cracks, face climbing also plays an important role on Tennessee rock.

The sandstone is solid, often as hard and trustworthy as sedimentary rock ever comes (short of being metamorphosed into something as tough as quartzite). Indeed, the rock here is much more compacted and offers far better fault block cracks than do other sites on the surrounding Cumberland Plateau. Face holds are common and range from tiny edges to major ledges. The blocky nature of the rock frequently permits, or requires, climbing that uses a wild language of body positions, with knee locks, stems, heel hooks and arm bars but a page from the local dictionary. Without such contorsionary antics, the relentlessly steep rock on many routes would soon outwit the merely muscular climber.

Suck Creek, Point Park and Bee Rock Cliffs (a.k.a the Markhams) are three "Nooga" areas that have seen extensive climbing development for a number of years. However, the two crags from Chattanooga's immediate vicinity that were chosen for this book are representative of the finest southern sandstone available. The top of Sunset Rock is accessible in thirty seconds of downhill walking from the car. Getting to the base takes another minute. This extremely popular cliff is 60 to 100 feet high and little more than a hundred yards long. However, there are numerous excellent routes on superbly sound rock on this cliff, while a short walk along the trail in either direction will provide numerous other less extensive outcrops with equally good climbs. Though Sunset Rock is ideally suited to top-roping, leading is most popular here. Just minutes from downtown, Sunset can't be beat for sheer convenience of access. And the view should not be missed either.

Twenty minutes by car from town and twenty minutes by foot from the parking lot is the mid-South's premier cliff: the Tennessee Wall. Not discovered until 1984, it has since become popular with those in quest of new routes or just fine climbing. The cliff averages about 100 to 120 feet high for its two or more miles of unbroken length. More discontinuous cliffs extend for additional miles, while another band of rock lies immediately above. Cracks split the cliff every few tens of feet, with the wall featuring many smooth faces, open corners, narrow aretes. And roofs; above all, roofs. One would be hard pressed to find a greater concentration of overhangs anywhere in North America than are found on the Tennessee Wall. Some of these overhangs, notably **Celestial Mechanics'** 35 feet, are possibly the longest horizontal roofs yet discovered on the continent – at least the longest with free-climbable cracks splitting them. Despite the proliferation of roofs, there are certainly many fine routes whose climbing is less athletic and less difficult.

Seventy miles south, Alabama's Yellow Creek Falls is another area dominated by cracks and overhangs. The cliff is smaller in potential than the Tennessee Wall because it extends for only about a hundred yards, but it is 200 feet high and relentlessly overhanging. Here horizontal roofs are less frequently an obstacle than walls that simply tilt outward. Frequently the two are combined. Few routes are less than 5.10. This area is on private property and special care must be taken to not in any way jeopardize the right of climbers to return here over the years.

Sand Rock is an incredible collection of fantastically shaped boulders about fifty feet in height. Roped lead climbing can be good here, and one 25 foot horizontal roof crack, **Champagne Jam** (5.12 +), is truly awe inspiring. But bouldering is the area's principle calling card, with a vast potential available.

ENVIRONMENT

Climbers may refer to the mid-South as the "Sandstone Belt," but the rest of the world knows it as the "Bible Belt." Religious publishing is one of nearby Nashville's main industries, while the city's "country" musicians belt out harmonious ways to save your soul. Chattanooga is better known for its famous Choo Choo, while the town's industry is simply industry. Yet this is Tennessee's fourth largest city, with a current population of over 170,000, and for those who have never visited the southern United States, Chattanooga offers a taste of its culture.

But the heart of the South lies in its rural environment, for it is here that the region's unique spirit is born. Between the strong accents noticeable at any stop for directions and a subtle change in the architecture of buildings and roads, initial impressions of the South are made.

The physical environment is in many ways distinctive as well. The landscape is heavily forested with deciduous trees (whose leaves remain far longer than those up north). Mixed coniferous forests are common as well, especially on the sandy soil along some ridgetops. This is the Cumberland Plateau, and its rolling terrain has many streams and rivers that have cut sharp, if shallow, canyons and valleys. Because these rivers have also sliced the cliffs out of the sedimentary plateau, water is almost inevitably seen from every climbing area.

The climate is one of the region's great attractions, for while most of the nation lies wrapped in a frozen blanket of snow, the Chattanooga region usually enjoys mild and comfortable weather. Winters have occasional chilly spells that render the rock unappetizing to free climbers, but more often than not the cliffs can be eagerly devoured. As on most of the East Coast, spring can be wet here. Though summers can get hot and humid beyond the liking of most climbers, locals will be found plying the rock at any time of year.

A visiting climber's deeper contacts with the local population might be limited to chatting with fellow climbers, who seem invariably to live up to their reputation for friendliness and hospitability. This appears to be not only a natural Southern trait, but is also born out of a genuine desire to share local climbing with the all-too-rare visitor. The visitor, by his very presence, seems to place Southern climbing on the map – where it deserves to be.

CLIMBING HISTORY

According to Cherokee legend, the mountains surrounding Chattanooga were formed when a great buzzard's wings touched the wet earth. The Cherokees named Chattanooga, which means "Rock Rising to a Point," then suffered when the area's great beauty and development potential attracted so many whites that in 1839 the Cherokees were murderously driven off along what came to be known as "The Trail of Tears." The road to the Tennessee Wall follows this sorrowful trail.

During the Civil War, Lookout Mountain – on which Sunset Rock is found – was the scene of the well known "Battle Above the Clouds," in which the defending Confederates were overrun by Union troops.

But a century passed before rock climbing arrived in Tennessee. In the 1950's and 60's a few widely scattered individuals began practicing the sport, while the Army base in Georgia trained some climbers as well. Still, most Southern climbing took place on the granite walls of the Carolinas; climbers didn't take the South's sandstone belt seriously until the 1970's.

The sandstone climbers were in many ways a separate camp from the granite climbers further east and they brought strong arms to the short cliffs of the Chattanooga region. The cliffs at Yellow Creek Falls were not climbed until 1977, though so much energy was immediately applied that most of the cliff's 50 odd routes (to 5.12) were established by the early 1980's. The Tennessee Wall was not discovered until late 1984 and not climbed until 1985, yet in that year alone 130 routes were established. This might seem like many climbers were at work on the Tennessee Wall; in fact, 90 percent of the routes were established by the same person.

While a few climbers at the top levels can be found down South, the numbers are still small in comparison with most climbing communities. The vast majority of climbers operate at or below the 5.10 level and in fact, most of them have done most of their climbing on trips out West or further east and north – to the Carolinas and Seneca.

Partly in an attempt to pull together the widely scattered and disconnected Southern climbing community, the Tennesee Climbing Association was formed in 1985. Their first two semi-annual meetings were held on weekends in Chattanooga because this area offers the major concentration of Southern climbing (though not climbers). Through the TCA, it was discovered that several hundred climbers exist in the Tennessee/Alabama/Georgia tri-State region. Perhaps once the inevitable world attention begins to turn to the region's incredible roof climbing and mild winter climate, more locals will begin attempting the harder routes here. The first detailed guidebooks to the Chattanooga region appeared in 1986 and will inevitably increase the local standards and number of climbers.

CAMPING

Camping at Yellow Creek Falls traditionally takes place on the road where climbers' cars are parked. Remember that this is private property and special respect must be shown for the environment – and possibly the noise level – to maintain both camping and climbing privileges.

In the Chattanooga region one can camp about half a mile up the trail to the Tennessee Wall. This is a lovely spot with a small stream nearby that has reputably safe drinking water and is on State Forest land. Camping here is legal, but it may be wise to not leave extra belongings in the car (see *RESTRICTIONS AND WARNINGS*).

Another option is the Mountain Air Campground (and hotel) on Lookout Mountain very near Sunset Rock. McFarland Rd; call for reservations: 615-820-2354. Just outside Chattanooga is the Raccoon Mountain Caverns and Campground (I-24 exit 174, then 1½ miles northwest on Highway 41). Telephone: 615-821-9403.

SEASONS AND WEATHER

Approximate Months	Typical Temperatures High	Low	Likelihood of Precipitation	Frequency of Climbable Days
Dec-Feb	50's –	30's	medium	medium
Mar-May	70's +	50's	med-high	med-high
Jun-Sep	90's –	60's	med-low	med-high
Oct-Nov	70's –	50's	medium	med-high

Comments: The Chattanooga vicinity often seems to enjoy better weather than the surrounding region. Rain can usually be avoided by climbing under overhangs. In the case of Yellow Creek, the whole wall overhangs and light rains are irrelevant. In the summer, heat and humidity are the limiting factors.

RESTRICTIONS AND WARNINGS

It cannot be overemphasized that Yellow Creek Falls is on private land with provisional permission to climb. The cliff was only included in this book because of its extremely high quality and historical value. Climbers visiting this area should bear in mind that their actions will determine whether Yellow Creek Falls remains open to climbers.

Be mindful when climbing "in the outback" (cliffs such as the Tennessee Wall and Sandrock) that one should take care to conceal valuables and secure the car against theft. Fortunately, no problems with climbers' cars have yet been reported.

GUIDEBOOKS

Southern Sandstone A Climber's Guide to Chattanooga, Tennessee (1986) by Rob Robinson. This guide covers Sunset Rock and most Chattanooga cliffs except the Tennessee Wall (which was discovered too late for inclusion). Available from Concord Investments, Inc. Suite 175, 3401 West End Building, Nashville, TN 37203. Guides to Yellow Creek Falls and the Tennessee Wall are planned for 1986 by the same author and publisher.

Sunset Rock and miscellaneous other areas (not including Yellow Creek Falls) are also included in *A Climbers Guide to the Mid-South* (1982) by Jim Detterline (Earthbound Enterprises, Rt. 4 Box 667, Chapel Hill, NC 27514) and *Southern Rock* (1981) by Chris Hall (East Woods Press Books, 820 East Boulevard, Charlotte, NC 28203).

GUIDE SERVICES AND EQUIPMENT STORES

No established local guide services are currently available. Contact the Tennessee Climbing Association, P.O. Box 3344, Nashville TN 37219-0344 for help in arranging a partner, instructor, or information on finding a private guide.

Canoeist Headquarters, 4825 Hixson Pike in Chattanooga is the nearest appropriate equipment outfitter.

EMERGENCY SERVICES

For emergency help, dial 911.

The nearest hospitals are the Erlanger Medical Center at 975 East Third Street, telephone: 778-7000; and the Downtown General Hospital at 709 Walnut Street, telephone: 266-7721.

GETTING THERE

Both Greyhound and Trailways serve Chattanooga. Chattanooga also has an airport, though Atlanta, two hours away by car, has the major airport for the region. Sunset could be reached by hitch-hiking, as could Yellow Creek Falls. The Tennessee Wall would have to be hiked into if one didn't have a car.

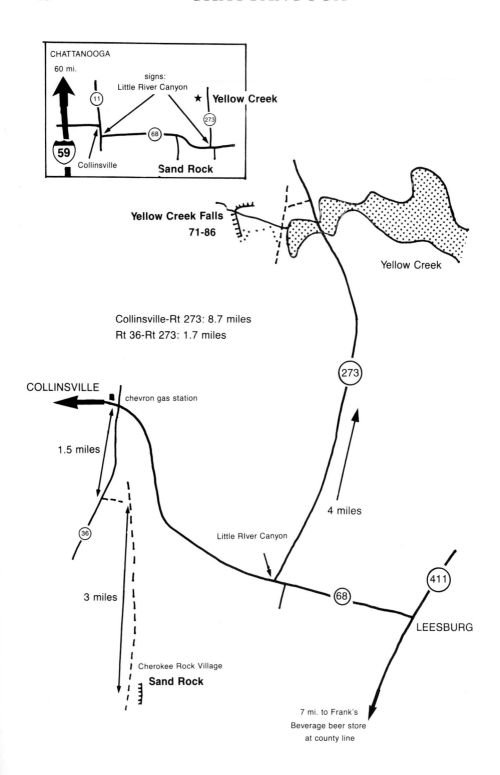

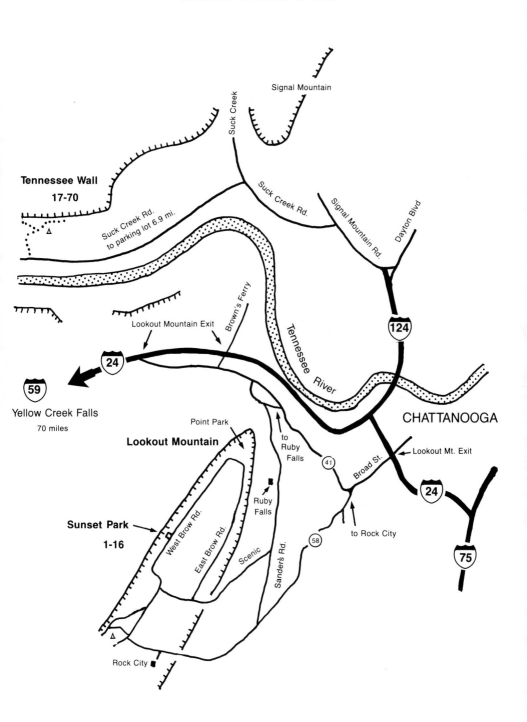

Signal Mountain

Suck Creek

Tennessee Wall
17-70

Suck Creek Rd.
to parking lot 6.9 mi.

Suck Creek Rd.

Signal Mountain Rd.

Dayton Blvd

124

Lookout Mountain Exit

Brown's Ferry

Tennessee River

24

59

Yellow Creek Falls
70 miles

CHATTANOOGA

Point Park

Lookout Mt. Exit

Lookout Mountain

to
Ruby
Falls

41

Broad St.

24

Ruby
Falls

Sunset Park

1-16

West Brow Rd.

East Brow Rd.

Scenic

Sander's Rd.

58

to Rock City

75

Rock City

Sunset Rock

1 **The Diamond** **5.7** Crack with diamond-shaped hole.

2 **Righthand Crack** **5.7** The corner.

3 **Lefthand Crack** **5.8+**

4 **Prisoner of Zenda** **5.11** First lead: Marvin Webb, 1982. Usually top-roped. Start from top of large boulder, wander up face.

5 **Rattlesnake Route** **5.9** FFA: Steve Jenkins, mid-1970's. The outside edge past one bolt, then keep right of two more.

6 **The Headwall** **5.10** First lead: Forrest Gardner, 1981. Usually top-roped. Start 15 feet left of the outside edge with a pebble-studded wall.

7 **Yellowbrick Road** **5.6** Start at right-facing flake.

8 **Alpha Omega** **5.10** FFA: Stan Wallace, early 1970's. Starting at main dihedral, stay left up several corners with small overhangs.

9 **Flagstone** **5.10+** FFA: Rob Robinson and Forrest Gardner, 1981. Ten feet left of main dihedral, climb right-facing corner, large flake, then past two bolts on upper face.

10 **Carte Blanche** **5.11+** Rob Robinson and Forrest Gardner, 1984. Start with the large black roof with finger crack above (**Total Eclipse**), then the **Flagstone** flake, then go right to a rounded groove.

11 **Scream Wall** **5.10−** Dennis Holland and Stephen Lepley, 1974. Climb to and past the short crack 20 feet up. The left variation is even more sustained.

12 **Euphoria** **5.11** Forrest Gardner, Rob Robinson and Marvin Webb, 1981. Stay ten feet left of **Scream Wall Direct**.

13 **Rusty's Crack** **5.9+** The prominent off-width-sized crack through roof.

14 **The Prow** **5.11+** Rob Robinson and Forrest Gardner, 1980. Climb the edge to the ledge, then just left of upper edge, finally traversing back to the prow.

15 **The Pearl** **5.11** FFA: Rob Robinson and Steve Goins, 1978. Start up left-facing corner, then the overhanging dihedral and slot above.

16 **Girdle Traverse** **5.11+** Rob Robinson 1980. Start at **The Pearl** and stay five to fifteen feet above the ground to **Alpha Omega**.

Robyn Erbesfield on Margin of Profit

Robyn Erbesfield on Margin of Profit

Tennessee Wall

All routes, 1985 unless noted.

17 **Magnum Crow** **5.10+** Rob Robinson and Bruce Rogers.

18 **Tough Guys Don't Dance** **5.12** Rob Robinson and Robyn Erbesfield.

19 **Crankenstein** **5.11−** Rob Robinson and Peter Henley.

20 **Tiers for Beers** **5.12−** Rob Robinson and Eric Janoscrat.

21 **Death by Boobalooboo** **5.12−** Forrest Gardner and Peter Henley. FFA: Rob Robinson and Robyn Erbesfield. Twenty foot roof.

22 **Space Sequential** **5.11** Rob Robinson and Robyn Erbesfield. Traverse across black face to crack.

23 **Sugar in the Raw** **5.11−** Rob Robinson, Shannon Stegg and Robyn Erbesfield. Roofs linked by cracks.

24 **March Hare** **5.9+** Marvin Webb and Steve Kerchner. Corner and overhang.

25 **Prerequisite for Excellence** **5.8** Bob Ordner, Roy Briton and Rob Robinson. Orange corner.

26 **No More Tiers** **5.11−** Rob Robinson and Forrest Gardner. Roofs linked by cracks.

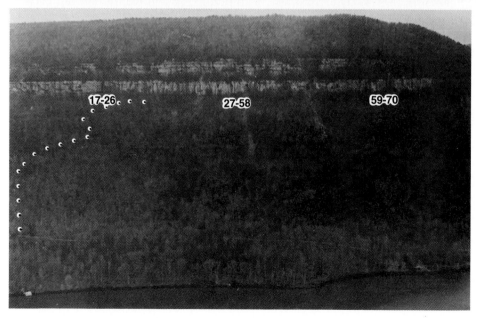

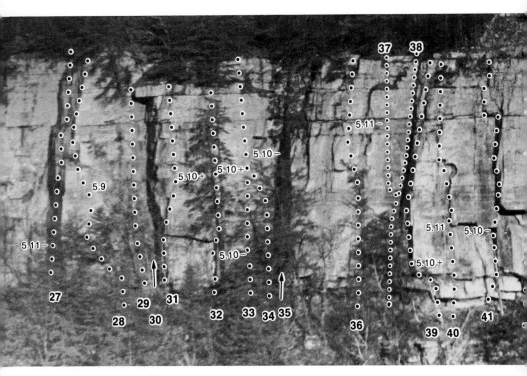

Tennessee Wall

27 Clip and Trip   5.11 –   Robyn Erbesfield, Shannon Stegg and Rob Robinson. Corner to thin cracks.

28 Finagle   5.9   Robyn Erbesfield, Shannon Stegg and Rob Robinson. Face.

29 Dirt Bag   5.8   Peter Henley and Rick Beckman. Crack.

30 In Pursuit of Excellence   5.8 +   Bob Ordner and Rob Robinson. Orange corner.

31 Guardian of the Gate   5.10 +   Rob Robinson and Tom C. Orange arête.

32 Points O' Contact   5.10 +   Rob Robinson, Bob Ordner and Roy Briton. Past roof to parallel cracks.

33 Slay Ride   5.10 +   Rob Robinson and Robyn Erbesfield. Face.

34 Finger Locking Good   5.10 –   Rob Robinson and Jay Dautcher. Finger crack.

35 Jay Walker   5.7   Jay Dautcher (solo). Corner.

36 Fly With the Falcon   5.11 –   Marvin Webb and Steve Kerchner. Crack.

37 The Heaven of Animals   5.11 –   Rob Robinson and Bruce Rogers. Crack, smooth overhang.

38 Puppy Ride   5.9   Peter Henley and Rob Robinson. Corner

39 Steel Puppies   5.10 +   Forrest Gardner and Rob Robinson.

40 Calves of Steel   5.11   Rob Robinson and Jay Dautcher.

41 Reptile Analysis   5.10 –   Forrest Gardner, Bob Ordner and Rob Robinson.

42 Hold Your Horses 5.10− Rob Robinson and Arno Ilgner. Direct start: Forrest Gardner and Robyn Erbesfield.

43 Stone Wave 5.11− Rob Robinson and Peter Henley. FFA: Gene and Laura Smith.

44 Crooked Checkers 5.9 Arno Ilgner and Rob Robinson. Corner.

45 Defcon Five 5.11− Rob Robinson and Tim Cumbo.

46 Mean Cuisine 5.10 Rob Robinson and Peter Henley. Crack to face.

47 Over the Hills and Far Away 5.9 Forrest Gardner and Peter Henley. Slab to high corner.

48 Blind Date 5.6 Sherburne Sentell and John Gore. Wide crack.

49 Digital Macabre 5.10 Marvin Webb and Steve Kerchner. Finger crack above roof.

50 Fill in the Blanks 5.9 Rob Robinson and Peter Henley. Face to arête.

51 Razor Worm 5.9+ Peter Henley and Forrest Gardner. Crack.

52 Cake Walk 5.10− Rob Robinson and Peter Henley.

53 Golden Locks 5.8 Rob Robinson and Marvin Webb.

54 Gravity Creeps 5.10 Rob Robinson and Forrest Gardner.

55 Greenwich Garden Party 5.9+ John Harlin and Rob Robinson. Corner to crack.

56 Nutrasweet 5.7 Robyn Erbesfield and Rob Robinson.

57 Margin of Profit 5.9+ Rob Robinson and Robyn Erbesfield. Thin crack to arête.

58 Hidden Assets 5.10− Rob Robinson and Peter Henley. Hidden corner.

Tennessee Wall

59 People's Express 5.10− Arno Ilgner and John Harlin. Corners. Initial roof poorly protected.

60 Espirit Nuvo 5.10 Rob Robinson and Bruce Rogers. Face. corners.

61 Crackattack 5.10− Rob Robinson and Bruce Rogers.

62 Ravin' Maniac! 5.11+ Rob Robinson and Robyn Erbesfield, 1986. Eight foot roof.

63 Open Sesame 5.8 Steve Goins and Rob Robinson.

64 Skinner Box 5.7+ Rob Robinson and Bruce Rogers.

65 Saddle Light 5.7+ Bruce Rogers and Rob Robinson. Four inch crack.

66 Solar Circus 5.10 Rob Robinson, Curt Merchant and Pat Perrin, 1986.

67 Celestial Mechanics 5.12+ Rob Robinson. Thin crack to 35 foot roof crack; one pitch. The leftmost of parallel roof cracks.

68 Space Dancer 5.10− Rob Robinson and Peter Henley.

69 Self Control 5.11 Mike Artz, Eric Janoscrat and Rob Robinson.

70 Tunnel Vision 5.7+ Eric Janoscrat, Mike Artz and Rob Robinson. Chimney capped by roof.

5.10 —

70

69

67

66

68

Rob Robinson attempting Supernova

Rob Robinson in a "Rambo hang" on Grand Dragon

Rob Robinson on Grand Dragon

Yellow Creek Falls

71 **Feats Don' Fail Me Now** **5.7** Kyle Leftkoff and Tim Snipes, late1970's. Traverse under large roof to vertical corner.

72 **Sweetleaf** **5.9** Shannon Stegg and Jim Okel, 1982.

73 **Grand Dragon** **5.12 −** Shannon Stegg and Jim Okel, 1980. FFA: Rob Robinson, 1983.

74 **Weak Duck** **5.10** Shannon Stegg and Rob Ordner, 1982.

75 **Lords of Discipline** **5.11** Rob Robinson and Gene Smith, 1983.

76 **Firecracker** **5.9** Shannon Stegg and Rich Gottlieb, 1979.

77 **Royal Crown** **5.10** Chick Holtkamp and Rich Gottlieb early 1980's.

78 **Sultans of Swing** **5.10 +** Rich Gottlieb, Shannon Stegg and Jan Shwarzberg, 1980.

79 **The Honeycomb Hangout** **5.11 +** Rob Robinson and Gene Smith, 1983.

80 **Bombs Away!** **5.10 −** Rich Gottlieb and Chick Holtkamp, 1980.

81 **JB Stoney** **5.10 −** Shannon Stegg and Larry Miers, 1980.

82 **White Supremacy** **5.10** Chick Holtkamp and Rich Gottlieb, 1980. Considered one of the finest routes in the East.

83 **Genetic Drift** **5.10** Chick and Chris Holtkamp.

84 **Creepin Jesus** **5.10 +** Rob Robinson and Forrest Gardner, 1983. Somewhat dangerous, but the normal start for Fire Wall.

85 **Quest for Fire** **5.11 +** Rob Robinson and Gene Smith, 1984. Start from the block.

86 **Fire Wall** **5.11** Rob Robinson and Forrest Gardner, 1981.

Looking Glass Rock

LOOKING GLASS WHITESIDES

HIGHLIGHTS

Both Looking Glass Rock and Whitesides Mountain protrude like distorted bubbles from the surrounding hardwood forests. Looking Glass is the primary attraction to climbers who visit deep into North Carolina's Appalachian Mountains. Its rounded granite flanks rise upwards of 400 feet and offer a gamut of routes including crack, face, friction, and aid. Most memorable is a unique feature called "eyebrows" – odd horizontal pockets – which require a unique style of climbing. Whitesides is one of North Carolina's largest cliffs and offers the only Grade V/VI route in the South. Climbing Whitesides is not very popular, however, as its flanks have very few cracks and even fewer bolts. A lack of protection has resulted in few routes.

CLIMBING

Looking Glass rises in a graceful sweep of granite, like a giant snake's head lifting out of the hillside. Following the flanks from the South End, past the Sun Wall, around the northwestern Nose Area and to the North Face, one traces an undulating path about a mile long. Though the rock everywhere on the Looking Glass is extremely solid and smooth, different facets and flanks each offer a unique character.

The South End is most popular in the cool of autumn through spring.

It receives plenty of sun, and its 200 foot height, set at a moderate angle, provides the greatest concentration of continuous cracks and corners. This area has the only extensive collection of moderate routes.

The Sun Wall offers some straight-in cracks, but this section of cliff has a unique character involving watergrooves through wavelike overhangs and "eyebrows." These "eyebrows" are horizontal flaring pockets and are generally climbed by friction/mantling. Occasionally an eyebrow will have a crack in the back which accepts a nut or Friend (#1 Tri-cams are frequently useful), but more often mantling the eyebrow is free of distracting protection. The lower 200 feet of the Sun Wall is steep, above which the angle kicks back radically. Most climbers traverse to rappel trees after the steep section.

The Nose Area holds the most extensive collection of eyebrows and the single most popular route on the Glass: **The Nose.** Four hundred and fifty feet at moderate angle and 5.8 in difficulty, this route features much friction, some crack, and plenty of climbers.

The North Face is almost a separate head on the Looking Glass snake, both in its slightly detached location and in its radically different character. Two-hundred foot crack climbs from 5.9+ to 5.11+ grace the left side, while wildly overhanging 400+ foot A4 and A5 routes blight the right side. Some of the most horrendous aid routes have been put up in 1984 and 1985 by a Tennessee climber who invented a special bashie for horizontal back-of-the-"eyebrow" cracks. These "duckbills" are swaged with a lip (the "bill") on a ring of cable. Placed with a chisel, they provide security that a normal bashie or copperhead couldn't. They should sometimes be backed up and equalized with a set of RURPS. Many "duckbills" have been left fixed by the first ascentionist, but they should probably not be trusted without the RURP backup.

After a rain, certain routes on the Glass can stay wet because of runoff from the vegetation above the cliffs. Most routes, however, dry off quickly in southern sunshine. The first couple of pitches of the **Seal** always stay dry because they lie under an overhang, and are therefore good for rainy day activity. Doing an aid route is another alternative.

The approach for each aspect of the cliff is different, though all are easy 20 minute walks. Alternatively, any part of the cliff can easily be reached from any other via a trail along the base of the cliff.

Whitesides is included in this book not for its breadth of good routes or its popularity, but simply because it offers the largest wall in the South on which climbing is currently legal. It has been popular among rappellers and cavers-in-training because they can make a 400 foot free rappel down the overhanging mid-section of the cliff (where the **Volunteer Wall** goes up). Several shorter routes skirt each edge of the main cliff, while three routes tackle the main 700 foot central section. Most routes to date are predominantly free climbs, while the **Volunteer Wall** is mostly aid. Because the wall is virtually devoid of cracks and very few bolts have ever been placed, all routes tend to be extremely runout. The **Volunteer Wall** requires extensive, sometimes overhanging, hooking, while some other routes don't even have adequate belay anchors.

Whitesides rock is knobby, with many rough face holds. The first ascent party believes that the **Volunteer Wall** could be climbed completely free; however, it will involve 70 foot runouts between bolts on a thin and overhanging face. The falls are said to be safe. If boldness and European limestone climbing skills are ever put to use here, Whitesides might someday provide truly incredible free climbs. Potential first ascentionists are urged to recognize the current tradition of minimal bolting – many local climbers view this issue very seriously. As usual, no bolts should be added to established routes.

Numerous other crags, many with fine cracks, will be found near Whitesides in the Cashiers Valley. To date, guidebooks to this region have been resisted by local climbers.

ENVIRONMENT

The scenic beauty, the wilderness, the hiking trails, waterfalls, river rafting and rock climbing potential of this region of North Carolina are perhaps unexcelled on the East Coast. When one combines these qualities with the southern climate, which permits activity almost throughout the year – and at higher elevations includes a brief ski season – one finds a mecca for outdoor enthusiasts. The summit of Looking Glass is almost 4,000 feet, while nearby mountains reach 6,500 feet; on the East Coast, that's about as high as they come.

The Great Smoky Mountains National Park is a short distance to the northwest, while the Shining Rock Wilderness Area is adjacent. However, Looking Glass and Whitesides are both on National Forest Land – the Pisgah and Nantahala respectively. Interestingly, the Pisgah contains the first land purchased into the National Forest system east of the Mississippi (in 1914). Even before its sale, this forest – part of Vanderbilt's 125,000 acre estate – was also the first land in the U.S. managed by a professional forester. George Vanderbilt wanted a working estate, with controlled use of its forests, water and other resources. His mansion, finished in 1895 as a replica of a 16th century chateau from the Loire Valley of France, is near Asheville. Called Biltmore, it is perhaps more famous than all of the region's scenic attractions combined. Tours are available.

Surrounding the hilltop locations of Looking Glass Rock and Whitesides one will find hardwood forests (sometimes clearcut, as the region is still managed for timber use) and fantastic rhododendron and laurel thickets that bloom profusely in May and June. During the summer months, great flocks of tourists come to play in the many well known waterfalls and swimming holes that abound in the cool mountain streams. The incredibly scenic Blue Ridge Parkway affords an excellent view of Looking Glass's Nose. Four hundred and fifty miles long, the Parkway reaches its southern terminous near here in Great Smoky Mountain National Park. Despite the southern latitude, this section of the road shuts down for much of the winter and is used as a cross-country ski trail.

CLIMBING HISTORY

The origins of climbing in the Looking Glass area were later than, and independent from, developments elsewhere in North Carolina. In the early 1960's kids were taught to rappel from trees at a camp near Hendersonville, but rock climbing began at the nearby Devil's Courthouse in 1964. The instigators of both tree and rock antics went to the Rocky Mountains to learn more about climbing, and brought back with them a new perspective on the Looking Glass. In 1966 **The Nose** was climbed. Taking a superb line in a fantastic position on outrageously good rock, this route has never been outclassed on the Glass. At a 5.8 standard, it is accessible to most climbers and yet is still a challenge; thus it has remained the area favorite. In fact, no additional routes were even put up until the end of the 1960's.

During the early 70's, when climbing took on new popularity along with all the outdoor wilderness activities in North Carolina, many new routes quickly appeared on the Glass. The **Original Route** on Whitesides was also established – an impressive accomplishment for its era. In 1975, a whirlwind visit by a New England rock star introduced 5.11 to the Looking Glass, while simultaneously a small group of climbers were developing an extremely bold style. **Free Man in Paris,** which connects poorly protected "eyebrows" and has been nicknamed "Dead Man in Pisgah," and routes on Whitesides, where sometimes even belays lack adequate anchors, were climbed at this time.

Locals put up a few more routes to 5.11+ on the Glass during the ensuing years, but activity slowed dramatically as the 1970's closed. The lack of natural lines undoubtedly played a role, along with the small number of climbers. Also, vast quantities of little publicized rock in the region, especially in the Cashiers Valley, diverted attention.

A few hard aid climbs were established on the overhanging section of the North Face during the 1970's, while sections of the long routes on Whitesides also required some aid. Not until the mid 1980's was there an awakening to the aid potential of unclimbed lines on both cliffs. Two Tennessee climbers independently sized up lines that had been deemed unclimbable and brought new techniques to bear. On the Glass, "duckbills" were part of the solution, while on Whitesides it involved a willingness to move up the overhanging wall on hooks. Both solutions also involved fresh perspectives and boldness.

CAMPING

Many climbers camp where the cars are parked for the trail accessing the **Nose** area. A prettier site can be found a short walk up the trail from the South End parking spot. Water can be found here as well, though it should be treated. A number of motels and all the city conveniences can be found in Brevard.

SEASONS AND WEATHER

Approximate Months	Typical Temperatures High	Low	Likelihood of Precipitation	Frequency of Climbable Days
Dec-Mar	40's +	20's	Low-med	med-high
Apr-Jun	70's −	40's	medium	high-med
Jul-Aug	80's +	60's	med-high	high
Sep-Nov	70's −	40's	med-low	high

Comments: Afternoon thundershowers are common in the summer. This area of the Pisgah National Forest is second only to the Pacific Northwest in annual precipitation. Sunny faces allow winter climbing despite a low ambient temperature.

RESTRICTIONS AND WARNINGS

Observe the usual environmental precautions to maintain the beauty of this National Forest. Switchbacks should not be shortcut.

Be sure not to venture onto Whitesides routes unless confident and qualified for extremely long runouts.

GUIDEBOOKS

The Climber's Guide to North Carolina (1986) by Thomas Kelley. Earthbound Books, P.O. Box 3445, Chapel Hill, NC 27515.

Southern Rock: A Climber's Guide (1981) by Chris Hall, is out of date. East Woods Press, 820 East Boulevard, Charlotte, NC 28203.

GUIDE SERVICES AND EQUIPMENT STORES

The Looking Glass Guides, P.O. Box 5292, Asheville, NC 28813, telephone: 704-258-4571.

In Asheville, stores include: Mountaineering South, 791 Merrimon Avenue and Black Dome Mountain Shop, 2 Biltmore Plaza.

EMERGENCY SERVICES

In an emergency, call 911. The Transylvania County Rescue Squad is little experienced at cliff rescues.

The nearest hospital is the Transylvania County Hospital on Highway 64 just north of Brevard. Telephone: 884-9111.

GETTING THERE

There is an airport near Asheville, which can also be reached by bus or train.

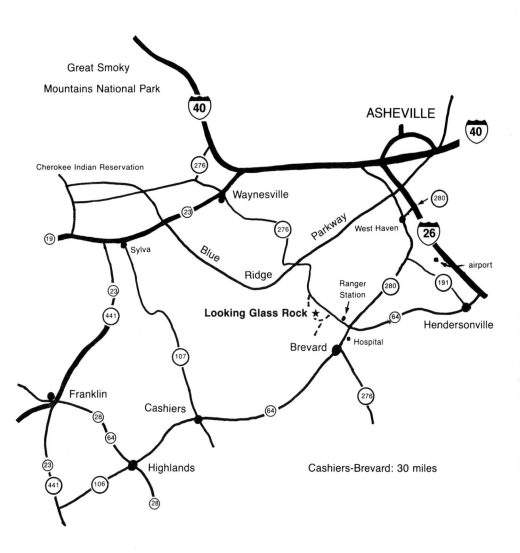

Great Smoky Mountains National Park

ASHEVILLE

Cherokee Indian Reservation

Waynesville

West Haven

airport

Sylva

Blue

Ridge

Parkway

Ranger Station

Looking Glass Rock ★

Hendersonville

Brevard

Hospital

Franklin

107

Cashiers

Highlands

Cashiers-Brevard: 30 miles

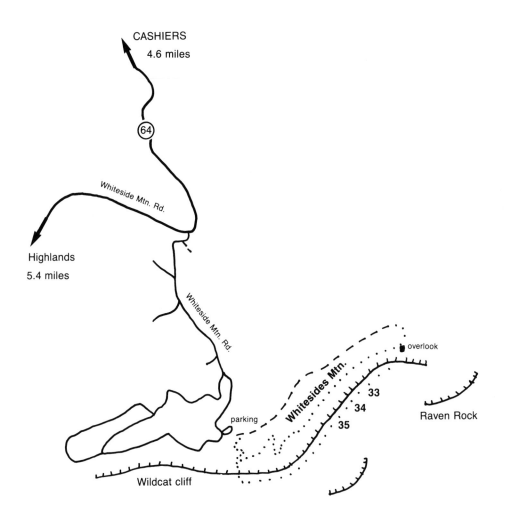

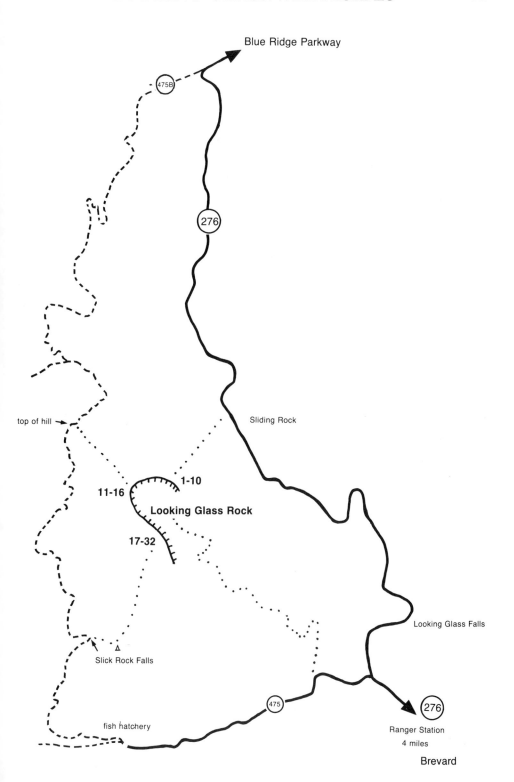

Blue Ridge Parkway

475B

276

Sliding Rock

top of hill →

1-10

11-16

Looking Glass Rock

17-32

Looking Glass Falls

Slick Rock Falls

475

276

Ranger Station
4 miles

fish hatchery

Brevard

North Face
1-10

11

Nose Area
12-16

Sun Wall
17-21

South End
22-32

Looking Glass Rock – North Face

1 **The Sperm** **5.9+** Brad Shaver and Bob Mitchell, 1971. FFA: Brad Shaver and Grover Cable, 1976.

2 **The Womb** **5.11+ or 5.9+ C1** Steve Longenecker and Bob Gillespie, 1970. FFA: Brad Shaver and Diff Ritchie.

3 **Safari Jive** **5.11+** Jeep Gaskin and Don Hanley, 1979

4 **Cornflake Crack** **5.11−** Art Williams and M. Holloway, 1972. FFA: Henry Barber and Rick Hatch, 1975.

5 **The Seal** **5.10** Bob Mitchell and Will Fulton, 1969. FFA: M. James. The first pitch is a good rainy-day route

6 **Invisible Airwaves** (first pitch) **5.10+** Jeff Burton, Whitney Hevermann, 1985

7 **The Brain Wall** **5.10+ A5** Forrest Gardner, Greg Allen and Bob Ordner, 1985

8 **Secret Alloys** **5.10 A5** Forrest Gardner and Rob Robinson, 1985. This is a direct finish to the **Rollins Route** A4 Chris Rollins (rope solo), 1984

9 **Glass Menagerie** **5.11 A3+** Jeep Gaskin and John Borstelmann

10 **Chieftains of Creep** **5.11 A4** Forrest Gardner and Rob Robinson, 1985.

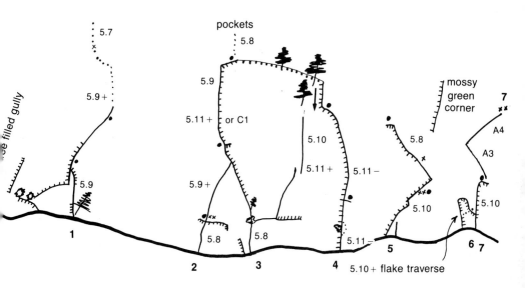

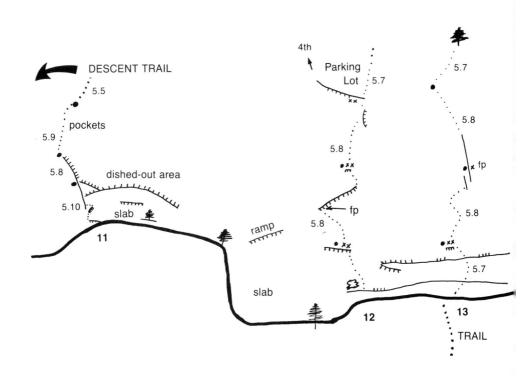

The Nose Area

11 Dum De Dum Dum   5.10 Brad Shaver and Bob Gillespie, 1972. FFA: Bob Mitchell and Ron Cousins, 1972.

12 The Nose   5.8 Bob Gillespie, Steve Longenecker and B. Watts, 1966. The Looking Glass classic.

13 Sundial   5.8 Bob Mitchell and Will Fulton, 1972.

14 Hyperbola   5.10 Percy Wimberly and J. Seay, 1975. FFA: Diff Ritchie, Jeep Gaskin and Bob Rotert. Very bad fall potential on 5.9 friction traverse.

15 Psychedelic Delusions of the Digital Man?   5.9 A3 Jeff Burton, Mark Stroud and Bill Tennent, 1985.

16 Odyssey   5.11 Bob Mitchell and Art Williams, 1972. FFA: Jeep Gaskin.

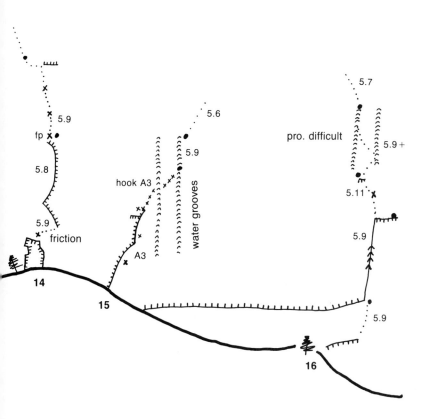

5.7

pro. difficult

5.9 +

fp

5.9

5.8

hook A3

5.9

5.11

water grooves

5.9

5.9

friction

A3

14

15

16

5.6

5.9

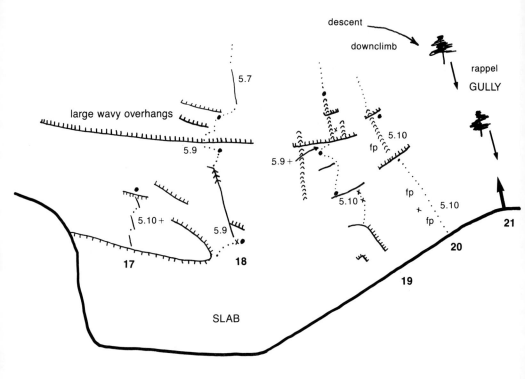

Sun Wall
17 Out To Lunch   5.10 Henry Barber and Rick Hatch, 1975.
18 Tits and Beer   5.9 Bob Rotert and partner.
19 Pat Ewing   5.10 Jeep Gaskin.
20 Nick Danger Third Eye   5.10 Jeep Gaskin.
21 Southender   5.8 Steve Wallace and Ron Cousins, 1972.

David Hessler on T and B

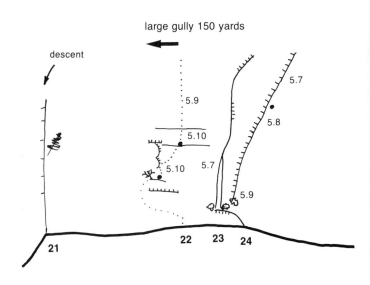

South Side

22 Dinkas Dog 5.10− Jeep Gaskin, Charlton Durant and Jeff Burton, 1979.

23 Fat Dog 5.7 Stan Wallace (solo), 1973.

24 Unfinished Concerto 5.9 P. Farram and H. Foreshipps.

25 Rat's Ass 5.8 Stan Wallace, Ron Cousins, Jim McEver and Art Williams, 1973.

26 Second Coming 5.7 Stan Wallace, Ron Cousins, Jim McEver and Art Williams, 1972.

27 First Return 5.8 Ron Cousins and Art Williams, 1972.

28 Gemini Cracks 5.8 Jim McEver and D. Broemel, 1973.

29 Zodiac 5.8+ Follow pockets.

30 Left Up 5.7 Stan Wallace and Jim McEver, 1973.

31 Right Up 5.8 Jim McEver, M. Woussey and Blair Ritter, 1974.

32 Bloody Crack 5.8 Stan Wallace, Jim McEver and Ron Cousins, 1973.

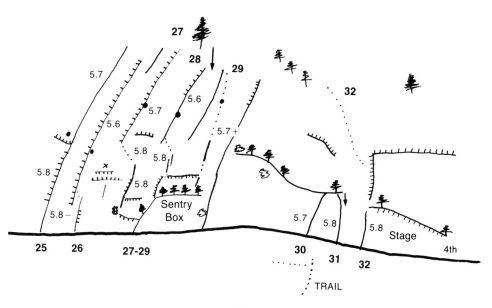

Eddy Whittemore on Volunteer Wall photo: Arno Ilgner

Whitesides   photo: Arno Ilgner

Whitesides   photo: Arno Ilgner

Whitesides   photo by Arno Ilgner

All routes are very runout, especially on the easier climbing. The **Original Route** is the best introduction to Whitesides climbing.

33 Original Route   5.9 A0 or 5.10 John Lawrence, John Whisenant, Peter Young and Jim Marshall, 1971. FFA: Bob Rotert and partner, 1977.

34 New Diversions   5.10 Bob Rotert and Thomas Kelley, 1982. FFA: Arno Ilgner and Thomas Kelley, 1986. To the Escape, the first ascent was by Bob Rotert, Keith Robinson and Peter Young in 1981.

35 Volunteer Wall   V/VI 5.10 A4 Arno Ilgner, Mark Cartwright and Eddy Whittemore, 1985.

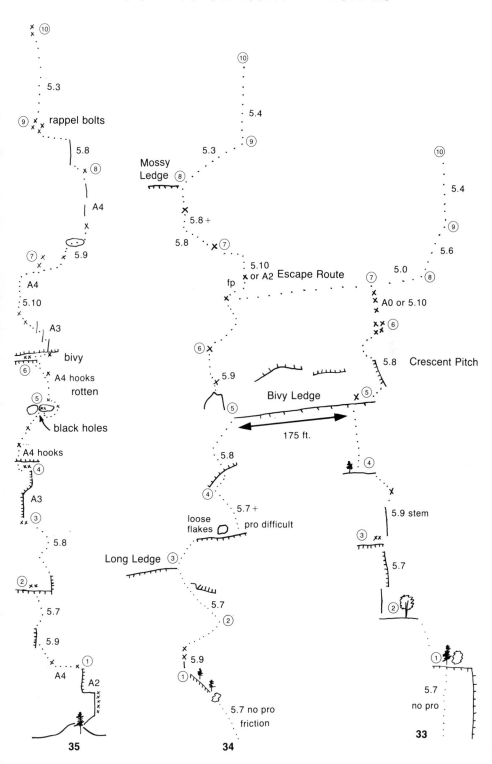

East Side of Table Rock

The Ampitheater

LINVILLE GORGE

HIGHLIGHTS
Nearly 2,000 feet from rim to river, North Carolina's Linville Gorge is the deepest canyon in the East. Because its flanks were too steep for early logging equipment, it is one of the few remaining virgin forests along the Eastern Seaboard. Timbercutters may have been repulsed by the rugged landscape, but climbers from throughout the South have made this one of the region's most popular rock climbing areas. Along the upper reaches of Jonas Ridge, 200 to 600 foot cliffs rise out of jungles of laurel, rhododendron, brambles and alder. Most popular among climbers and picnickers alike is Table Rock Mountain, which lifts into the Blue Ridge sky, providing views that extend east to the Piedmont and west to ridge after ridge of Appalachian mountains. The rock is a peculiar metamorphosed sandstone or quartzite that is universally steep, usually solid, and often crackless. Though access is simple, some cars will object to the last leg of the tortuous nine mile dirt road.

CLIMBING
The climbing experience varies greatly between the several cliffs along Jonas Ridge which form the Gorge's east rim. First encountered and dominating the ridge, is Table Rock Mountain. Table projects 500 feet above the ridge, with cliffs of half that height wrapping its eastern and northern exposures. Ledge systems, often forested, break the continuity of most of these walls, but between the ledges is clean quartzite.

  This quartzite has a unique character, one that might bring a moment of pause and an increased heart rate at critical times of the lead. The rock has been metamorphosed into slightly wavy shapes that look almost like shale, except that it is quite solid. Some mica schist and gneiss will also be found. The pause and adrenaline come when one notices that these wavy edges often tilt downwards, providing less agreeable footing than one might expect from the land of Southern Hospitality. Friendly routes that follow upward-trending cracks certainly exist, but the climbing is dominated by faces where only the occasional crack is encountered and many of those that are found are horizontal. Nevertheless, locating adequate protection is rarely considered a serious problem. A number of 5.5 to 5.7 routes that ascend a less steep section of Table Rock are entirely bolt protected and provide excellent routes that are perhaps the most popular climbs on the rock.

Table Rock is easily reached in ten minutes by a good trail from the parking area, and it can be descended by an even better picnicker's trail from the summit, though some people either scramble off or rappel down before reaching the top. And unless the crag intrudes into a rain cloud, as often happens in the winter and spring, the views from the belay ledges are some of the most expansive and magnificent in the South. Not surprisingly, Table Rock is the most popular cliff at Linville.

Equally accessible is the Chimneys, a fascinating jumble of rocks that are often top-roped. Not boulders, these miniature cliffs (averaging twenty to forty feet) are a confused mass of rocks that perch along a narrow section of the ridge. A hiking trail weaves through the Chimneys, and interested spectators are not uncommon while climbers dangle and thrash on any number of routes. Near the start of the Chimneys, one cliff has a large eye bolt on its summit that is used as a top-rope anchor.

From the far side of the Chimneys, narrow and barely noticable trails cut into the undergrowth. After a few minutes of walking through the dense shrubbery, the forest suddenly opens and the ground drops away beneath one's feet. The view across the Gorge clearly shows the ruggedness of this wild area and, by taking a right at the trail fork, one can catch a glimpse of the climbing objective: the North Carolina Wall. A steep scramble down a gully puts one at the base of the long wall.

Almost 500 feet high by 2,000 feet long, the North Carolina Wall has a number of fine routes that exploit the major weaknesses in the rock. But the weaknesses are few and often disconnected, making for sometimes devious climbing. First impressions can focus on a vegetated and disillusioning section of cliff, but in fact the crag is basically clean and has some fine and exposed climbing that presents a good feel for this wild area.

Just past the North Carolina Wall is the Ampitheater, a chasm cleaved out of the hillside and lined with cliffs. Most popular are the Prow (actually the southernmost extention of the NC Wall) and the Mummy Buttress. Both offer tremendously exposed climbing with a great diversity of difficulties, from airy and exciting 5.4 to overhanging 5.11. The Mummy Buttress is up to 600 feet high, and steep for most of the way. Both the North Carolina Wall and the Ampitheater area have rock that is more horizontally striated and has more cracks than that of Table Rock. Some large exfoliated sections will also be found; these, like the Bumblebee Buttress, provide occasional corner systems.

A word of warning for those in the Ampitheater who want to check out the North Carolina Wall – go over the top. Traversing under the cliff is a long and arduous bushwack through bramble-filled underbrush.

Table Rock, the North Carolina Wall, and the Ampitheater area offer the most popular climbing at Linville. Other cliffs exist as well, including Wiseman's View across the Gorge, Hawksbill further up the ridge, and Shortoff Mountain at the southern end of Jonas Ridge. These areas are disconnected from the areas included in this book, but some of them provide outstanding climbing.

CLIMBING HISTORY

The Linville area was named for William Linville and his son, who were scalped by Indians in 1766 while exploring the region. But the Linvilles had other concerns besides climbing, and it was not until the late 1950's or early 1960's that some preliminary crag exploration was done with hemp ropes. At that time North Carolina rock climbing was in its infancy and nothing significant to climbing history came of these explorations. Initial development in the state focused on the most accessible cliffs, including Moore's Wall, Stone Mountain and Looking Glass.

In the late 1960's, the North Carolina Outward Bound School was established within clear sight and a short hike of Table Rock. Its staff

helped to intiate the growth of climbing in Linville, and soon the
Appalachian State University in nearby Boone fielded climbers to the
Gorge as well.

During the early to mid 1970's, a suddenly blossoming number of
young climbers in the South initiated a spurt of climbing development
in the Gorge area. Interest in the Gorge flowered as a direct outgrowth
of the environmental movement of the period, and though new route
activity has not quite kept pace with the initial burst, interest in climbing
has continued unabated into the 1980's. Despite such interest in the
sport and the popularity of the Gorge, outright crowding is rare –
perhaps limited to the major college holidays.

ENVIRONMENT

The churning maelstrom of the Linville River flows 1,500 feet below the
Table Rock parking area on the east rim of the Gorge, while Wiseman's
View, on the opposite rim (the Linville Mountain side) is less than 6,000
feet away. The intervening space is rugged and wild – so rugged that it
avoided the timbercutters' axes and so wild that it was declared one of
the first Wilderness Areas in the East. The area was initially designated
"wild" in 1951, partly in recognition of the many rare plants that grow
in this unmolested valley. Rhododendrons of four species grow thick as
corn in Kansas, making a jungle of tangles away from the trails and a
riot of flowers in late spring and early summer. Mountain laurel, sand
myrtle and a healthy complement of very healthy thorny vines further
snare hikers who stray from the trails.

But vistas are spectacular where cliffs break the jungle's continuity.
Table Rock is especially impressive; from its promontory the eye travels
in a 360 degree sweep, from the hills that taper into the pancake-flat
Piedmont to the east, down past the Chimneys and the flow of the
Linville River to the south, to multiple ridges of the Appalachian
Mountains to the west (including the highest peak on the East Coast,
6,684 foot Mt Mitchell). In the north, one spies more Eastern-style
mountains (rounded and vegetated) and a peculiar monolith in the
distance. The monolith is a condominium complex at a ski area, and its
incredible visibility has since spawned laws restricting such developments
– unfortunately, the laws do not extend retroactively.

Vistas from the Linville area often show a bluish tint for which the
Blue Ridge Mountains were named. It results from the composition of
particulate matter in the air; however, industrial pollution is changing
that tint to white or brown in much of Blue Ridge country.

The North Carolina Wall to the Mummy Buttress is cut out of the
upper flank of the Gorge, and views are not quite as panoramic as those
from Table; still, one can trace the length of the Linville River flowing
a thousand feet below and clearly audible from the cliff.

On a cool day in the Ampitheater, one might hear the chattering of shivering teeth instead. The cleft seems to collect cold air, which breezes downwards past the climber with an unexpected chill.

Besides its official designation as a Wilderness Area, another indicator of the wildness of this region (at least by East Coast standards) is the location of the North Carolina Outward Bound School directly beneath Table Rock. OB students make frequent use of these hills, and classes sometimes fill the easier routes on Table Rock.

The only way to obtain a good view of Linville's cliffs is to drive to the other side of the Gorge. Wiseman's View is particularly easy to get to and might prove a good stop before driving up to Table Rock.

CAMPING

The Table Rock parking and picnic area is adjacent to the Wilderness Area border. Permits are required to camp within the Wilderness Area on weekends from May through October, and the picnic area is posted against camping, but one is allowed to camp almost anywhere in the National Forest on the east slope of the ridge. For permits, contact the District Ranger's Office in Marion, telephone: 704-652-4841, during business hours or by mail: P.O. Box 519, Marion, NC 28752. Permits are issued first-come first-served beginning on the first working day of the *previous* month.

Facilities at the picnic area include tables, outhouses and garbage cans. Water is available from a cistern a half-mile from the parking lot along a trail leading into the Gorge. Walk to the saddle betwen Little Table Rock and Table Rock, then go north. The cistern is not marked; until one is sure of finding it, it may prove safer to bring one's own. Be sure to have all supplies with you; few people will want to subject their cars or themselves to the dirt road drive more often than necessary.

SEASONS AND WEATHER

Approximate Months	Typical Temperatures High	Low	Likelihood of Precipitation	Frequency of Climbable Days
Dec-Mar	50's −	20's	med-high	med-low
Apr-Jun	70's +	40's	high-med	med-high
Jul-Aug	90's	70's	medium	med-low
Sep-Nov	70's	40's	med-low	high

Comments: Spring, when dry, is particularly beautiful because of blooming wildflowers. Fall foliage is also exciting. Winter is extremely variable – from shirt-sleeve to blizzard. Mid-summer can be very hot.

RESTRICTIONS AND WARNINGS

Permits were required to climb in the Linville Gorge Wilderness Area until it was determined that climbers had very little impact on the environment. At this time, no permits are required for day use, but are required for some overnighting (see *CAMPING*).

During hunting season (around the Thanksgiving holidays) the area is inundated with guns and their operators. Table Rock is relatively safe, but other areas require caution.

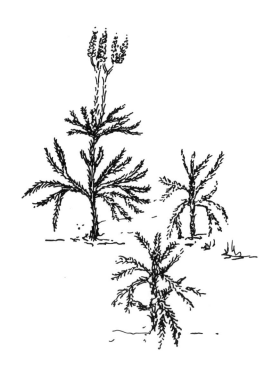

GUIDEBOOKS

The Climber's Guide to North Carolina (1986) by Thomas Kelley. Earthbound Books, P.O. Box 3445, Chapel Hill NC 27515.

  Southern Rock: A Climber's Guide (1981) by Chris Hall. East Woods Press Books, 820 East Boulevard, Charlotte, NC 28203.

GUIDE SERVICES AND EQUIPMENT STORES

The nearest equipment store is in the college town of Boone, an hour's drive north of Table Rock: Footsloggers, 835 Faculty Street. A guide could be obtained from The Looking Glass Guides, P.O. Box 5292, Asheville, NC 28813, telephone: 704-258-4571, or from the guiding service operating out of Paddling Unlimited, 6208 Yadkinville Road, Pfafftown, NC 27040, telephone 919-945-3744.

EMERGENCY SERVICES

The speediest rescue could probably be obtained by contacting the Outward Bound School a mile and a half from the Table Rock parking lot (also the nearest phone). The nearest hospital is in Morganton: Grace Hospital, 2201 South Sterling, telephone: 438-2000.

GETTING THERE

A car is almost mandatory for reaching the climbing areas at Linville Gorge. The last mile of a six mile dirt road is both steep and rutted; some cars may be inappropriate for this section.

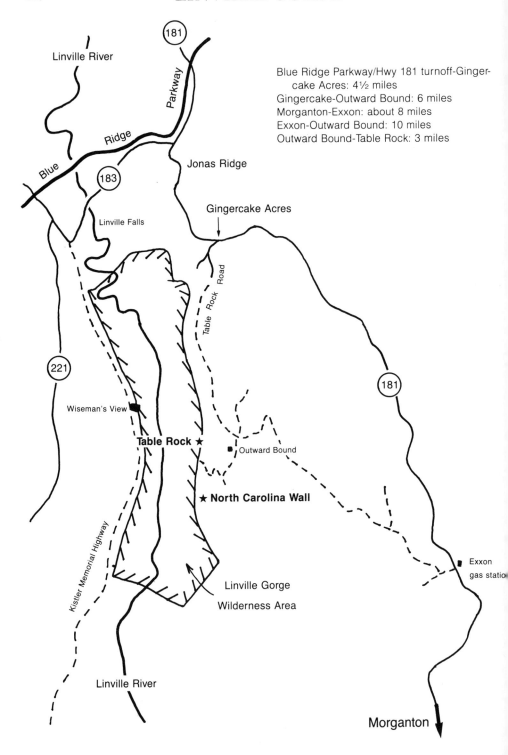

Blue Ridge Parkway/Hwy 181 turnoff-Gingercake Acres: 4½ miles
Gingercake-Outward Bound: 6 miles
Morganton-Exxon: about 8 miles
Exxon-Outward Bound: 10 miles
Outward Bound-Table Rock: 3 miles

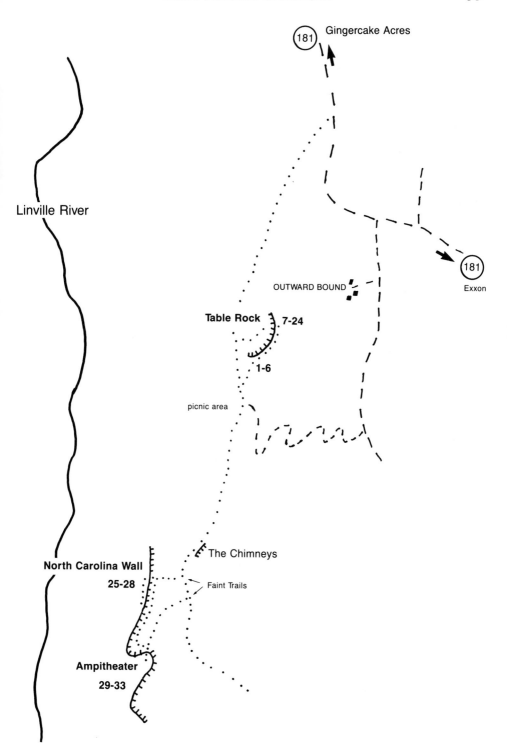

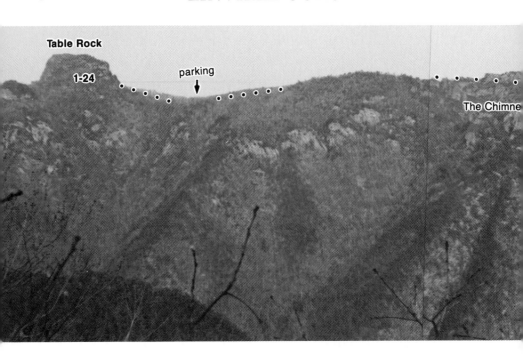

Monster Buttress

25-28
North Carolina Wall

29-35
Ampitheater

Table Rock – South Side

1 **Fresh Garbage** **5.10 –** Bob Rotert and Diff Ritchie, 1976.
2 **Crackerjack** **5.8**
3 **Hang 'Em High** **5.9** G. Jacobson and Porter, 1972. FFA: Brad Shaver and Mick Craig, 1974.
4 **Hang Hog variation** **5.9** Tom Howard and Jim Okal, 1981.
5 **Morning Woman (Mourning Maiden)** **5.10 –** Brad Shaver and Diff Ritchie, 1976. The first pitch has cut ropes if not belayed where indicated.
6 **Two Pitch** **5.3** Jim Anthony et al, 1948. Follow bolts.

Table Rock – East Side

7 Blood, Sweat and Tears 5.7 Jim Daly et al, 1973.

8 Wedding Present 5.10 Pete Nobles and Lyle Dean, 1980.

9 Rip Van Winkle 5.7 Tim McMillan and P. Cobb, 1972.

10 Wasp 5.5 Mickey Craig, Charlie Page and Jim Anthony, about 1974.

11 Peek-A-Boo 5.5 Bob Gillespie and Bob Mitchell, 1970.

12 Peek-A-Boo Left 5.10 – Joe Coates et al, 1978.

13 Jim Dandy 5.5 FA: Outward Bound, late 1960's. Follow bolts.

14 Skip to my Lou 5.6 FA: Outward Bound, late 1960's. Follow bolts.

15 Helmet Buttress 5.6 Tom Howard, Jim Daley and Mickey Craig, 1973.

16 No Workman's Compensation 5.6 Roy Davis and Andy Damp, 1970.

17 Cave Route 5.5 Bolts.

18 Northeast Passage 5.11 Jim Downs and Tom Howard, 1980.

19 Block Route 5.6

20 Opa 5.9 + Arno Ilgner and John Harlin, 1985. Runout.

21 My Route 5.6 Follow bolts.

Table Rock – North End

22 Second Stanza 5.9 John Lawrence and C. Sproull, 1968. FFA: Bob Gillespie, Roy Davis and Steve Longenecker, 1970. Excellent route.

23 White Light 5.8 + Peter Young and John Lawrence about, 1972. Left start is the popular **True Grit** start (5.9 –).

24 North Ridge 5.5 Bob Gillespie and Bob Mitchell, 1970. The classic.

Arno Ilgner on Opa

Arno Ilgner on Table Rock

Monster
Buttress

North Carolina Wall

25 Rinky Dink 5.10 Bob Mitchell, Brad Shaver and Art Williams, 1972. FFA: Jim Okall, Shannon Stegg and Tom Howard, 1980. Excellent mostly 5.8 climbing. Crux is on second pitch, with the traverse very unprotected for follower.

26 Bumblebee Buttress **5.8−** Bob Mitchell and Bob Gillespie, 1970. The classic.

27 The Corner **5.7** Art Williams and Mike Holloway, 1971.

28 Mitzeitzusparen **5.9+** Tom Howard and Dan Perry, 1980.

photo: Thomas Kelley

Ampitheater

29 Prow   **5.4**   Art Williamson, M. Calkins and Andy Damp, 1970.

30 Openbook   **5.11 or 5.10 A0**   G. Jacobson and G. Harder, 1972. FFA: Bob Rotert and Anderson, 1978. The stunning right-slanting dihedral. The first move into the dihedral is the crux; the rest is 5.10 and is possibly the best pitch in the Gorge.

31 Trinidad   **5.9+**   Thomas Kelley, Ralph Fickel and Aric Kast, 1985. #1 Friend useful at third belay.

32 Brothers   **5.7+**

33 Mummy   **5.6**   Bob Gillespie, Bob Mitchell and Steve Longenecker. A local classic.

34 Daddy   **5.6**   First known ascent: Art Williams and Mike Holloway, 1972. One of the longest and most classic routes in the Gorge.

Mummy Buttress photo: Thomas Kelley

South Face

Strawberry Preserves

STONE MOUNTAIN

HIGHLIGHTS

Stone Mountain fulfills all dreams and expectations of climbing in the South. A gentle 600 foot granite dome, its flanks are comfortably laid back in the foothills of the Blue Ridge Mountains, with expansive views extending eastward over the Piedmont. Across an open meadow, a park bench faces the glimmering white cliff, while nearby picnic tables sit under the shade of tall green trees. South facing, the smooth friction slabs hold the sun's warmth and climbers often ascend shirtless in winter. But the Rebel spirit lurks beneath Stone's smile. Winter's comfort becomes summer's inferno, and sweaty palms in any season can precipitate horrendous grounding sliders if friction is lost. Stone Mountain slabs have a unique character, with wavy ridges for holds that are almost face but definitely friction. Bolt protection often seems widely spaced unless you are as familiar with this style of climbing as the locals who, when put on the sharp end of the rope, belie their seeming geniality.

CLIMBING

It has been said that Stone's slabs rest at the perfect angle. Because most holds are rounded and the climber relies on friction to stay put, the rock could not be much steeper without making climbing impossible. On the other hand, if it were any lower angled, most climbs would become mere walk-ups. Indeed, other slabs found near Stone are not climbed because of their low angle.

Six hundred feet high (as measured on the rock) and over 2,500 feet wide, Stone's great South Face sports less than fifty routes, while the North Face holds but a dozen. Climbs tend to follow the few natural lines, such as the prominent brown water streaks, occasional dikes, and rare cracks and corners. Where features are absent, routes follow the lines of least resistance past widely spaced bolts.

Bolts are, in fact, the principal method of protection on almost all Stone Mountain routes. Though the tremendously popular **Great Arch** follows a crack for four pitches, it is unique. Most routes, whether they involve identifiable features or blank rock, rely almost exclusively on bolts. These bolts are actually maintained by local climbers; older, less safe bolts are usually, but not necessarily, replaced. Visitors should still inspect bolts and hangers because, like bolts anywhere else, they can never be completely trusted. *NEVER* hit a bolt or hanger with a hard object and don't add any new bolts.

Runouts have developed for several reasons, not the least of which is simply a tradition for boldness. Though one might think of Southerners as laid-back and easy going, there is often an underlying competitiveness that demands expression.

Just as inducive to runouts, however, is the type of climbing at Stone Mountain. The rounded friction-edges (on rock that is completely solid and non-granular, yet was never glacially polished) are basically variations on a theme. They take getting used to, but soon seem repetitive. Many North Carolina climbers find that once they have developed the knack, the climbing at Stone can become boring if repeated too often. The occasional completely unprotected routes might never become boring, but they lack a certain appeal.

In fact, though climbs are often runout, groundfall-potential routes are rare. On friction slabs, long falls rarely result in more than scrapes and burns. To minimize these – while the belayer takes in rope quickly – the falling leader tries to stay on his feet, even running downhill.

For falls that take place above a bolt but still on the first pitch, there is a special belaying technique used extensively at Stone Mountain. The rope is run through a carabiner attached to a sling at the base of a tree. The belayer is not anchored in any way, allowing him to run into the woods during a fall, thus pulling up all the slack. With sufficient skill, the leader can be stopped at the bolt! It helps to have a clear path to run on that has been pre-planned and to use a mechanical belaying device.

This isn't to say that all routes are frighteningly runout. Climbers of most temperaments will find enjoyable climbing at Stone, though the timid will have to choose routes especially carefully. Needless to say, the advent of sticky rubber shoes has made climbing much more secure. Ratings on older routes have retained their traditional grading in this book. The newest routes were put up with sticky rubber and graded as such.

Stone is ideal as a winter area because the climbing requires delicacy and balance instead of strength. Thus out-of-shape climbers from the frozen North will find their bodies don't limit them – only their minds.

A few comments must be made concerning equipment needs. Most important is that many bolt hangers will not accept "blind gate" carabiners. Be sure to have at least several 'biners with narrow gates, or bring wire stoppers that can be threaded through hangers. For some routes a light rack is useful, though often carabiners and slings suffice.

Climbing new routes is currently officially banned by the Park administration.

ENVIRONMENT

With 10,000 acres of rolling, forested hills, Stone Mountain is the largest State Park in the North Carolina system. Several of these hills have granite dome outcroppings, though only Stone itself is steep enough to be of interest to climbers. Stone Mountain has a circumference of about four miles, with rock replacing the wooded slopes only on the north and south sides. While trail systems lace the State Park and provide beautiful hiking, no major trail serves the north side of the rock, and consequently, it receives much less visitation.

One of Stone's special delights is its typically mild winter climate. Unlike Looking Glass and Linville Gorge, Stone sits below the nearby Blue Ridge Mountains, not in them. The crag's most popular face has a southern exposure, which allows climbers on the reflecting white cliff to be quite comfortable even when the ambient temperature is below freezing. Unfortunately, the same factors that make Stone so pleasant in winter convert the South Face into a solar oven in summer. This drives most people to climb only in the early morning and late evening. The North Face, though much less popular due to the walk, can be climbed at this time of year with only a moderate amount of sweat dripping from one's fingertips.

Unless one is travelling on popular weekends or at night, the nearby Blue Ridge Parkway is an idyllic road to travel when visiting Stone. This incredible ridgetop road (a National Park for its entire 450 mile length) offers magnificent views. It extends from Shenandoah National Park in Virginia, past Linville Gorge and Looking Glass Rock, to end at Great Smoky Mountain National Park. Sections, however, are closed during poor winter weather.

CLIMBING HISTORY

The first routes at Stone Mountain were climbed in the mid-1960's by a self-taught group of climbers who had developed their skills in Hanging Rock State Park (including Moore's Wall). On investigating Stone, they quickly climbed the half dozen or so "natural" lines – those that followed crack systems, more or less – and concluded that there was little left to do on this huge chunk of rock.

It wasn't until 1971, when **Grand Funk Railroad** was climbed, that people started looking more closely at less obvious lines. Then a rappeller was killed at Pilot Mountain State Park, which resulted in a climbing ban in all State Parks in 1973. Nevertheless, the north side was first explored then. In 1974 climbing was allowed on a "trial basis" and climbers returned to new route activity in force, sometimes at a runout 5.10+ standard. By the end of the 1970's, standards had reached 5.11+, but soon activity started waning again, with only the occasional new route being established.

Ironically, the wide spacing of the bolts on typically runout routes may contribute to a reduction of new route potential: without a line of bolts delineating the route, who would want to stray from the best holds? And with the precedent of infrequent bolts, who would put in the new line? Currently, development continues at a slow pace on the popular South Face. The North Face received a burst of new routes by a single determined pair of climbers in the spring of 1985. Climbers might note that the Park administration officially forbids new route activity.

CAMPING

The old informal campsites along a creekside have been closed; now campers must stay in a modern, groomed campground with toilets and showers (conveniences in season only). Beware that the campground gates are locked at night, preventing arriving or leaving by car. Check at the campground for gate times. Prices are moderate.

The nearest small grocery store is McGrady's, about one mile northwest of the entrance to the park. This country store is something of an institution among local climbers. There is a small restaurant in Traphill, but otherwise most services are found in Elkin, 20 miles south.

SEASONS AND WEATHER

Approximate Months	Typical Temperatures High	Low	Likelihood of Precipitation	Frequency of Climbable Days
Dec-Mar	50's +	30's +	low-med	high-med
Apr-May	80's	50's	med-high	med-high
Jun-Sep	90's	70's	med-low	low
Oct-Nov	70's +	40's	med-low	high

Comments: Even on cold days, the South Face can be pleasantly warm. On hot days, watch out. The North Face is generally too cold in winter, but reasonable when the South Face is excessively hot.

RESTRICTIONS AND WARNINGS

Climbing at Stone is currently allowed on a "trial basis" only. Any flaunting of the Park rules will only endanger climbing access. Current rules are posted by the parking lot and/or the climber's access trail. In 1986 they include the following: climbers must be off the cliff a half-hour before closing time; the crag is closed to climbing when wet (but it dries quickly); no new routes are permitted; climbers using "unsafe" practices will be barred from the Park. The Park administration can be contacted at: Stone Mountain State Park, Route 1 Box 17, Roaring Gap, NC 28663, telephone: 919-957-8185.

GUIDEBOOKS

The Climber's Guide to North Carolina (1986) by Thomas Kelley. Earthbound Books, P.O. Box 3445, Chapel Hill, NC 27515.

Dixie Crystals: A Climber's Guide to Stone Mountain North Carolina (1983) by Roid Waddle. Earthbound Books.

Southern Rock: A Climber's Guide (1981) by Chris Hall. Much less complete and accurate. East Woods Press Books, 820 East Boulevard, Charlotte, NC 28203.

GUIDE SERVICES AND EQUIPMENT STORES

No nearby equipment stores are available. Though based several hours away, the guides at Paddling Unlimited, are familiar with Stone Mountain: 6208 Yadkinville Road, Pfafftown, NC 27040, telephone 919-945-3744. The Looking Glass Guides, are also familiar with Stone's climbing: P.O. Box 5292, Asheville, NC 28813, telephone: 704-258-4571.

EMERGENCY SERVICES

In case of emergency, the State Park should be contacted at 957-8185. The superintendent lives just up the valley from the campground. Otherwise call the Wilkes County Sheriff at 838-9111. The nearest hospital is in Elkin: Hugh Chattam Memorial Hospital, Parkwood Drive, telephone: 835-3722.

GETTING THERE

No public transportation serves Stone Mountain State Park.

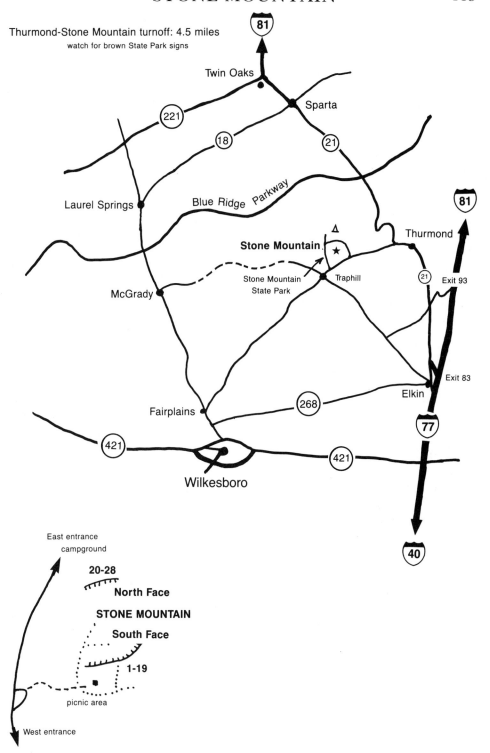

Thurmond-Stone Mountain turnoff: 4.5 miles
watch for brown State Park signs

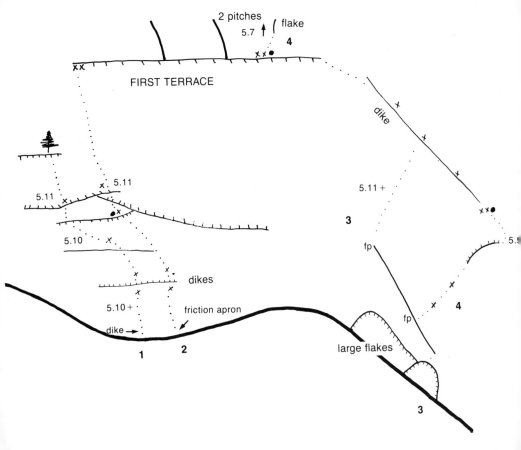

South Face

1 **The Discipline** **5.11** Sandy Fleming and Steve Pachman. Good protection.

2 **Disco Dance of Death** **5.11** Jeff White.

3 **Last Dance** **5.11+** Jim Byer and Bill Hoadley, 1979. One of the most difficult routes at Stone.

4 **Fantastic** **5.9** Gerald Laws and Buddy Price, 1974. Excellent and unusually varied climbing. Bring some nuts.

Middle Section

5 **Block Route 5.8, 5.9 var.** Begin in crack with small pine tree.

6 **Great White Way 5.9** Gerald Laws and Buddy Price, 1974. Need wire stopper for head of first bolt.

7 **Great Brown Way 5.10+** Chris Rowins and Chris Wychowski, about 1978. The first double bolts are not the belay. Runout.

8 **The Great Arch 5.5** B. Chatfield and F. Green, late 1960's. Nut protection.

9 **Mercury's Lead 5.9** Bob Rotert and Tom McMillan, 1974. First bolt 30 feet up.

10 **Rainy Day Women 5.10−** Bob Rotert, Tom McMillan, Gerald Laws and Jim McEver, 1974. First bolt 30 feet up—just **above** the crux climbing.

11 **Yardarm 5.8** J. Dailey and Steve Wallace, late 1960's. Start up a left-facing flake.

12 **No Alternative 5.6** George DeWolfe, R. Wright and Palmer, late 1960's. Classic introduction to Stone Mountain. Bring nuts.

13 **Deception Crack 5.9−**

Strawberry Preserves

Middle Section

14 Entrance Crack 5.4 Often jammed with beginners.

15 The Pulpit 5.8 Will Fulton et al, late 1960's. Begin at left-facing flake.

16 Strawberry Preserves 5.10+ Eric Zeeschi, Robin Hinkle and Lindsay Broom, 1979. Protect in the tree. Runout.

17 Electric Boobs 5.9+ Bob Rotert and Tom McMillan, 1974. Bulges in the rock; first bolt 25 feet high.

18 Grand Funk Railroad 5.9− Bob Mitchell and Will Fulton, 1971. Classic.

19 Saturday Night Fever 5.10 Protect in the tree.

Perry Williams on Grand Funk Railroad

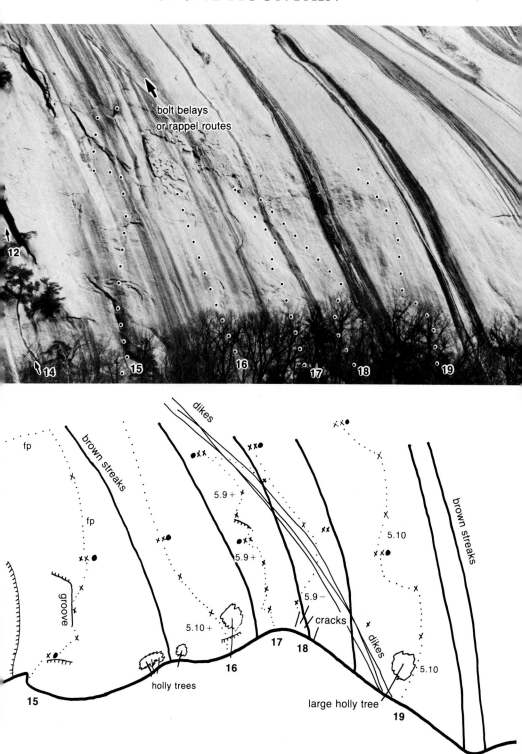

bolt belays
or rappel routes

12

14 **15** **16** **17** **18** **19**

fp

brown streaks

dikes

fp

5.9+

×× ●

5.9+

5.10

brown streaks

groove

5.10+

5.9−

cracks

17 **18**

dikes

5.10

16

holly trees

large holly tree

15 **19**

North Face

Access: Go over the top of the South Face, then traverse the top of the North Face until directly above the pine tree and crack on **Stainless Steel.** Descend easy slabs to the tree and rappel. Rappels also possible from anchors on **Teardrop** and **Bowl Games.** Two ropes make it much easier. Can also be approached from below via bushwacking.

20 Indian Lookout 5.8, direct var. 5.8+ Gerald Laws, Mike Fischesser, Jerry Laws and John Davis, 1973. The unprotected traverse makes the regular route unsafe for the second.

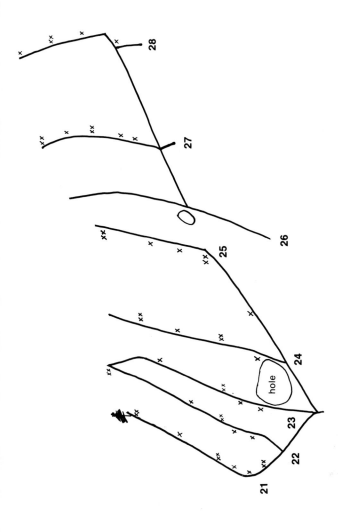

21 **Stainless Steel 5.9+** Gerald Laws and Mike Fischesser, 1973. Classic.
22 **Quinn the Eskimo 5.10+** Jeff Tucker and Vince Davis, 1985.
23 **Defeat 5.11** Vince Davis and Jeff Tucker, 1985.
24 **Chapped Green 5.11** Jeff Tucker and Vince Davis, 1985.
25 **Road Show 5.9** Vince Davis and Jeff Tucker, 1985.
26 **Teardrop 5.9−** M. Dumic, J. Botkins and T. Cook, 1976.
27 **Bowl Games 5.9** Jeff Tucker and Vince Davis, 1985.
28 **Merkin' Man 5.10** Gerald Laws.

Moore's Wall

MOORE'S WALL

HIGHLIGHTS

Rising out of the tobacco farming lowlands of central North Carolina is an isolated quartzite cliff of surprisingly high quality. Moore's Wall, in Hanging Rock State Park, is complex, steep, and up to 300 feet high. The solid sandstone is notorious for its incredible, arm-pumping verticality that is often graced with good handholds. Primarily a weekend area for residents of the heavily populated surroundings, Moore's would undoubtedly see more visitors were it closer to the traditionally beaten tourist path along the Blue Ridge Mountains.

CLIMBING

Though occasional sections of rock are of a softer sandstone, most of the wall has been metamorphosed into almost solid quartz – hard and angular. Still, the original horizontal bedding is maintained and these layers have yielded sometimes incredible face holds that can lead, ladder-like, straight off the deck and into the terrifying realm above. The fright factor can be inversely proportional to one's ability to hang onto good holds on an overhanging – or perhaps merely vertical – wall . . . and hang on . . . and hang on . . .

But it is not always so; sometimes the holds are less obvious. In addition to hanging on, one must quickly figure out complex moves with occasionally sparse protection. Lest a false impression be given that Moore's is nothing but steep face climbing, it must be pointed out that cracks are also common here, though rarely are they continuous for any great length. Slings can be important items to help improve the protection while weaving the rope up the sandstone tapestry.

For those who wish to spice their mildly overhanging walls with a real overhang, a number of roofs can be found as well. These are liberally sprinkled on routes from all difficulty grades, 5.7 and up. Even though Moore's specializes in steep and difficult routes, there are certainly a few quality climbs that blow neither the mind nor the arms.

Another wall, located after a hefty walk past the Ampitheater, has seen some recent route activity.

Superb bouldering on large rocks can be found half way up the trail to the Sentinel Buttress.

Northerners escaping the winter cold may find Moore's Wall disappointing. It faces north and its hilltop location keeps it in the wind. If Moore's proves too chilly, one might consider nearby Pilot Mountain, which faces south and sits in a wind-pocket. The Big Pinnacle is closed to climbing, but the Little Pinnacle has boulder and top-rope problems. Sauratown Mountain also has a cliff that faces south and holds at least a half-dozen difficult crack routes 100 feet long.

ENVIRONMENT

The forested hillsides of Hanging Rock State Park, which features Moore's Wall, rise out of the surrounding lowlands. Spring and fall are the primary climbing seasons here, coinciding nicely with the leafing out of this primarily broad-leafed deciduous forest and then the spectacular demise of these same leaves. In the spring, rhododendron and laurel blooms add shades of purple to the pale green of the trees. In the fall, a patchwork of reds and oranges extends to the distant horizon. Hemlocks provide some greenery year-round.

Despite its northern aspect, summers at Moore's Wall suffer from the same sweltering heat that overwhelms the rest of the Carolina lowlands. At this time of year, a climber driving to Moore's Wall via nearby Winston-Salem might find the sickly-sweet tobacco smog especially unappetizing. This town, with its giant R.J. Reynolds factory, symbolizes the dominance of tobacco in the local economy; factory tours are a major tourist attraction.

CLIMBING HISTORY

In the late 1950's, a man from the nearby town of Eden saw the Walt Disney movie "Two for the Mountain." Fascinated, he checked out the classic book, *Mountaineering: The Freedom of the Hills*, taught a friend to climb, and in 1959 established the first route on Moore's Wall. Simultaneously, a small group from the University of North Carolina at Chapel Hill began climbing at Hanging Rock, in the same State Park. They all joined forces and became the earliest climbers in North Carolina. In ensuing years they continued to establish routes, and soon students from Duke University took up the sport as well. But no one seemed inclined to take climbing too seriously; new routes went up very slowly and their difficulty remained low.

It was not until the mid-1970's that routes harder than 5.6 were established. Then, suddenly, things changed. In 1976 a number of 5.7 to 5.8's were put up on the steeper sections of cliff. Within two years 5.10, 5.11, and the era of hard climbing had finally arrived. The new batch of climbers working the cliffs soon realized that highly improbable looking lines would go with reasonable, if strenuous, effort. By the early 1980's Moore's Wall was well known and had been visited by virtually every Southern climber and quite a few Northerners as well. Anyone attracted by the call of the apes had to come pay his respects to Moore's steep walls.

CAMPING

Vandalism at the traditional camping site near the water pipe has made it less attractive. A local climber, Tim Fisher, bought the land at the very end of Mountain Road, including the turnaround on the road, and encourages climbers to stay for free on his land. Obviously, great respect must be shown for his property. All that he asks is that no new fire pits are made and that trash is removed. From there it is but a ¼ mile walk to the cliff. There is a drinking water spring just below the campsite, with water running from a pipe. The other camping possibility is in the official (moderately priced) Hanging Rock State Park campground. Access from here to the cliff is somewhat longer, as one must walk across the hill and down to the wall's base.

Nearby is the Moore's Springs Restaurant, on Moore's Spring Road, which features country-style cuisine.

In the summer, slide-lectures are given twice each week by naturalists at the State Park campground. A lake for swimming can also be found there.

SEASONS AND WEATHER

Approximate Months	Typical Temperatures High	Low	Likelihood of Precipitation	Frequency of Climbable Days
Dec-Feb	40's	30's −	medium	low-med
Mar-May	70's +	50's	medium	high
Jun-Sep	90's −	70's	medium	med-high
Oct-Nov	70's −	50's	med-low	high

Comments: In the summer, heat and humidity are the limiting factors. Lack of sun renders winters especially cold.

RESTRICTIONS AND WARNINGS

Respect must be shown for the private camping site to avoid having it closed down. No new fire pits should be made and trash must be removed.

GUIDEBOOKS

The Climber's Guide to North Carolina (1986) by Thomas Kelley. Earthbound Books, P.O. Box 3445, Chapel Hill, NC 27515.

Southern Rock: A Climber's Guide (1981) by Chris Hall. Years out of date concerning Moore's Wall even before it was published.

GUIDE SERVICES AND EQUIPMENT STORES

The nearest equipment store is just northwest of Winston-Salem: Paddling Unlimited, 6208 Yadkinville Rd, Pfafftown, NC 27040. A guide service operates out of the store as well, telephone: 919-945-3744.

Not quite as close is Carolina Outdoor Sports, 844 West Lee St, Greensboro, NC 27403. The Looking Glass Guides, based out of Asheville, could also field guides to Moore's Wall. P.O. Box 5292, Asheville, NC 28813, telephone: 704-258-4571.

EMERGENCY SERVICES

For rescues contact the Stokes County Sheriff at telephone: 293-8787. The nearest hospital is the Stokes Reynolds Memorial Hospital at the intersection of Highways 8 and 89, 7 miles from Moore's Wall. Telephone: 593-2831.

GETTING THERE

Winston-Salem, twenty miles away, is easily reached by major airline. From there, a car should be rented. Hitchhiking may, eventually, get you there as well.

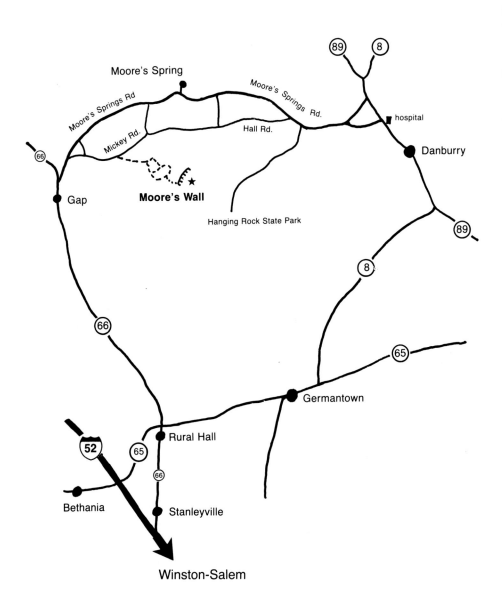

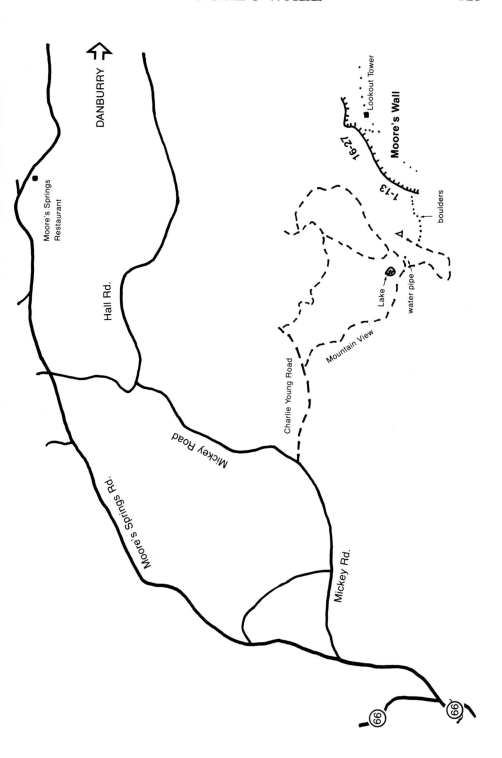

Lookout Tower

Moore's Wall

16-27

1-13

boulders

Lake

water pipe

Mountain View

Charlie Young Road

DANBURY

Moore's Springs
Restaurant

Hall Rd.

Mickey Road

Moore's Springs Rd.

Mickey Rd.

66

66

Descents 1) Downclimb **Sentinel Chimney** or face to left (**Scrambled Eggs** 5.4), 2) go south to trail from Hanging Rock State Park, then take the fork just before the lookout tower, continue down a gully to the base of the wall.

Tim Fisher on Air Show   photo by Tim Schneider

Wall of Fire

1 Riders On the Storm   5.10+ FA: Tom Howard et al, about 1978. Large Friend helpful on second pitch. Has never been climbed through the top roofs.

2 Wild Kingdom   5.11+ Tom McMillan et. al. about 1977. FFA: Tom McMillan and Rob Robinson, 1978. Runout.

3 Edge of Fire   5.11 Munson brothers, about 1979. First pitch: top rope the arête right of the wide crack (5.11).

Sentinel Buttress

4 Sentinel Super Direct   5.9 At the low point of Sentinel Buttress, the obvious thin crack in corner with several overhangs. Climb up to and around right side of overhang forty feet up, then left to another overhang with a crack.

5 Sentinel Direct   5.5 Robert Mosely and Minor Davis, 1963. Several variations possible. Most common start: thirty feet left of the low point, climb deep corner to overhangs and up right past overhangs past pine tree forty feet up.

Circus Wall

6 Bimbo Bulge   5.10+ Rich Gottlieb and Jack Carter, about 1977.

7 Zoo View   5.7+ Tom Howard and Bruce Meneghin, 1976. Left variation is 5.8.

8 Break On Through   5.10 Tom McMillan and Tom Howard, 1978.

9 Air Show   5.8+ Tom Howard and Bruce Meneghin, 1976.

10 Sentinel Chimney   5.4 Mostly used as access to other routes.

11 Herdie-Girdie Girdle   (traverse)   5.9− Tom Howard and Jim Okle, 1981. Start from near top of Sentinel Chimney, traverse under Circus Wall roofs (above Bimbo Bulge crux), cross Fire Wall at base of Wild Kingdom second pitch (poor pro—small brass nuts).

12 Too Much Fun   5.9 (no photo) Tom Howard and Bruce Meneghin, 1976. 75 feet east of Sentinel Buttress is a forty foot left-facing corner. Climb the corner, move right to thin corner and up past a bolt to ledge. Continue up and left (5.9) or off right (easy). **Descent** scramble down right.

13 Blue Chock   5.10 Canard brothers about 1974. Climb the main **Too Much Fun** corner, continue to overhang which is passed on left (crux), traverse right to the left-facing corner (runout on thin face) and up.

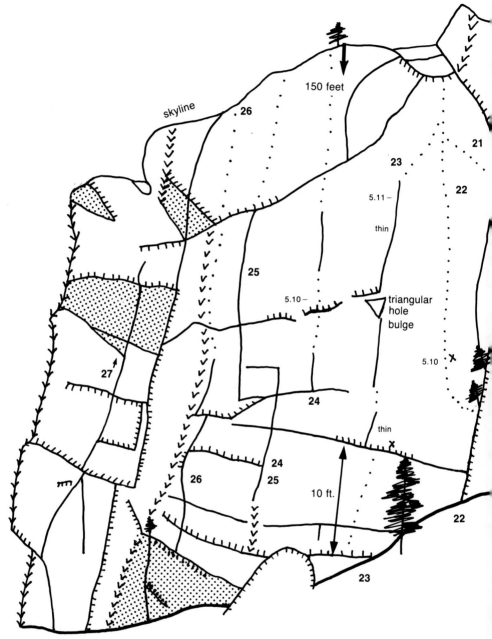

23 Quaker State 5.11 − Rob Robinson and Tom McMillan, 1978. Runout after crux and strenuous near top.

24 Do or Dive 5.10 − Tom McMillan, Lee Carter and Rob Robinson, 1978.

25 Raise Hell 5.8 Tom Howard and Bill Newman, 1974.

26 Five Easy Pieces 5.10 + Lee Munson, 1984.

27 Aid Raid 5.11 − FA: Bob Rotert, about 1976. The roof crack.

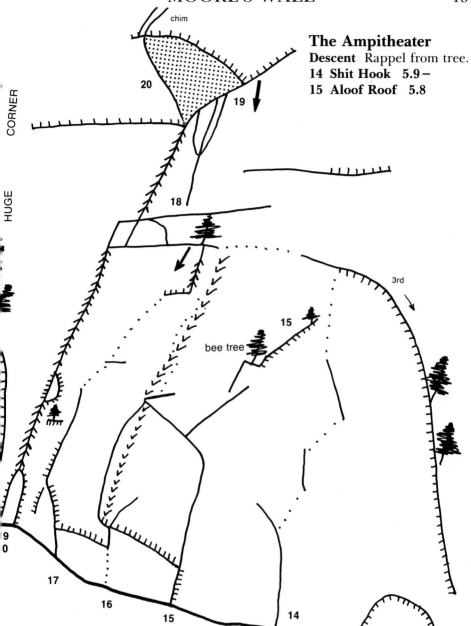

The Ampitheater
Descent Rappel from tree.
14 Shit Hook 5.9−
15 Aloof Roof 5.8

chim

20

19

18

3rd

15

bee tree

CORNER

HUGE

9
0

17

16

15

14

16 **Stab in the Dark** **5.11−** Tom McMillan et. al., 1978. Poor pro on upper (5.8) arête.

17 **Breaking Rock is Hard to Do** **5.9−** Rich Gottlieb and Jack Carter, 1978.

18 **Finger Love** **5.10** Tim Fisher and Jon Regelbrugge, 1984.

19 **Doan's Pills** **5.9** Right side of roof; very awkward.

20 **Zombie Woof** **5.10** Carlton Ramm and partner, 1978.

21 **Almost Seven** **5.7** Tom Howard and Bruce Meneghin, 1976.

22 **Nuclear Crayon** **5.10** Jeff Lauschey and Jon Regelbrugge, 1985.

Tom Howard on Direct Finish to Supercrack photo: Bruce Burgin

NEW RIVER GORGE

HIGHLIGHTS

Shrieks of pleasure can frequently be heard rising from the whitewater rapids 800 feet below. But these rafters are oblivious to the gasps of a climber struggling on the vertical sandstone cliffs that rim the New River Gorge. Thick stands of trees hide most of the cliff bands, yet the modest 50 to 150 foot high bluffs provides some of the finest steep crack and face climbs that could be wished for. Though several sections, primarily on the North Rim, have received especially intense development in the past few years, the cliffs in fact extend for miles on both rims of the gorge. Access could hardly be more convenient, with approach walks to the more popular cliffs taking between fifteen seconds and fifteen minutes. With an ability to absorb as many people as choose to come here – from partyers to solitude seekers, from those who must connect the chalk marks to those who want to go where the hand of man has never set foot – the New River Gorge is a climbing area that can delight any skilled enthusiast.

CLIMBING

Though climbing is well behind river rafting in popularity at the New River Gorge, it is attracting an increasing following. Many Pittsburgh and Washington, D.C. climbers who used to spend their weekends at Seneca now come to the "New" instead. North Carolina climbers play a leading role in New River climbing as well. Beyond the excellent routes, the attractions are less developed crags and the adventure of exploration.

Fresh discoveries are often just around the bend.

All the climbing takes place along the uppermost rim of the canyon, where a single bed of sandstone caps the steep slopes below. This bed varies from 50 to 150 feet (mostly 100 feet) in height and runs for mile upon mile. Though breaks in the continuity of the rock bed are frequent, some of the exposed cliffs extend for more than two miles without an ascent route easier than 5.7.

In fact, very little climbing at all will be found that is less than 5.7. The cliffs here tend to be steep; between 80 and 90 degrees is the norm. The rock is usually excellent, frequently impeccable. The Nuttle Sandstone here has not been metamorphosed into quartzite as it has at nearby Seneca Rocks, but it is extremely monolithic, compact, hard.

On first examination of the cliffs, phenomenal cracks seem to completely dominate. Not until these obvious lines had been climbed did people begin scrutinizing the faces between. Frequently, small edges and other face holds were found where previously all looked blank. The New may eventually end up with as many face climbs as crack, but first impressions will always be the fissures. Some have said that vertical foot for vertical foot, the crack climbing here is as fine as can be found anywhere. This may well be true. Of course, the vertical cliffs only extend for one pitch, which for some people may be a disappointment. However, for the increasing number of climbers who only climb the first pitches of longer routes anyway, the lack of height won't matter.

Beauty Mountain, whose cliff is about ¾ of a mile in length, is one of the most scenic locations and also has the most consistently long climbs. Many routes are nearly a full ropelength. The Brain, different in character from the rest of the cliff and at its far end, dries out relatively quickly after a rain. Another great attraction of Beauty is the Boulderfield, a collection of monstrous boulders, thirty feet high and 100 feet across, that provide climbing of all types while specializing in overhanging faces. The views from here are outstanding. Unfortunately, the scenic qualities of the Boulderfield attract many teenage partyers, especially on Friday and Saturday nights.

The Endless Wall when combined with the Fern Buttress is over four miles long and is the longest continuous cliff band yet discovered — consequently it has the most potential. Diamond Point has perhaps the finest 200 foot stretch of rock in the Gorge. Its cracks are simply outrageous.

The Bridge Buttress lies directly under the northern terminous of the New River Gorge Bridge. The walls here are mostly buried in the trees just above the road and can be especially sticky on the many humid days that plague the region. But access is convenient and the routes are great. Walking west from here, past an abandoned garbage dump, one finds the Junkyard Wall. Some excellent climbs lie here, often poking high enough out of the trees to receive good sun exposure.

The junkyard is symbolic of a lack of environmental concern by local (non-climbing) residents. More wordly and concerned visitors will surely not emulate the natives' littering habits. Leave only footprints.

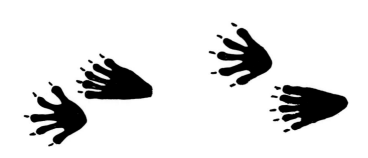

ENVIRONMENT

Despite its name, the New River is claimed to be the oldest river in America, and the second oldest in the world (behind the Nile). From its North Carolina source, it flows oddly northward and becomes one of the few rivers to cross the Appalachians from east to west. The river has flowed through the region since the Appalachians were a mountain range taller than the Rockies, but during the last ice age its progress was blocked in the midwestern plains. While at one point the Mississippi was considered to be a tributary to the New River, now the New joins the Kanawa, then the Ohio River before finally reaching the massive Mississippi.

The landscape continues to be rugged by East Coast standards, while the New River is wild by nearly any boater's criteria. It has one of the most concentrated stretches of whitewater in the U.S., with twenty-one major rapids (many Class 5) in one fifteen mile stretch. The canyon is up to 1,300 feet deep and the 50 mile section upriver from the New River Gorge Bridge was designated a National River, administered by the National Park Service. Those interested in river rafting with a professional outfit should expect to pay about $50 weekdays, $60 weekends, and need to make reservations for weekends. Four companies are: North American River Runners (304-658-5276), New River Adventures (304-574-3008), West Virginia River Adventures (304-658-5277) and Eastern River Expeditions (207-695-2411, collect).

The canyon's ruggedness had kept it free of development until 1873, when the Chesapeake and Ohio Railroad completed laying tracks up the valley floor. Soon the Gorge experienced a boom of coal mining activity, with 20 villages and thousands of people, all completely dependent on the railroad. During the Great Depression, activity in the Gorge folded up, only leaving the town of Thurmond – a dwarf of its former self. The railroad tracks are still occupied, though now the trains chug on by, not stopping at the ghost depots.

In West Virginia's "mountainous" highlands, the New River Gorge can be cold and snowy in the winter. But midsummer is often so maddeningly hot and humid that one eagerly looks forward to the cool, crisp days of autumn when the hardwood forest takes on many brilliant hues. On the second Saturday in October there is the Annual Bridge Day, when cars are kept off one lane on the famous bridge – the world's longest single span bridge, 1,700 feet across – and people swarm on. This is perhaps the largest sanctioned yearly gathering of BASE jumpers; parachutists and bungie-cordists alike dive towards the water, 870 feet below.

Climbers will appreciate the unspoiled beauty of the New River Gorge from their belays atop the cliff. With the wide open valley all around, the river rapids relatively tame below and often no-one in sight, one can get a magnificent feeling of wilderness just a few minutes from the car. After the climb, or to pass the midday summer heat, one can drive to the water and take a refreshing swim. The New River Gorge is simply a jewel.

CLIMBING HISTORY

Adventure is not a recent phenomenon at the New River Gorge. This region of West Virginia fielded many Confederate soldiers during the Civil War (in fact, General Robert E. Lee's famous horse "Traveller" came from here), while the town of Thurmond was known as the "Dodge City of the East." But climbers only recently discovered the vast expanses of sandstone. Not until the 1980's did the word start getting out about the potential of the New River Gorge.

Though there was occasional evidence of someone having been on the cliffs before, it appears that the first serious climbing occured in 1975. A small group of river guides climbed mostly at the Bridge Buttress – the long bridge had not yet been built, but the road leading down to the rafters' take-out passes immediately beneath the cliff. In 1978 a local motorcycling enthusiast discovered Beauty Mountain and rock climbing at about the same happy time.

About 1980 the tempo quickened. The locals discovered that they could lead Beauty Mountain's incredible **Supercrack** (solid 5.9), which they had already top-roped several times. They not only gained confidence in themselves, but also in their area as more people gradually filtered in and confirmed the quality of New River's cracks. By 1983 the New had developed a loyal following, with people regularly commuting long distances to climb there – from North Carolina, Virginia, Pennsylvania and Ohio.

Still, the New River Gorge was only known to a small band of climbers until a spectacular cover shot on *Climbing* magazine brought it to national attention in 1984. Then people outside of the word-of-mouth group started dropping by. The nucleous of regulars remained small, perhaps one to two dozen people, but because many of these climbers were already solid at 5.11 climbing, there was little time lag before difficult routes were being done. The area's first guidebook, listing over 250 climbs, came out in the spring of 1986.

With the inevitable increase in numbers of climbers at the New, some of the myriads of classic routes will finally receive more traffic. Before the guidebook, routes had often seen few repeat ascents because the active climbers had been in quest of virgin territory. Because solitude has also been an appeal to some of these climbers, it is fortunate for everyone that the sandstone extends for so many miles that unfrequented cliffs will always be available for those who look for them.

CAMPING

The local sanctioned camping is at the New River Gorge Campground, just northeast of the Bridge. Fairly expensive, they do have showers. Slightly further away, but more moderately priced and also with showers, is the Pattyhill Campground near Ansted.

Near the Boulderfield or the parking lot at Beauty Mountain is another possibility for overnighting. This location is free, but can be disturbed by partying teenagers on Friday and Saturday nights. On the road leading down to the river below Bridge Buttress is a pipe with running water. This is considered drinkable by most climbers and rafters.

The Comfort Inn, two miles south of the Bridge, offers more luxurious quarters (800-228-5150 or 304-574-3443). Laundry facilities can be found in Fayetteville, three miles south of the bridge.

On the west side of the road leading to Fayetteville is the Western Pancake House, a favorite breakfast place for rock climbers and river rafters alike.

SEASONS AND WEATHER

Approximate Months	Typical Temperatures High	Low	Likelihood of Precipitation	Frequency of Climbable Days
Nov-Mar	40's −	20's −	high	med-low
Apr-May	70's	40's	med-high	med-high
Jun-Aug	80's +	60's	med-high	high
Sep-Oct	70's	40's	low-med	high

Comments: In the summer, afternoon thundershowers are common, as is extremely high humidity.

RESTRICTIONS AND WARNINGS

Poison ivy is common in some locations; copperhead snakes are also found in the area.

GUIDEBOOKS

New River Rock (1986) by Richard V. Thompson II. Available from the author at Box 387, Sewickley, PA 15143.

GUIDE SERVICES AND EQUIPMENT STORES

Guiding and limited equipment are available from North American River Runners Outfitter Shop on Route 60 West, seven miles north of the Bridge. P.O. Box 81, Hico, WV 25962, telephone: 304-658-5276.

EMERGENCY SERVICES

In case of emergency, contact the Fayette County Sheriff, telephone: 574-1200. The nearest hospital is the Plateau Medical Center, Oak Hill, telephone: 465-0551.

GETTING THERE

Greyhound serves Beckley, thirty miles south. Hitch-hiking will get you to the Gorge fairly directly.

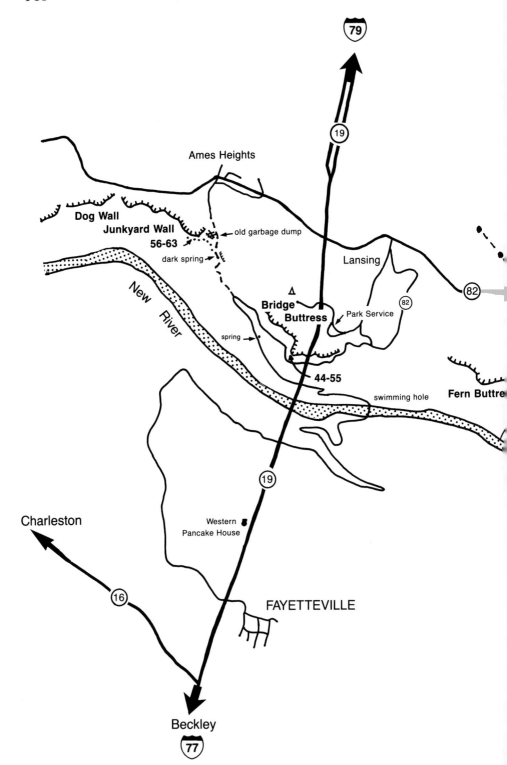

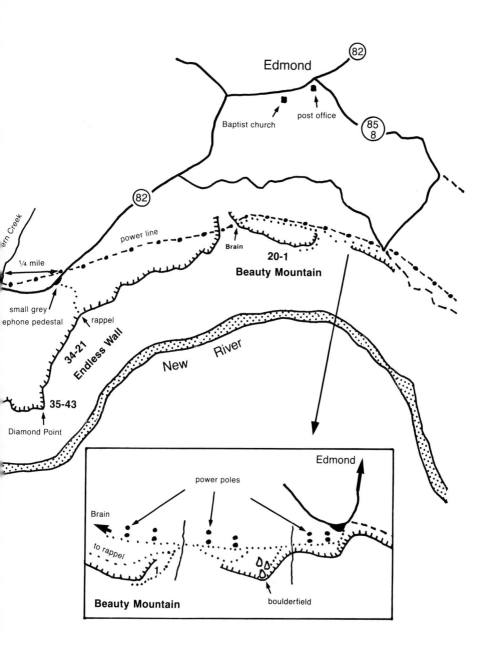

Beauty Mountain

Rick Thompson on Brain Death

Andrew Barry on Right Son of Thunder

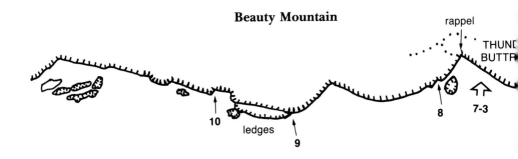

Beauty Mountain

rappel

THUND
BUTTR

10

ledges

9

8

7-3

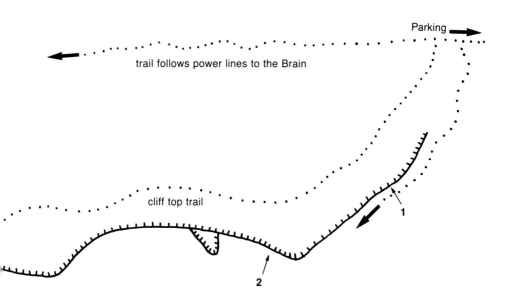

Parking

trail follows power lines to the Brain

cliff top trail

1

2

Beauty Mountain

1 **Throw Down Those Childish Toys** **5.7** Rick Thompson, Nick Brash and Tom Howard, 1985. The right-curving flake about fifty feet from the start of the wall.

2 **Welcome to Beauty** **5.11** (**Right Hand Variation 5.11+**) Steve Erskine, Hobart Parks, Tom Horton and Rick Skidmore, 1978. FFA: Pete Absolon and Chris Guenther, 1983 (Right Var. Cal Swoager and Greg Phillips, 1983). On the steep orange wall, climb either right-hand crack to roof, then left or right diverging finger cracks above.

3 **Momma's Squeeze Box** **5.8** Tom Howard and Bill Newman, 1981. Chimney, with small crack protection inside.

4 **Right Son of Thunder** **5.11** Cal Swoager and Ed McCarthy, 1985. Climb the obvious crack, step right to a bolt, up to a horizontal, left 10 feet, and up.

5 **Left Son of Thunder** **5.11** Cal Swoager 1985. Climb discontinuous crack to end, then finish on **Right Son of Thunder.**

6 **Mushrooms** **5.10−** Phil Wilts and Ed McCarthy, 1983. The crack system just right of the offwidth crack. Often dirty.

7 **Screamer Crack** **5.8+** Nick Brash and Bruce Burgin, 1979. Large corner-crack.

8 **Super Crack** **5.9+** Nick Brash and Chuck Basham, 1980. The long corner-crack. **Photo Finish** traverses left after crack to roof at outside corner (5.9).

9 **Chasin' the Wind** **5.11** Mike Artz and Cal Swoager, 1985. The crack high on a grey wall. Climb to the ledge via corner 30 feet right of upper crack.

10 **Fat Man's Folly** **5.9** Tom Howard, Nick Brash and Bill Newman, 1981. The left corner to square roof, followed by squeeze chimney.

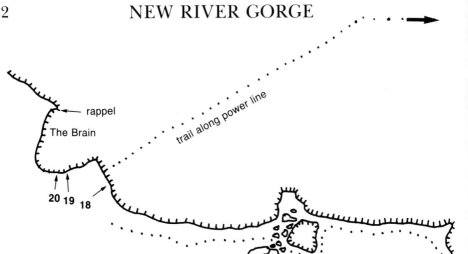

rappel

The Brain

20 19 18

trail along power line

Andrew Barry and Rick Thompson on Right Son of Thunder

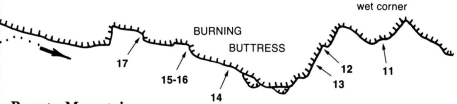

wet corner

BURNING

BUTTRESS

17

15-16

14

12

13

11

Beauty Mountain

11 Quick Robin, to the Bat Crack (a.k.a. Bat Crack)   5.10– The inside corner, moving right to blunt arête below roof.

12 Rod Serling Crack   5.10 Jim Okel, Tom Howard and Dan Perry, 1981. The left-facing dihedral to triangular roof and thin crack above.

13 Steve Martin's Face   5.11 Andrew Barry, Mike Artz and Rick Fairtrace, 1985. From a small ledge, climb the orange face past a bolt that requires a wire nut to clip. Intricate and bold.

14 Burning Calves   5.10 Phil Wilt and Ed McCarthy, 1983. Thin crack past "pods." Starts with a thin left-facing corner 30 feet left of large block.

15 Spider Wand   5.10 Tom Howard, Doug Reed and Vernon Scarborough, 1983. The flared left-facing corner. Pass triangular roof on right.

16 Wham Bam, Thanks for the Jamb   5.10 Phil Wilt and Ed McCarthy, 1983. After 20 feet of the **Spider Wand,** move right to handcrack.

17 Happy Hands   5.9 Steve Erskine, Hobart Parks, Tom Horton and Rick Skidmore, 1980. The hand crack.

18 Hot Flash   5.10 Rick Thompson and John Harlin, 1985. Start under small low roof. Climb the right-arching flake on overhanging wall above, followed by solution pockets angling left. Hidden fixed pin near top; #3 and #4 Friends useful in pockets.

19 Brainteasers   5.10– Tom Howard and Bill Newman, 1981. Climb crack, move right below roof to right-facing corner and face above.

20 Journey to the Center of the Brain   5.8 The grooves and solution pockets with many variations. Bolt at summit for top-roping. Friends useful in leading.

floating block

29

28

Endless Wall

21 Imperial Strut 5.10− A0 Rick Thompson and Scott Garso, 1985. Right-facing corner about 250 feet from rappel. A0 refers to tree.

22 Oyster Cracker 5.10 Mike Artz, Andrew Barry and Bruce Burgin, 1985. Right-leaning orange flake system.

23 Purity Made 5.7 Tom Howard and Bill Newman, 1981. Wide crack.

24 Tuna Fish Roof 5.11+ Andrew Barry and Mike Artz, 1985. Corner to large roof 40 feet up. A hanging belay above the roof reduces rope drag.

25 Celibate Mallard 5.10 Mike Artz and Andrew Barry, 1985. Right-facing flake/crack system past roof.

26 Roy's Lament 5.9 (Direct Finish 5.9+) Dan Perry, Jim Okle and Tom Howard, 1985; Direct: Scott Garso, Rick Thompson and Bruce Burgin, 1985. Right-facing flake past ledge. Move right below final roof for normal finish, straight up for Direct.

27 The Undeserved 5.10 Tom Howard, Jim Okle and Dan Perry, 1980. Climb prominent crack to its end, move left around outside corner to left-facing dihedral, then up.

28 New Fangled Dangle 5.10 Tom Howard and Bill Newman, 1980. The flared dihedral.

29 The Orgasmatron 5.11− Andrew Barry and Mike Artz, 1985. Climb left-facing corner, roof and crack, then roofs above ledge.

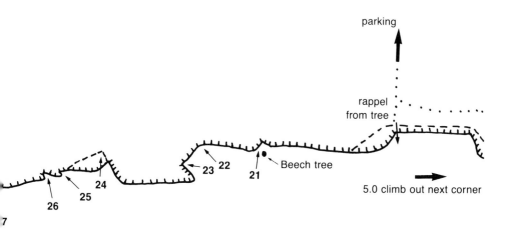

parking

rappel
from tree

Beech tree

23 22 21

24

26 25

5.0 climb out next corner

7

Glenn Thomas on Brain Death photo: Richard V. Thompson

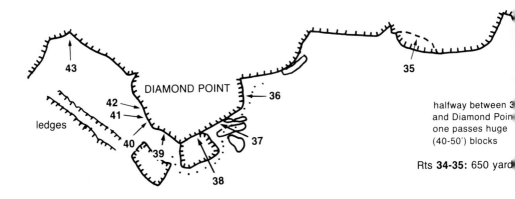

DIAMOND POINT

43

42
41

ledges

40

39

36

37

38

35

halfway between 3
and Diamond Poin
one passes huge
(40-50') blocks

Rts **34-35:** 650 yard

Andrew Barry on Right Son of Thunder

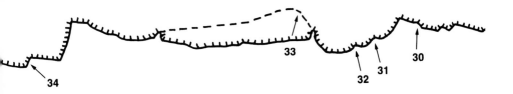

Endless Wall

30 Fantasy 5.8 (Direct Finish 5.9+) FA Direct: Mike Artz and Mike Cote, 1985. Prominent handcrack/corner to ledge. Normal exit is right of roof, Direct is left.

31 Doce Doe 5.9 Tom Howard and Bill Newman, 1981. Climb right-leaning ramp/dihedral, then right through roofs.

32 The Mystery 5.10− The wide, orange dihedral.

33 Permission Granted 5.10− Mike Artz and Mike Cote, 1985. Face climb out right side of 40 foot roof. Belay just above roof because of rope drag. Good for rainy days.

34 The Grafenberg Crack 5.9+ Tom Howard and Rick Thompson, 1985. Climb a short handcrack followed by a right-facing corner/flake, then left at its end.

35 Nestle Krunch Roof 5.10− Mike Cote, Mike Artz and Rick Thompson, 1985.

36 Leave it to Jesus 5.11+ Cal Swoager and Stuart Kuperstock, 1985. Climb spectacular thin crack up orange wall to left jog, then traverse to and up left side of arête.

37 Ovine Seduction 5.10 Andrew Barry and Mike Artz, 1985.

38 Supersymetry 5.7 Andrew Barry and Mike Artz, 1985.

39 Raging Waters 5.10+ Rick Thompson and Tom Howard, 1985. A few feet left of yellow pine, climb short corner, then flake system to large flake which turns into a ledge. From the ledge, move right to face of large detached flake.

40 Can I Do It Till I Need Glasses? 5.10 Rick Thompson and Mike Artz, 1985. Climb from either side to reach a steep crack with light streak to its right. Follow the crack 40 feet, then traverse right to another crack and hanging belay. Climb to top.

41 Remission 5.10 Mike Artz, Mike Cote and Rick Thompson, 1985. The obvious crack with a left jog half way up.

42 Zygomatic 5.11− Maurice and Doug Reed, 1985. Climb the pink left-facing corner, the roof and the face above.

43 The Diving Swan 5.10+ Mike Cote and Mike Artz, 1985. Climb an orange right-facing flake to the roof, then the right-facing corner, moving right near the top to a flared crack.

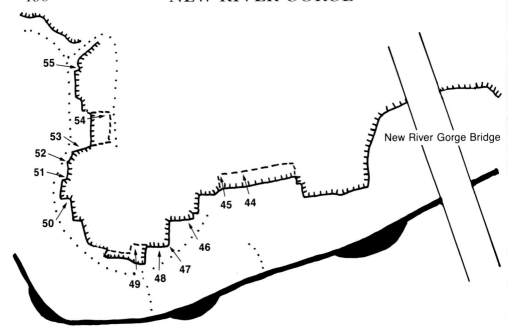

New River Gorge Bridge

Bridge Buttress

44 Slant Crack Direct 5.11 − Rick Skidmore, Hobart Parks and Steve Erskine, 1980. FFA: Andrew Barry and Eric Anderson, 1985. 30 feet right of the stone shelter, climb the crack to a pair of bolts (5.10, good rainy day climb) then roof system above.

45 Labor Day 5.10 Doug Reed and Tom Howard, 1984. Just right of the stone shelter, climb right side of detached flake, then left past roof.

46 The Layback 5.9 − Rick Skidmore and Hobart Parks, 1975. The right-facing flake.

47 Angel's Arete 5.10 − Steve Erskine and Tom Horton, 1979. The beautiful pink arête.

48 Zag 5.8 Hobart Parks and Rick Skidmore, 1975. The wide crack. Possibly the first route in the Gorge.

49 Handsome and Well Hung 5.11 − Rick Skidmore, Hobart Parks and Steve Erskine. FFA: Rich Pleiss and Ron Augustino, 1983. The orange dihedral to the roof, followed by bolts leading right.

50 Jaws 5.9 Rick Skidmore, 1977. The prominent right-facing corner.

51 Tree Route 5.9 The left-facing corner with large hemlock at its base.

52 Marionette 5.11 Kris Kline and Mike Artz, 1983. The thin crack in the corner leading to a roof and handcrack.

53 Skid's Route 5.9 Rick Skidmore and Hobart Parks, 1976. On the right wall of the "Trashcompactor," climb the high thin crack to the right-facing corner and up.

54 Underfling 5.10 Tom Howard, 1983. Undercling out the left side of the "Trashcompactor" roof.

55 Easy Money 5.10 − Hobart Parks, Steve Erskine, Tom Horton and Rick Skidmore, 1978. The black offwidth.

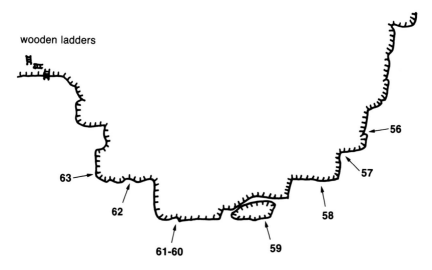

wooden ladders

Junkyard Wall

DO NOT PARK YOUR CAR ON THE SWITCHBACK! River rafting company buses need lots of space to make the turn. Above or below is okay, but park well to the side of the road. There is lots of poison ivy on the trail past the garbage dump.

56 Rap Scallion's Blues 5.10 Doug Reed and Tom Howard, 1984. Climb the obvious right-facing corner, pass the roof and move left to crack.

57 Brain Death 5.9 Tom Horton and Rick Skidmore, 1979. Climb the wide crack, then the corner past a series of overhangs.

58 CUI (Climbing Under the Influence; a.k.a. New Yosemite) 5.9 Steve Erskine and Tom Horton, 1979. The beautiful hand crack.

59 New River Gunks 5.6 Ed McCarthy and Cal Swoager, 1985. Starting just left of the edge, climb up then right to vertical crack leading to ledge. Continue up right-facing corner then move to the right wall, climbing over a roof with a wide crack.

60 Curtains 5.10+ Hobart Parks and Rick Skidmore, 1980. Climb the right-facing corner until the crack splits into a "Y," then follow the right-hand crack and face above.

61 The Entertainer 5.10− Wes Love and Tom Howard, 1984. At the "Y" in Curtains, climb the thin left crack to the flake then go straight up the face.

62 Rhododendrom Up Your Bum 5.9+ Andrew Barry and Steve Lancaster, 1985. A left-facing corner that starts 20 feet above the ground. Enter it from the right and pass the small roof on the left.

63 Stuck in Another Dimension 5.10 Climb the right-hand of two cracks and the offwidth roof crack above.

Seneca Rocks – This bridge was washed out in 1985

SENECA ROCKS

HIGHLIGHTS

Above a pastoral valley high up the Potomac River rises a fin of rock that looks like the serrated edge of an old cross-cut saw. This unique quartzite crag, about 300 feet high and topping out 900 feet above the valley floor, holds some of the East Coast's finest and best known rock climbing. Seneca Rocks, West Virginia, has long been one of the few Eastern areas to be included on a foreign visitor's U.S. climbing tour. Its rock is infamously steep and its routes graded stiffly, yet there are climbs here for everyone. This is truly an area that no travelling climber will want to miss.

CLIMBING

Two of the most visited climbing areas in the East are the Shawangunks and Seneca Rocks, 600 miles apart. Despite their separation, they are both comprised of a similar quartzite-like sandstone – in Seneca's case, it is Tuscarora Sandstone. However, at the "Gunks" the sedimentary bed is horizontal, while at Seneca the bed has been tilted vertically. The only other popular climbing area in the country to have such vertical slivers of rock is the Garden of the Gods, in Colorado. That fact noted, comparisons end. Seneca rock is solid quartzite. Its solidity is demonstrated by the amazing rock splinters that somehow remain upright despite being tilted outward from, and barely attached to, the main cliff body.

Yet sandstone, even in such a highly metamorphosed state as it is here, can rarely be completely trusted. Sometimes gravity has its way, converting potential energy to kinetic energy with Seneca's rock just as forcefully as it does with Seneca's climbers. Several routes were eliminated on the Thais Face when the entire upper section peeled off in 1972. Loose rock in smaller doses is a more common problem and is the principal disadvantage incurred from tilting the Tuscarora upward (compared with the Shawangunk's more staid and stable horizontal bedding). Beware when climbing beneath another party and be sure to test handholds.

But occasional loose rock is a small price to pay for the unique character of Seneca's climbing. This is one of the few places where summiting can sometimes be more hair-raising than climbing the route – because on reaching the top, one suddenly sees down the vertical backside of the sandstone sliver. Vertigo is a typical response.

Many cracks are found at Seneca, far more than at the Shawangunks, though face climbing is also common. In fact, most routes blend the two types of climbing in a diverse mixture. On routes where face predominates, protection is often more widely spaced and more difficult to place than some might like. The proverbial "long neck" can be as useful as more literal long arms. And perhaps more useful than long arms are strong ones, as the one truly unifying theme among Seneca routes is their steepness. Roofs are not common, but dead-verticality is, even at the lower grades.

For some reason, difficulty ratings have tended to be lower than a visitor might anticipate. Stiff ratings seem to be a Seneca tradition, and first time visitors – especially those without a gorilla's forearms – will likely want to keep this in mind.

The distinct east and west sides at Seneca Rocks are a clear advantage on hot or cold days. To find preferred temperatures, one needs simply to climb on the sunny or the shady side – whichever is appropriate for the season – then switch sides when the sun does. Wind whistling along the exposed ridgeline can cool things off, no matter what the season.

Routes are usually two or three pitches in length, each pitch being less than 100 feet on average. Frequently, however, a particular route will start high on the cliff, with the access being from another, often easier route. In this case, the climb one is after might only be one pitch. Likewise, there are many one pitch climbs that only ascend the lower sections of cliff or shorter cliffs. Descents usually involve one or more rappels and some downclimbing. They can be more difficult and important to locate than the climb up.

On rainy days, climbers can shop and socialize at the local climbing store, the Gendarme, or mingle with the other tourists at the Forest Service visitor center. Here films are frequently shown, including a few on climbing. Running water, sometimes hot, is also found here. Perhaps the finest rainy day activity is to investigate the excellent spelunking to be found in the region. Fishing is also popular, as are all the other outdoor activities including hiking, boating and bicycling.

ENVIRONMENT

Running in parallel ridgelines that stretch due north and south, the Allegheny Mountains of West Virginia were once a major barrier to the westward progress of early American settlers. One of the best passages into the heart of the wilderness was the valley carved by the North Fork of the Potomac River. Here settlers followed the trail of the Seneca Indians to a beautiful open valley and founded the small community of Mouth of Seneca.

The tiny hamlet currently consists of two general stores, a couple of restaurants (some with hotels), a post office, and a few widely scattered homes. The pastoral countryside and the peaceful community has remained little changed since the Civil War which, in fact, also did little to change Mouth of Seneca.

The river lost its gentle Eastern flavor due to a large flood in 1985. Now the stream looks like a western Montana floodplain, complete with gravel bars. It will take years for the vegetation to regrow.

East of Seneca Rocks, the hills are forested with both hard and softwood trees. Fall foliage here easily rivals that of the better known forests of New England. A popular song goes, "Almost Heaven, West Virginia ..." Sitting on the summit of the South Peak on a quiet weekday evening, with the sun low in the western sky, one might strike the word "almost."

CLIMBING HISTORY

There is a legend that the South Peak was first ascended by an Indian princess named Snowbird. She led a group of braves to the rock, promising herself to whoever followed her to the summit. Only one brave made it, while the others either fell to their deaths or turned back, insufficiently brave.

A surveyor is rumoured to have made the next ascent, in 1908. Undocumented accounts of early technical climbing on the rocks have been reported by the owner of one of Seneca's general stores. Included in these accounts is the story of a vandal who attempted to blow up the Gendarme formation.

Recorded roped ascents began in the mid-1930's, as climbers from Washington D.C. discovered Seneca to be the nearest major rock outcrop. Though they must drive nearly four hours on today's modern roads, Washington area residents continue to be the primary "locals" at Seneca.

The only time that a population of climbers lived near the cliffs was during World War II when the 10th Mountain Division used the rocks as their training base. Upwards of 75,000 pitons were placed in Seneca's hard sandstone; the recruits are said to have been given five pitons per day and told not to come back with them. One face still memorializes these efforts: the "Face of a Thousand Pitons." Such skills as silent belay signals and muffling the sound of piton hammering were taught here. Though the value of the troops has been contested, some claim that a decisive battle in Italy was won by the Division after it climbed a cliff to take the enemy by surprise. The Army did play a decisive role in the future of climbing as a sport, for it was here that nylon ropes, angle pitons and aluminum-alloy carabiners were developed.

Some veterans became leaders in the next stage of Seneca climbing, with free climbing taking a somewhat higher priority when the climbing became purely recreational. Climbers soon began coming from Pennsylvania as well as Washington D.C., with the first listing of routes being published by the Explorer's Club of Pittsburgh. Still, D.C. climbers dominated the Seneca "locals," or at least the standards. Most of the mid-range classics were established during the period that extends to the mid-1960's, with "Triple S" (**Shipley's Shivering Shimmy**) being the hardest, at a stiff 5.8 (it is still considered one of the finest corner/crack pitches on the East Coast).

By the mid-1960's, pressing the limits of difficulty took on a new level of importance. A number of extremely steep and sustained routes were climbed to a standard that was labeled 5.9, albeit conservatively. The term "Seneca 5.9" quickly gained notoriety. 5.10 didn't officially arrive until 1966, and was firmly established during the early 1970's when the quest for hard routes continued to heat up. By the late 70's the challenge of extreme seriousness in both difficulty and sometimes hazard was taken up by an expanding influx of climbers. Despite being one of the leading East Coast climbing centers, Seneca has always been delayed in establishing the hardest contemporary grades, at least as recognized by local ratings. It was 1979 when 5.11 was officially brought to fruition, though it probably should have been assigned to routes put up in 1971, or at least 1975 (**Totem** and **Terra Firma** respectively). 5.12 arrived in 1982.

By the mid-1980's, the main cliffs had been pretty well scoured for route potential, with activity beginning to shift to smaller outlying crags. A number of climbers formerly active at Seneca also began turning their attention to exploring the New River Gorge, also in West Virginia. While the New River Gorge is less known to the international climbing community, Seneca Rocks has been long established as one of *the* places to visit on the East Coast. And among climbers of the Northeast, it has become *the* place to extend the climbing season later into the fall and start it earlier in the spring.

CAMPING

Camping along the riverside used to be popular; however, in November of 1985, a major flood wiped out everything near the river, including the footbridge. The bridge was rebuilt, and a campground was planned for the river bend south of the Gendarme. There is also inexpensive camping on the flats behind the Gendarme climbing shop. Hotel options are limited to Yokum's (telephone: 304-567-2351) and Hedricks 4-U (304-567-2111).

The swimming hole survived the flood. A drinking water spring is located where the trail to the West Face of South Peak leaves the dirt road.

The most popular restaurants with climbers are the Valley View and the Rocks View.

SEASONS AND WEATHER

Approximate Months	Typical Temperatures High	Low	Likelihood of Precipitation	Frequency of Climbable Days
Dec-Feb	40's −	10's +	med-high	low
Mar-May	60's +	30's	med-high	med-high
Jun-Sep	90's −	70's	medium	high
Oct-Nov	60's +	40's −	med-low	high

Comments: During summer, afternoon thundershowers are common. September-early October can be rainy. Sudden brief storms often come from the west, while long sessions of rain come more gradually from the south. Summer heat and winter cold can often be avoided by judicious choice of east versus west faces.

RESTRICTIONS AND WARNINGS

VERY IMPORTANT: Take care to stay on the switchbacking trail that runs through loose talus shortly after leaving the dirt road. Locals are attempting to minimize the visual and erosional blight that occurs when irresponsible people shortcut on the slope.

It is wise to learn the usually intricate descent route before being stranded on the summit in the dark. Carrying a flashlight is highly recommended.

Loose rock dropped by people climbing overhead and occasionally encountered on route is perhaps the greatest hazard at Seneca. Wind and pigeons can also be a nuisance, as can uneducated tourists hiking to the top of the North Peak Trail.

GUIDEBOOKS

Seneca Rocks W. Va. A Climber's Guide (1980) by Bill Webster.

Seneca (A fold-out photo guide.) (1976) by John Stannard. Mail order either guide from The Gendarme, P.O. Box 53, Seneca Rocks WV 26884. A new guidebook has been in the works for a number of years. Anticipated publication date is spring, 1987. Authors: Mike Artz and John Markwell. Mail order from The Gendarme.

GUIDE SERVICES AND EQUIPMENT STORES

The Seneca Rocks Climbing School is run by John Markwell, as is The Gendarme, the local climbing store. Both have become Seneca institutions. The Gendarme is the place to go for new route information, socializing and a complete selection of gear. In fact, many climbers from throughout the Southeast do their shopping here, mail order or in person. Seneca Rocks Climbing School, Gendarme, Seneca Rocks WV 26884. 304-567-2600 day; 703-474-2335 evening.

EMERGENCY SERVICES

Rescues are currently handled by climbers and coordinated by the Gendarme store staff. The evening telephone number is 703-474-2335. The Franklin County Sheriff can be reached at 304-358-1114. The nearest hospital is a half hour away by car: the Grant Memorial Hospital on Route 28 just south of Petersburg, telephone: 304-257-4488. The Davis Memorial Hospital in Elkins is about an hour's drive away, but is larger.

GETTING THERE

The nearest air service is to Elkins, West Virginia, 37 miles away.

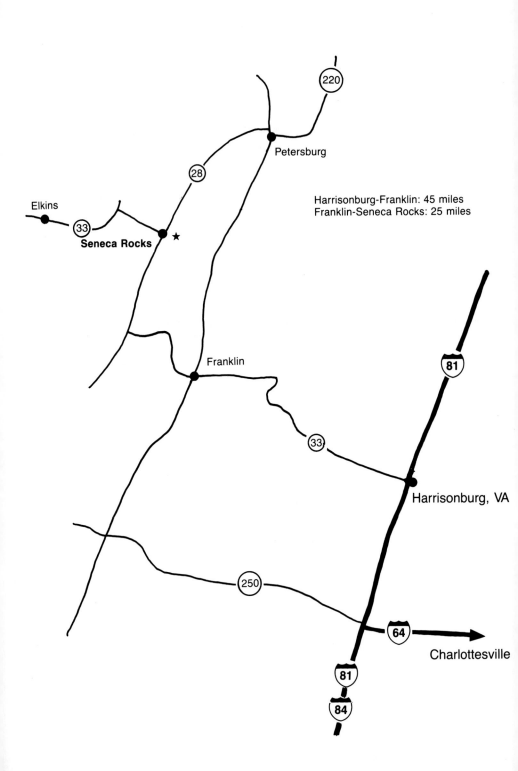

Harrisonburg-Franklin: 45 miles
Franklin-Seneca Rocks: 25 miles

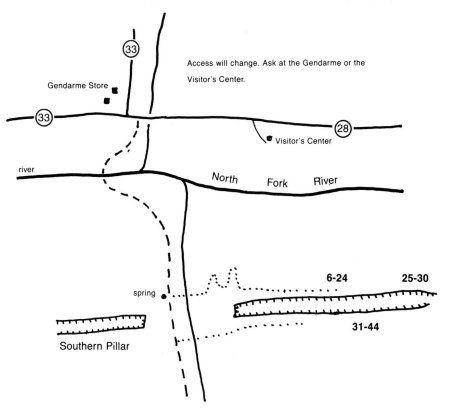

4 Muscle Beach 5.10+ Ray Snead and Matt Hale, 1975. Strenuous but good pro and superb location.

5 Ecstasy 5.7 FA: unknown. Classic.

South End

1 Ye Gods and Little Fishes 5.8 Arnold Wexler, John Reed and Earl Mosburg, 1953. FFA: unknown.

2 Totem 5.10 FA: Ivan Jirak. FFA: John Stannard, 1971.

3 Simple J. Malarky 5.6 FA: Jim McCarthy and Arnold Wexler. Somewhat runout.

South Peak – West Face

6 Breakneck 5.4 FA: Ivan Jirak.

7 Triple S (Shipley's Shivering Shimmy) 5.8 Jim Shipley and Joe Faint, 1960. Supreme classic.

8 Marshall's Madness 5.9 – Tony Marshall and John Christian. The main crack system splitting the left side of the "Face of a Thousand Pitons."

9 Cottonmouth/Venom Flake 5.10 – Matt Hale and Tom Evans, 1969/Hunt Prothro, Herb Laeger and Charlie Rollins, 1975. Strenuous. Start in the right-most short dihedral.

10 Sidewinder 5.11 – Howard Doyle and Eric Janoscrat, 1983.

11 Le Gourmet Direct Start 5.6 FA: unknown. Runout.

12 Projected Futures 5.12 Pete Absolon, 1984.

13 Traffic Jam 5.7 FA: unknown. Superb location.

14 Crispy Critter 5.7 Gary Aitken and Charlie Fowler, 1973.

15 Poor Man's Critter 5.7 Gary Aitken and Steve Piccolo, 1973.

16 Critter Crack 5.6 Dave Garman, Mike Murphy and John Markwell, 1972.

17 Prune 5.6 FA: John Markwell, John Christian and Arnold Wexler. Difficult route finding. Very runout.

18 Conn's West 5.2 N.C. Hartz, Henry Schulter and Earl Richardson, 1944.

19 West Pole 5.7 George Bogel and Jim Payznski, 1970. FFA: Tim Beaman and Larry Myer, 1971. Not nearly as hard as it looks.

20 Bring on the Nubiles 5.9 Hernando Vera and Kevin Stephens, about 1982. Fantastic position and climbing.

21 Thais Direct 5.8 FA: unknown. Follow corner. A Fritz Wiessner route was destroyed when the upper part of the face fell down in 1972.

22 Pleasant Overhangs 5.7 FA: Joe Shipley. Spectacular second belay.

23 Greenwall 5.6 John Christian, Jim Shipley and Alan Talbert, 1956. Classic.

24 Tomato 5.7 Tom Evans and Matt Hale, 1969.

South Peak – West Side

Old Man descent

North Peak – West Face

25 Madmen Only   5.10– FA: Jim Shipley and Joe Faint. FFA: George Livingstone and Roger Craig, 1966. Seneca's first 5.10.

26 Psycho Killer   5.11 Jack Beatty and Alex Karr, 1981.

27 The Bell   5.12– FA: Jeff Burns. FFA: "The Over Thirty Club": Cal Swoager, Alex Karr, Hunt Prothro and Mel Banks, 1983.

28 Malevolence   5.10+ Hunt Prothro and Charle Rollins, 1974. Poor protection.

29 Negative Feedback   5.11 Jack Beatty and Lieth Wain, 1979.

30 Circumflex   5.9 Dennis Grabnegger and Neil Arsensault, 1974. Runout.

Perry Williams on Triple S

South Peak – East Face

31 Soler 5.7 Tony Soler and Ray Moore 1951.

32 Conn's East 5.4 John Stearns, George Kolbucher, Bob Hecker and Jim Crooks, 1944.

33 The Changeling 5.11 Jack Beatty and Jim Woodruff, 1980.

34 Terra Firma Homesick Blues 5.11 Herb Laeger and Eve Uiga, 1975.

35 Castor 5.9 Pat Milligan and George Livingstone, 1971.

36 Pollux 5.9+ Pat Milligan and George Livingstone, 1971

37 Conn's East Direct Start 5.6 Arnold Wexler, 1954. The first moves may b

38 Spock's Brain 5.11– Leith Wain and Jack Beatty, 1979.

39 High Test   5.9 Herb Laeger and Eve Uiga, 1974.

40 Nip and Tuck   5.10 Herb Laeger and Eve Uiga, 1974. FFA: Bob Richardson, Rich Perch and Herb Laeger 1974. Runout.

41 The Gendarme   5.4 Paul Bradt, Sam Moore and Don Hubbard, 1940. Several harder variations are possible.

42 Eeyor's Tail   5.3 FA: unknown.

43 Orangeaid   5.9 Mark Carpenter and Barry Wallen, 1966. FFA: John Stannard, 1971.

44 Alcoa Presents   5.8 FA: Joe Faint and Mike Nicholson. FFA: Tom Evans, Bob Lyons and Bob Williams, 1968.

Stuart Pregnall on Lost Arrow, Great Falls

CARDEROCK GREAT FALLS

HIGHLIGHTS

Just a few minutes' drive from downtown Washington, D.C., Carderock and Great Falls provide rock climbers with delightful little crags. The tallest cliffs are only about 70 feet high, but their quantity, quality and the beauty of their natural setting make them ideal for afterwork training by bureaucrats, politicians and other Washington residents. The cliffs and their surroundings – the Potomac River and the C & O Canal – are also a delight to climbers who pass through Washington.

CLIMBING

Ironically, weekends at Carderock and Great Falls are sometimes less crowded than weekday evenings. This is because Washington residents can easily reach Seneca Rocks for the weekend, while the New River Gorge and the Shawangunks are accessible as well. Carderock and Great Falls can thus be used for weekday training, leaving the body honed for bigger action on weekends.

Over the last several decades, tradition has called for top roping, not leading, at both Carderock and Great Falls. The short cliffs, ranging from 30 to 70 feet in height, are ideal for this, as are the convenient upper anchors (usually sturdy trees). Top roping allows the cliffs to be scoured for routes – even where there is no potential protection – while maintaining safety and fun for afterwork climbers seeking relaxation and physical training. Many younger climbers, not yet in need of relaxation, choose to solo, sometimes very competitively. Leading is discouraged not only because nut placements are frequently absent, but also because the rock frequently deforms under stress – causing nuts and even pitons to pop out.

Free-soloing is made especially hair-raising by the nature of the rock. Though very compact and almost always solid (especially on the travelled routes), it is a mica-schist where wavy and downsloping holds are common. The schist tends to be slippery, especially on the frequent humid days that Washington is famous for. Popular Carderock routes are notoriously slick, some taking on a polished sheen. For diversity, tiny quartz inclusions that require delicate edging are sometimes found.

The Carderock and Great Falls climbing areas, both situated on the banks of the Potomac River within a few miles of each other, are distinctly different in both access and popularity. Carderock is the easiest place for a Washington resident to sandwich a couple of hours of climbing between work and dark, and, as a consequence, it usually packs about five times as many climbers into one tenth the quantity of rock. Nevertheless, Carderock is still attractive to all but the most crowd-hating of persons. It is a fine place to boulder, with good landings on smooth ground. The area is compact, with a well used trail along the cliff's base, and is ideally suited to meeting potential partners for weekend trips or simply for a belay on the higher problems.

Due to the intense use and top roped climbing, routes have been densely squeezed onto the better sections of cliff. Many routes are so contrived that one must carefully monitor "on" versus "off" route holds. Some climbs have moved a few inches left or right over the years, with a common Carderock scene running: "Don't use that foothold! BEEP – off route, get down and try it again." Locals used to pride themselves on sandbagging, leading to gradings that bore little resemblance to reality. Sandbagging is less common now, but many routes have kept their offbeat grades as a "humorous" tradition.

Great Falls takes a bit more time to get to, and its cliffs are scattered over a far broader area: a couple of miles along both sides of the Mather River Gorge of the Potomac. Because of the scattered climbing, because the bouldering is less attractive (poor landings) and because climbers tend to go there with partners, this not such a good place to meet people. However, if the object is solitude, Great Falls offers a remarkably remote experience considering its proximity to such a major metropolitan area as Washington, D.C.

Good cliffs can be found on both banks of the Potomac below the Great Falls themselves. The eastern (Maryland) side is the most frequented by tourists and picnickers, who find the old C & O Canal and trails spurring to the river's edge a fascinating attraction. There are a few interesting cliffs here, but by far the greatest number and diversity lie on the Virginia side. Only Virginia cliffs have been included in this book, but the Maryland side is recommended for its delightful walk along the C & O Canal and for some climbing as well. (To see the Virginia cliffs from the Maryland side, start at the Great Falls Tavern visitor center, then take the Billy Goat Trail to the river's edge).

Experienced local climbers have developed an excellent top rope anchor system. They use a long section of rope – preferably nonelastic caving rope covered with one inch tubular webbing – to extend from the cliff edge back the sometimes considerable distance to a good tree anchor. The webbing acts as an extra sheath that both protects the anchor rope from cutting over the sometimes sharp edges, and is replaceable when damage does show up. Be sure to check thoroughly for people below before dropping the rope over the cliff.

ENVIRONMENT

Carderock's cliffs lie in the woods at the edge of a quiet side channel of the Potomac River. A short trail, little more than a hundred yards long, leads from the parking lot and picnic area to the top of the cliff, from which an easy scramble (or another short trail) leads to the base of the cliffs. Heavily foliated from spring through autumn, the deciduous forest canopy keeps most of the cliffs well shaded during the hot summer months – though hardly free from the almost omnipresent humidity.

To non-climbers, "Carderock" does not refer to the cliff itself; instead, it is the name of the 100 acre recreation area that is a part of the Chesapeake & Ohio (C & O) Canal National Historical Park administered by the National Park Service. Lately, climbers have also had a hand in managing the area around the cliffs, with the trail and belaying area at the base being renovated by a group of volunteers that include members of the Potomac Appalachian Trail Club, the American Alpine Club, and many individuals unaffiliated with clubs.

Great Falls, though quieter in terms of climbing activity, is far more boisterous in its physical environment than is Carderock. The cliffs line the open bank of the Potomac River, sometimes dropping straight into the water. And the water here is churning, as the Potomac plunges over the Great Falls and races through the narrow channel of the Mather Gorge. It is a favorite place for kayakers, who usually outnumber the climbers. On a hot day, few climbers would not eagerly change places with a kayaker playing in the standing waves at the head of the Gorge. Fortunately, the cliffs on the Virginia side (included in this book) are generally shaded in the afternoon because of their eastern orientation. Visitors on a cold midwinter afternoon would do better to explore the Maryland side or, even warmer, stay at Carderock.

Perhaps Carderock and Great Falls would have been preserved as parks for their physical beauty alone, but the principle reason for their preservation is the presence of the historically fascinating canals: the C & O and the Potowmack. The Potowmack is a short canal that bypasses the Great Falls on the Virginia side. The C & O, however, extends for 185 miles, from tidewater to Cumberland. Built between 1828 and 1850, the canal was conceived at a time when boat traffic was vital to opening the West, and completed by the time the railroad had rendered canals almost obsolete. It was never financially successful, but was still maintained despite occasional floods until 1924. Now, it is a dinosaur kept in superficial order for the benefit of great numbers of tourists, Washington picnickers and walkers. In fact, its banks provide multi-day hiking and bicycling trails, complete with campgrounds every five miles.

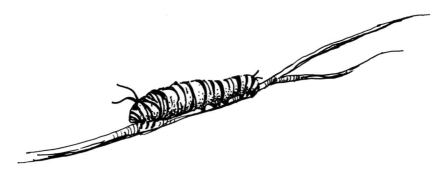

CLIMBING HISTORY

Roped climbing at both Carderock and Great Falls dates almost from the origin of the sport in North America. In the late 1920's and during the 1930's, a few climbers plied many of the cliffs of the region. During that period, lead climbing was prefered to top roping, and multi-pitch climbs up to six pitches long were ferretted out of the small cliffs, mostly by heavy reliance on traversing and short ropes. Some top roping was done as well, with standards at an extraordinary level when compared with lead climbs elsewhere. At least one 5.9 route was top roped as early as 1936. Aid climbing was never popular here, though it was certainly practiced on occasion.

It was during World War II that Carderock became the primary climbing area. Gas rationing cut back on mobility by automobile, so climbers took the trolley to Glen Echo, then walked an hour through sometimes jungle-like terrain to Carderock. From the War on, Carderock's popularity has been maintained by its ready convenience to the urban masses. One can now drive to within a two minute walk to the cliff, allowing literally hours of climbing after work or school.

For decades the cliffs were used principally as training grounds by mountain clubs. The largest of these, the "Washington Climbers," transformed into the Mountaineering Section of the Potomac Appalachian Trail Club (a mostly hiking/nature-oriented group). But by the 1960's, the club members visiting the cliffs started to be outnumbered by non-members. Still, the PATC plays a valuable role in organizing trail maintenance and publishing the Great Falls guidebook. There are also a number of schools and other organizations that use the cliffs for teaching and training. Popular routes, even some difficult ones, often become quite polished through repeated attempts and successes.

With today's ease of mobility, Carderock, and to a lesser extent Great Falls, are firmly entrenched as weekday climbing areas, with weekends reserved for multi-hour drives to Seneca or further flung areas.

CAMPING

Just a mile north of Carderock is one of the "Hiker-Biker" campgrounds (Marsden Tract), but it must be hiked into, carrying all of one's gear; a free permit must be obtained from the Great Falls Tavern (a.k.a. Visitor's Center) at the end of McArthur Boulevard on the Maryland side of Great Falls – open daily 9-5, ask for legal places to park overnight. Another option, about ten miles from the climbing areas, is Lake Fairfax Park Campground in Virginia (telephone: 703-471-5415). The Bennett Regional Park is a 20-30 minute drive from Carderock, moderatly priced and has showers: 23701 Frederick Road, off I-270 in Clarksburg, MD, telephone 301-972-9222. Hotels in Washington D.C. are notoriously expensive, though some good buys can be found. The Washington International Youth Hostel/Franklin Park Hotel is at 1332 I Street, NW (telephone: 202-347-3125).

SEASONS AND WEATHER

Approximate Months	Typical Temperatures High	Low	Likelihood of Precipitation	Frequency of Climbable Days
Dec-Feb	50's –	30's	medium	med-high
Mar-May	70's	40's +	med-high	med-high
Jun-Sep	90's	70's +	medium	high-med
Oct-Nov	70's	40's	medium	high

Comments: Humidity is very high from late spring to late summer.

RESTRICTIONS AND WARNINGS

A voluntary registration system is available at the visitor's center on the Virginia side of the Great Falls Park. Climbing on that side is prohibited below overlooks and between the overlooks and the falls. Climbing on historic buildings is prohibited. The parks close at dark. No alcoholic beverages are allowed. Poison ivy is thick in some approach gullys at Great Falls. Copperhead snakes are occasionally encountered. The river drowns an average of seven people a year – be careful at the water's edge!

GUIDEBOOKS

Climber's Guide to Carderock (1980) by John Forrest Gregory. Available from local stores or from John Forrest Gregory, 4114 Davis Place, N.W. #105, Washington, D.C. 20007.

Climber's Guide to the Great Falls of the Potomac (1985) by James A. Eakin. Available from local shops or from the Mountaineering Section of the Potomac Appalachian Trail Club, 1718 North Street, N.W., Washington, D.C. 20036.

EMERGENCY SERVICES

In an emergency, the Park Service should be contacted by calling 301-426-6680. The police and other emergency services can be reached by calling 911.

GETTING THERE

To negotiate the freeways and urban traffic, a car is almost mandatory.

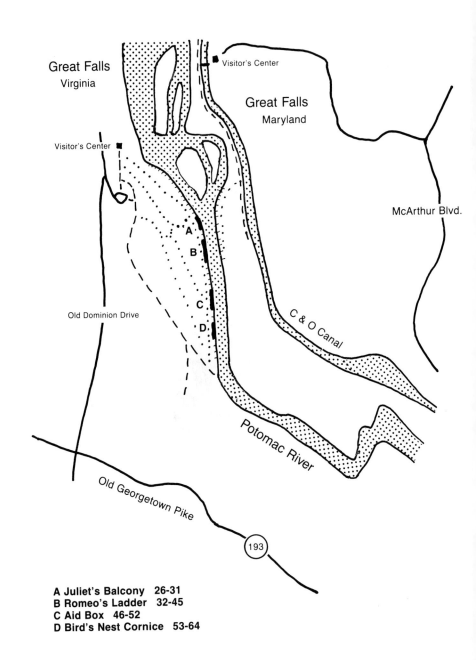

Great Falls
Virginia

Visitor's Center

Great Falls
Maryland

Visitor's Center

McArthur Blvd.

A

B

C

Old Dominion Drive

D

C & O Canal

Potomac River

Old Georgetown Pike

193

A Juliet's Balcony 26-31
B Romeo's Ladder 32-45
C Aid Box 46-52
D Bird's Nest Cornice 53-64

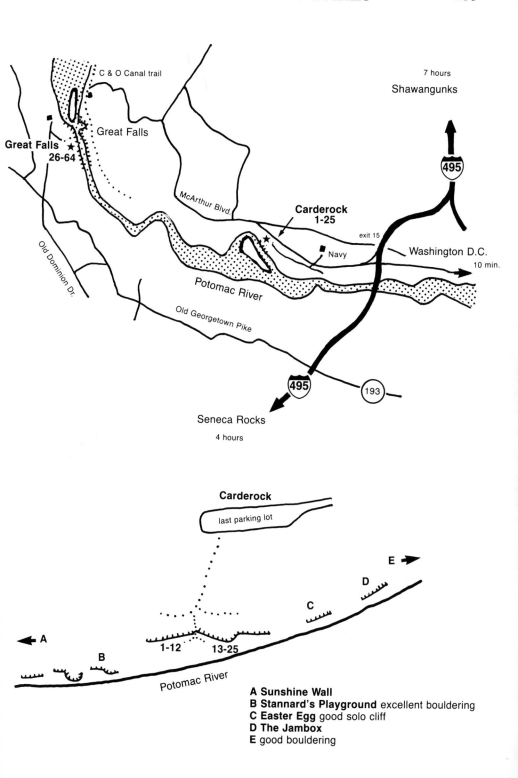

A **Sunshine Wall**
B **Stannard's Playground** excellent bouldering
C **Easter Egg** good solo cliff
D **The Jambox**
E good bouldering

John Forrest Gregory at Carderock

Stuart Pregnall on Cripple's Face, Carderock

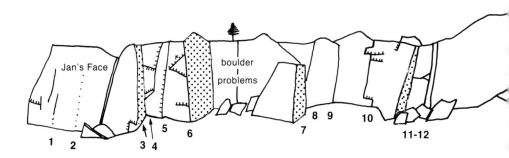

CARDEROCK

1 Stannard's Flake   5.10 Don't step outside of cracks.

2 5.4 route up Jan's Face.

3 The Dream and variations   5.10 to 5.12 The easiest route starts from the block under the outside of the overhang; the most difficult starts using a knee jam and goes directly out overhang.

4 The Rack   5.6   (Direct 5.9+) The Rack starts from the top of the block; the Direct climbs the right edge through the two overhangs.

5 Stirling's Crack   5.5 The layback crack.

6 Schmoe's Nose   5.11− Several variations possible.

7 Back of Impossible   5.9 The overhanging arête.

8 Swayback Layback   5.7 The right-facing layback from the left edge of the face to a crack.

9 Ronnie's Leap   5.7 The left-facing ramp. Named after Herb and Jan Conn's dog, who walked off the top.

10 Beginner's Crack   5.0 Greasy but good.

11 Meenahan's   5.7 Face climb up the low angle side of the flake, staying within one foot of the right edge.

12 Back of Meenahan's   5.10 Brute laybacking and heel hooking up the severely overhanging side of the flake.

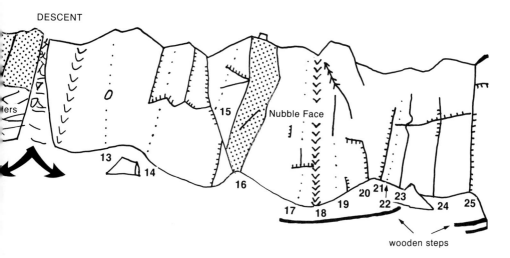

wooden steps

13 Silver Spot   5.12/5.13 Start on nubbins to the right of the dead tree. Currently the hardest climb at Carderock.

14 Biceps Bulge   5.8 Undercling over roof.

15 Green Buckets   5.7 Start on ramp and go up through middle of bulge.

16 Crack   5.1 The original Golden Staircase.

17 Incipient Crack   5.9 Climb the incipient crack at the overhang using only the holds within six inches of the crack.

18 Chris' Goat   5.6 The outside corner.

19 Cripple's Crack   5.9 The most prominent right-slanting crack. A classic.

20 Cripple's Face   5.8 The face right of the main crack.

21 Butterfly   5.8 Climb the river-facing wall without using the corner.

22 Merv's Nerv   5.9 Very small face holds between **Butterfly** and **Easy Layback**.

23 Easy Layback   5.4 Classic.

24 Triple A   5.7 Up a face to three "A" shaped holds, then over roof.

25 Trudy's Terror   5.3 The prominent inside corner.

GREAT FALLS

Juliet's Balcony
26 **Mantelpiece** **5.10+** Avoid using the arête and the inside corner.
27 **Right Stuff** **5.7**
28 **Left Stuff** **5.7**
29 **Balcony Corner** **5.5**
30 **Backslider** **5.7**
31 **Possibilities** **5.9**

Romeo's Ladder/Seclusion
32 **Zig-Zag Edge** **5.5**
33 **Stan's Lead** **5.5**
34 **Sickle Face** **5.10**
35 **Snowflake** **5.6**
36 **Flaky** **5.8**
37 **Great Beginnings** **5.7**
38 **Nylons** **5.9+**
39 **Romeo's Ladder** **5.6**
40 **Ergometer** **5.11**
41 **Lunging Ledges** **5.9**
42 **Entropy** **5.11−**
43 **The Demon** **5.12+**
44 **Oyster** **5.12−** Follow the bolt ladder.
45 **Delivery Room** **5.5**

Aid Box
46 **P.V. Wall (Potomac Valley Wall)** **5.12−** Stay left of crack in upper wall.
47 **P.V.O. (Potomac Valley Overhang)** **5.12−**
48 **Lost Arrow** **5.10**
49 **Splinters** **5.7**
50 **Diagonal** **5.9−** The crack.
51 **Monkey Fingers** **5.12−**
52 **Dark Corner** **5.6**

Bird's Nest/Corners

53 Eagle's Nest   5.9−
54 Fair Square   5.11
55 Bird's Nest   5.7
56 Plumb Line   5.12
57 Two Lane Highway   5.10−
58 One Lane Highway   5.10
59 Shoulder of the Road   5.9
60 Z Slash (a.k.a. Lightning Bolt)   5.11+
61 Armbuster   5.9
62 The Nose   5.6
63 Crank Up   5.10
64 Tiparillo   5.11+

Karen Roussell on Right Stuff, Great Falls

Sky Top Cliff and the A.K. Smiley memorial tower

SHAWANGUNKS

HIGHLIGHTS

By remarkable coincidence, this most extensive of East Coast crag complexes is also within a short drive of New York City, the greatest metropolitan area in the country. Its climbing culture is profoundly shaped by that proximity. The sheer number of climbers would easily overwhelm almost any other area, but the scope and unique nature of the "Gunks" welcomes the weekend crowds with class and distinction. Horizontally layered, the impeccably solid quartzite/conglomerate provides face holds and fracture lines that lead climbers onto improbable faces and overhangs. This is one of the rare places where a 5.4 route can provide the high quality of a 5.10. With over 1,000 routes to choose from, on cliffs that average 200 feet in height, it is possible to find peace on even the most popular weekends. And the serenity is not limited to the climbs: 5,000 surrounding acres of wooded hills are preserved by the Mohonk Preserve. They are of a gentle beauty that is rendered especially memorable by their proximity to the New York City area.

CLIMBING

For seven miles, the Shawangunk Mountains have an escarpment that faces southeast. Occasional breaks pierce the escarpment, cleaving it into separate cliffs.

The Trapps is a 200 foot high cliff that extends continuously for over a mile. A carriage road runs near the base of the cliff, and climbers stroll along the unpaved road, reading the guidebook and matching photos while scanning the rocks above. The Trapps absorbs most of the climbers who visit the Gunks, offering them hundreds of routes at all levels of difficulty. Here are found the largest number of easy climbs, with good routes down to 5.3 that ascend vertical faces on large, clean holds. Many of these easier climbs have ledges that divide the cliff into comfortable sections, helping to keep a beginner at ease. At levels only a couple of grades harder, climbers tackle horizontal roofs that are intimidating from below, but which supply magic handholds above. Of course, on other roofs a climber doesn't feel quite as serendipitous, and the difficulty skyrockets. Most climbing at the Trapps, however, does not involve roofs – it is simply steep, with sharp edges. The grade is usually determined by the size of those edges and the distance between them.

Because of the massive scope of the Trapps, this book excerpts two sections that are particularly good, diverse, and easy to locate. Topos of the cliff are keyed into obvious features on the carriage road. Though routes at the "Uberfall" are not covered, this is the area one passes on the road where the standard descent takes place, where the bulletin board and emergency rescue box is located, where the ranger collects the day use fee and, most recognizably, where the largest crowds hang out. This is the great climber gathering point, where friends meet-up, plans are made, and climbing is avoided. The nearby section of cliff between **Belly Roll** and **Maria** (covered on the first topo) has one of the most popular collections of easy and moderate routes, with a few hard classics as well. The other section described stretches between **High Exposure,** a perfectly named 5.6 route that epitomizes the tremendous "air" that one finds at the Gunks on bucket-sized holds, and the **Yellow Wall** area, whose 5.11 and 5.12 routes project the climber out a series of overlapping roofs.

The neighboring Near Trapps cliff is much less extensive. The topo drawings cover the entirety of its solid, popularly climbed northern section, running from **Kansas City** to **Farewell to Arms.** If the Trapps has many roofs, the Near Trapps is a veritable maze of them. Fortunately, the maze has passageways between overhangs that allow moderate ascents. And naturally, some routes seek out difficulties instead of avoiding them, tackling the roofs directly. **Kansas City,** the first 5.12 at the Gunks, plasters the climber to the underside of a nearly horizontal roof for a dozen feet. Despite the amazing number of routes on the topos, even more exist that have not been drawn in. With some of the Shawangunk's finest rock, this section of the Near Trapps has few routes not worth recommending.

Sky Top, lying at the end of a gentle four mile walk along wooded carriage roads, is the least visited cliff in this chapter. Least visited by climbers, that is, because the fantastic – in the literal sense of the word – neighboring Mohonk Mountain House resort fields many walkers who explore the talus below the cliffs and investigate the Smiley Memorial

Tower above. Sky Top is unique at the Shawangunks because it doesn't simply face east, it wraps around to face southwest as well. Most of the routes in this book lie on the southwestern exposure. The 150 foot cliff may not be quite as tall as the Trapps, but since it rises out of bare talus, there are no trees to interfere with the expansive views or the blowing winds – which can be good or bad, depending on the temperature and number of bugs.

Parking for all three of these cliffs takes place between the hairpin turn and the pass at the southern terminous of the Trapps. On a spring or fall weekend, the visitor will be simply astounded by the number of cars: several hundred have been counted. The parking situation is likely to be changed soon, with a new lot being constructed over the hill.

In addition to the three cliffs covered in this book, there are others. Millbrook is the tallest at the Gunks, measuring over 200 feet, while several smaller cliffs traditionally left out of local guidebooks lie scattered over the region, often becoming weekend retreats for those in the know who want to escape the gathering crowds.

ENVIRONMENT

Just an hour and a half's drive north from New York City, the Shawangunk Mountains rise out of apple orchard country. In the fall, cider flows from the fruit stands nearly as freely as water from the spring at the Uberfall. Clifftop views extend eastward over the patchwork of farms, pasturelands and towns that comprise the fertile Hudson River Valley.

The crags themselves are set on the southeast-facing ridgeline of the wooded Shawangunk Mountain hills, whose deciduous trees highlight the four seasons that affect the East Coast so decisively. During the chilly days of winter, the leafless trees let the sun shine through to the cliffs, often warming them enough for comfortable climbing. In spring, the pastel greens of budding trees parallel the rising excitement of climbers who come from as far as Quebec for their traditional opening to the climbing season. In summer, the heavy foliage serves to shade the lower sections of the routes from the hot sun, and in the fall, the spectacular colors and wind-blown leaves can pull a belayer's attention away from his duties. Fall is when the two hour round-trip walk to Sky Top is worth doing for a half hour climb – or skip the climb, for that matter.

Five thousand of the wooded acres surrounding the cliffs are managed by the Mohonk Preserve, Inc., which is dedicated to maintaining the land in a natural state for recreational and educational purposes. The private land accumulation began in 1869 by the Smiley family, who built and continue to maintain the Mohonk Mountain House resort near Sky Top. The non-profit Mohonk Trust, later Preserve, was established in the early 1960's to protect the land in perpetuity. All outdoor lovers are thankful for the preservation effort of the Smiley family, with climbers especially grateful that the cliffs have never been threatened with closure – though the law-suit and liability insurance crises of the mid-1980's together pose an ominous cloud over continued access.

From the cliffs, the village of New Paltz is clearly visible just seven miles away, and the campus of the State University of New York can be seen in town. Surely no college students could have more accessible climbing; a few have enrolled here specifically for that reason – though all the schools of the New York metropolitan area are within easy reach of the Gunks and offer stiff competition for those whose academic interests rival their climbing ambitions. In fact, a wonder of the Shawangunks is the cross section of climbers that frequent the cliffs. The climbing population has exceptional urban sophistication, and on a weekend one is more likely to share a belay ledge with an art dealer or an investment banker than a mono-focused climber. While many high-powered businesspeople are weekend warriors fully capable of turning their energy and drive loose onto the hardest of climbs, more are climbers simply because of the friendly nature of the Gunks. Here non-demanding climbs are found that are clean, exposed and highly enjoyable. At the Gunks, a family can enjoy climbing as they might enjoy a mountain hike in the Rockies.

CLIMBING HISTORY

An intriguing claim to New Paltz is made by some Germans, who feel that the town's name was actually "New Pfaltz," after the Pfaltz forests of West German/French border region. The town, according to this theory, was named in memory of the prominent cliffs of the Pfaltz, cliffs which are among Germany's most popular for rock climbing.

True or otherwise, the cliffs of the Shawangunks were well known to the many wealthy vacationers who frequented the Mohonk Mountain House resort. The resort originated in the late 1800's and was popular in the early 1900's, the period when rock climbing was first gaining a toehold in America. Considering the fact that the Gunks has become the most popular climbing spot on the East Coast, if not in the country, it would be logical to think that rock climbing in North America had originated there.

It comes as a great surprise then, to learn that the Gunks were not discovered by climbers until 1935. While the sport was well into its first boom period in New Hampshire, with climbers ferreting out every crag they could find, Shawangunk rock lay untouched. The story of its discovery reads like melodramatic fiction. Thirty miles away, climbers were ascending another cliff which has now faded into obscurity. In the crystal-clear air that followed a thunderstorm, they spotted a line of cliffs on the horizon where normally only the hazy eastern atmosphere could be seen. One of the climbers had been active in exploring New Hampshire's crags and lost no time in checking out his new discovery, nearly a day's drive closer to his New York home than North Conway. Suddenly, the Gunks had arrived. As far as climbers are concerned, the cliffs might have materialized during a clap of the thunderstorm that preceeded their discovery.

Histrionics aside, early climbing at the Gunks was dominated by two immigrants from Germany and Austria who found here a pale substitute for the beloved mountains they had left behind. Until the 1950's they, with a few additional climbers who usually paired up with the leading two, set the tone of local climbing. With so much rock to explore, there was little quest for sheer difficulty. One 5.8 was climbed in 1946, but it became so legendary that no one considered approaching that grade again for eleven years.

Another irony of this early period is that for years only Millbrook and Sky Top were thought to be worthy of climbing. The Trapps and Near Trapps were ignored as being too scruffy to be of interest. Also worthy of note is that in the late 1940's and early 1950's, a woman was one of the leading climbers at the Gunks, helping to establish many of the most difficult new routes. This situation anticipated the 1980's, when women again took their place at the cutting edge of difficult route development – a situation unparalleled in North America, perhaps anywhere.

The increase in climbing popularity was gradual, building from two dozen people on a busy weekend in the early 1940's to twice that number ten years later. (Contrast that to over 1,000 people in the mid-1980's.) Most of the climbers during this period were members of the Appalachian Mountain Club, whose emphasis in climbing centered more on socializing than on physical or mental challenge. The laid-back approach began to change in the mid-1950's with the arrival of a few young, unaffiliated climbers. They delighted in negotiating difficult rock and in competition. Two in particular were hot on each other's heels, driving the standards quickly past the known realm of 5.6 routes and into increasingly uncharted territory. Enormous psychological barriers were passed with every milestone, as 5.8 proved possible in 1957, 5.9 in 1960, and 5.10 in 1961.

While for some climbers the quest to tumble barriers on the rock was its own reward, for others the freedom of climbing was a metaphor in their attempt to crumble the restrictions of social order. The Appalachian Mountain Club was a third group, an entrenched part of that social order. Conflict soon erupted, with some of the freedom-hunters being assigned, and eagerly accepting, the entirely appropriate name "Vulgarians." The AMC "Appies" and the Vulgarians fed off of each other's excesses, thus creating one of the most colorful chapters in American "climbing" history. This conflict between conservative club members and a younger, less bureaucratic generation bears a certain resemblance to the current situation in Quebec climbing as described in its chapters in this book.

Action on the cliffs did not stop for rearranging the social hierarchy on the ground. The late 1950's also saw a growing awareness of the national and international scope of the sport, with Gunks climbers venturing to the major areas of the West, and Westerners and Europeans visiting the Gunks. This activity crested in the early 60's, ebbed for a few years, and swelled again in the later 60's.

5.11 arrived with an eye-opening bang in 1970 with the free ascent of **Foops.** Though initially graded 5.10, the audacity of free climbing such an appalling ceiling shook climbers up. The next year the 5.11 grade was officially given to other climbs, while young climbers brought a level of intensity to the act of climbing that had not been seen to date. The 5.12 roof of **Kansas City** was climbed in 1973, and **Super Crack** went the following year. Though the pace of climbing continued unabated, the 5.13 grading didn't arrive for another decade, until the ascent of **Vandals** in 1983.

As the 70's progressed, climbers increasingly went at routes that were not only hard to climb, but were hard or impossible to protect. To some extent, this boldness was dictated by the clean-climbing precedent set during the hard-climbing explosion of the late 60's. This activity coincided with the advent and quick acceptance of nuts, and the local ethics boiled down to a philosophy of preserving the rock in its original form. Bolts were disapproved of, and to this day few will be found on the miles of cliffs at the Shawangunks. Given the fact that only the location of protection is dictated by cracks, not the location of holds, even the nearly 1,000 routes listed in the 1986 guidebook does not nearly exhaust the area's climbing potential.

CAMPING

Considering the private ownership of the Shawangunks area and the number of people who climb here, the camping is amazingly undeveloped. Many climbers roll out their bivouac sacks on the carriage road near the Uberfall. Others sleep next to or in their cars, especially on the dirt road below the hairpin. The parking parking between the hairpin turn and the pass is likely to change soon, as is the tenting area near the pass. Notice signs will appear.

Spring-fed drinking water (whose potability is not guaranteed) can be found from the pipe at the Uberfall and at the road directly below.

Numerous hotel options and all the other amenities of a small city can be found in New Paltz. A popular breakfast spot is the Plaza Diner, on the eastern side of town.

A good bed-and-breakfast establishement is Ujjala's, at 2 Forrest Glen, telephone: 914-255-6360. Least expensive (and possibly least attractive) is the Huguenot Motel, by the railroad tracks. More comfortable are the Thunderbird (914-255-6200) and 87 Motel (914-255-9220). The Anzor is considered by some to be the best of a poor lot (914-883-7373). Most expensive, but a memorable experience, is the Mohonk Mountain House (914-255-1000); try one of their murder-mystery weekends if you've tired of climbing.

Camping is not permitted deeper into the Mohonk Preserve, and is especially disapproved of near Sky Top. This is a day-use area that receives considerable traffic.

There is a fee campground in nearby Gardiner: Ganahgote Campsites (914 255-5193).

On selected Saturday nights in the spring and fall, the Mohonk Preserve provides a climbing lecture or film for a small fee at the university. They claim to do it, at least in part, to keep the climbers out of the local bars. Visit Rock and Snow for details on the programs and location.

SEASONS AND WEATHER

Approximate Months	Typical Temperatures High	Low	Likelihood of Precipitation	Frequency of Climbable Days
Dec-Mar	30's	20's −	med-high	low-med
Apr-May	70's	30's +	medium	high-med
Jun-Aug	80's +	60's	medium	medium
Sep-Nov	70's −	30's −	medium	high

Comments: Blackflies make their unpleasant appearance in spring, while mosquitoes can be a nuisance all summer. Chiggers can also prove to be pests, producing little itching welts. Morning sun can quickly warm sheltered walls in the winter, while summer heat and humidity can make the cliffs ridiculously muggy.

RESTRICTIONS AND WARNINGS

Anyone on Mohonk Preserve property must pay a small day-use fee. Alternatively, one can purchase a yearly pass. This fee provides much of the operating budget for maintenance of the Preserve and should not be avoided by climbers. Most climbers consider themselves fortunate that they have never been restricted in their use of the cliffs. They do everything in their power to maintain good relations with the management. The fee is usually collected on the carriage road near the Uberfall, though a ranger could come asking for it anywhere.

Always search out the most established approach trail and use it; indiscriminate wanderings on the shale-based talus slope leading to the cliffs from the carriage road can cause severe erosional damage.

Overnighting in the Sky Top area is not permitted.

Thefts of climbing equipment – from cars, tents and the cliffs themselves – are an inevitable result of the popularity of the Shawangunks.

GUIDEBOOKS
The Gunks Guide (1986) by Todd Swain. Alpine Diversions, Box 42, New Paltz, NY 12561.

Shawangunk Rock Climbs (1980) by Richard C. Williams. American Alpine Club, 113 East 90th Street, New York, NY 10028.

Shawangunk Rock Climbing (1985) by Richard DuMais. Stunning color action photos. Chockstone Press, 526 Franklin Street, Denver, CO 80218.

GUIDE SERVICES AND EQUIPMENT STORES
Rock and Snow in New Paltz is the major equipment outlet for many climbers throughout the New York area. The store is on the main street near the traffic light at the bottom of the hill.

Most of the numerous private guides can be contacted through Rock and Snow, 44 Main Street, New Paltz, NY 12561, telephone: 914-255-1311. Peak Performance Inc., operates independently: 130 Mountain Rest Road, New Paltz, NY 12561, telephone: 914-255-7017.

EMERGENCY SERVICES
In case of emergency contact a ranger if possible. The Mohonk Preserve can be reached at 255-0919, and the Mohonk Mountain House is good in an emergency at 255-1000. The New Paltz Rescue Service and the police can be reached at 255-1323. The Medical Associates of New Paltz are at 40 Sunset Ridge, telephone: 255-1200. The nearest hospital is Vasser Brothers Hospital, at Reade Place in Poughkeepsie, telephone: 454-8500. Alternatively, one could use the Kingston Hospital at 373 Broadway, Kingston, telephone: 331-8566.

GETTING THERE
Trailways buses serve New Paltz. From there, it should be no problem to hitch-hike to the cliffs or to bum a ride in Rock and Snow.

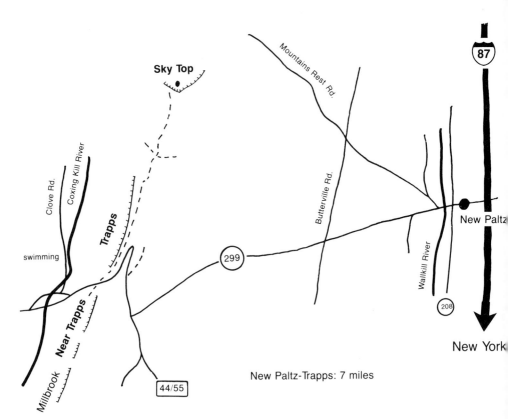

New Paltz-Trapps: 7 miles

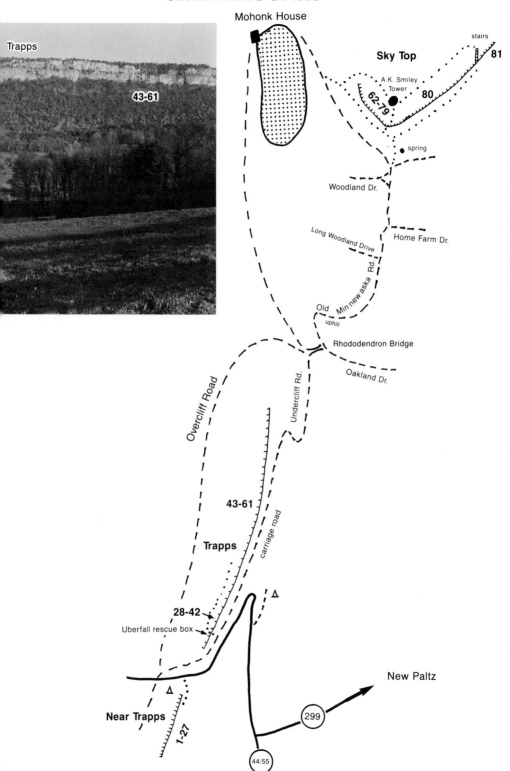

Mohonk House

Trapps

43-61

Sky Top

stairs

81

A.K. Smiley
Tower

62-79   80

spring

Woodland Dr.

Long Woodland Drive   Home Farm Dr.

Old   Minnewaska Rd.

uphill

Rhododendron Bridge

Oakland Dr.

Overcliff Road

Undercliff Rd.

43-61

carriage road

Trapps

28-42

Uberfall rescue box

New Paltz

299

Near Trapps

1-27

44/55

Near Trapps

1 **Farewell to Arms** **5.8** Jim McCarthy and Al DeMaria, 1960

2 **Bird Cage** **5.10** Dick Williams, Steve Arsenault and Wilbur Cain, 1971. FFA: Henry Barber and Bob Anderson, 1972.

3 **Birdland** **5.9** Jim McCarthy, John Rupley and Jim Andress, 1958.

4 **Transcontinental Nailway** **5.10** Joe Fitschen and Art Gran, 1961. FFA: Jim McCarthy, 1965.

5 **Roseland** **5.9** Jim McCarthy and Hans Kraus, 1958. FFA: Jim McCarthy, 1960.

6 **Gelsa** **5.4** Fritz Wiessner, Beckett Howorth and George Temple, 1942.

7 **Fat City** **5.10** John Stannard and Gary Brown, 1968. FFA: Dick Williams and Dave Craft, 1966.

8 **Baskerville Terrace** **5.7** John Wharton and Dave Isles, 1958. FFA: Jim McCarthy, 1961.

9 **Requiem for a Heavyweight** **5.12-** Russ Clune and Russ Raffa, 1982.

10 **Fat Stick** **5.7** Jim McCarthy and Hans Kraus, 1957.

11 **Yellow Ridge** **5.7** Fritz Wiessner, Edward and Ann Gross, 1944.

12 **Yellow Belly** **5.9** Jim McCarthy, Bob Larsen and Ken Prestrud, 1957.

13 **No Slings Attached** **5.10** John Bragg, Mark Robinson and Russ Raffa, 1977.

14 **Alphonse** **5.8** Ken Prestrud and Lucien Warner, 1948. FFA: John Turner.

15 **Grand Central** **5.9** Bonnie Prudden, Hans Kraus and Dick Hirschland, 1947. FFA: Jim McCarthy, 1963.

16 **Layback** **5.5** Fritz Wiessner and George Temple, 1941. The first route at the Near Trapps.

17 **Inverted Layback** **5.9** Dave Craft and Pete Geiser, 1959.

18 **Te Dum** **5.7** Hans Kraus and Roger Wolcott, 1949. FFA: Art Gran.

19 **Swing Time** **5.11** Ants Leemets and Elmer Skahan, 1964. FFA: John Stannard, 1968.

20 **Sling Time** **5.11** Dick Williams and Jim McCarthy, 1964. FFA: John Stannard, 1973.

21 **Disneyland** **5.6** Dave Craft and Pete Geiser, 1959.

22 **Broken Sling** **5.8** John Turner and Craig Merrihue, 1956. FFA: Jim McCarthy, 1962.

23 **Criss Cross** **5.10** Jim Andress and Doug Tompkins, 1959. FFA: Pete Ramins and John Stannard, 1971.

24 **Criss** **5.11** John Stannard and Willie Crowther, 1967.

25 **Le Plie** **5.7** Art Gran and Roman Sadowy, 1957. FFA: unknown.

26 **Outer Space** **5.8** Art Gran and Jim Geiser, 1959.

27 **Kansas City** **5.12** Dick Williams and DC, 1962. FFA: John Bragg, 1973.

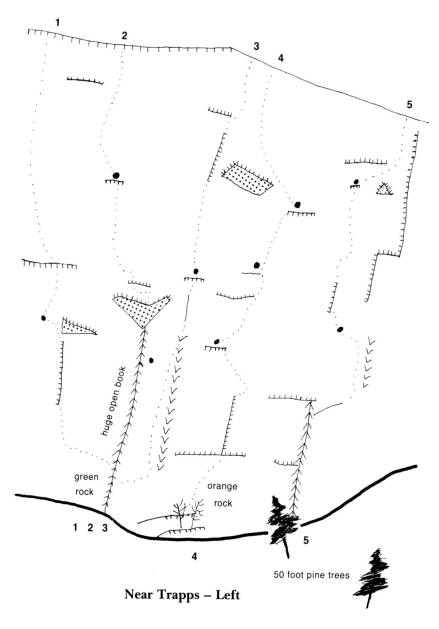

Near Trapps – Left

1 **Farewell to Arms 5.8**
2 **Bird Cage 5.10**
3 **Birdland 5.9**
4 **Transcontinental Nailway 5.10**
5 **Roseland 5.9**

These routes are on the far left side of the cliff. Start at route **27**, closest to the road.

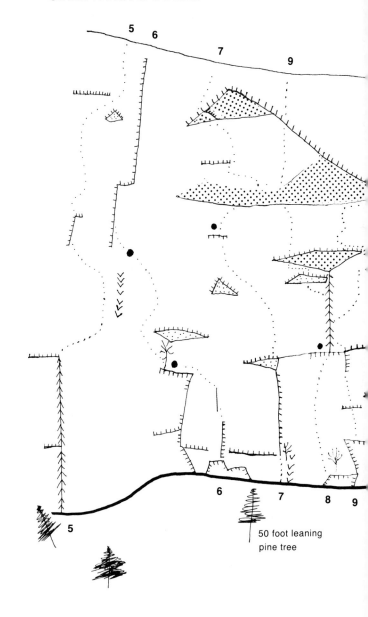

Near Trapps

5 **Roseland** 5.9
6 **Gelsa** 5.4
7 **Fat City** 5.10
8 **Baskerville Terrace** 5.7
9 **Requiem for a Heavyweight** 5.12 −

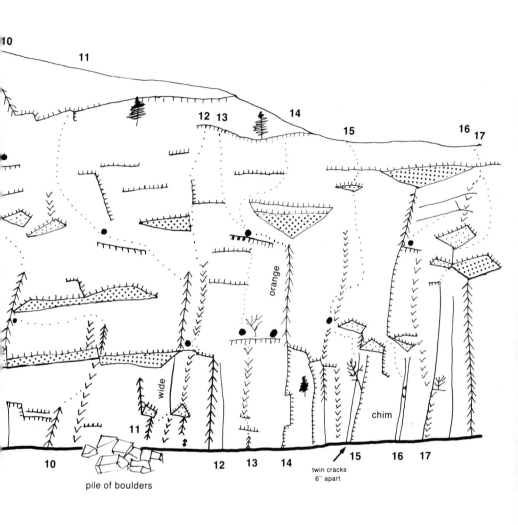

Near Trapps

10 Fat Stick 5.7
11 Yellow Ridge 5.7
12 Yellow Belly 5.9
13 No Slings Attached 5.10
14 Alphonse 5.8
15 Grand Central 5.9
16 Layback 5.5
17 Inverted Layback 5.9

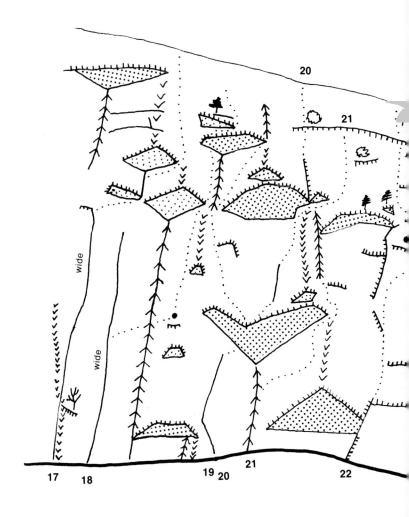

Near Trapps – Right

18 Te Dum   5.7
19 Swing Time   5.11
20 Sling Time   5.11
21 Disneyland   5.6
22 Broken Sling 5.8

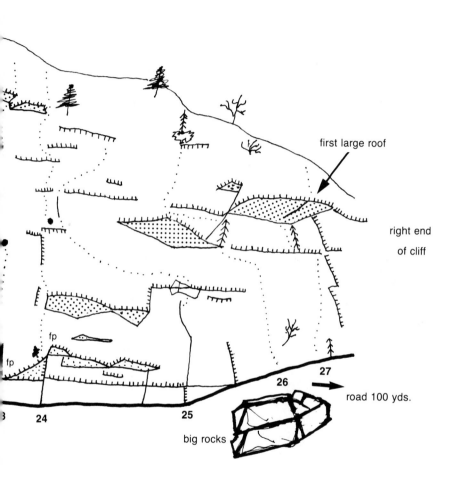

first large roof

right end
of cliff

fp

fp

27

26

road 100 yds.

25

24

big rocks

Near Trapps – Right

23 Criss Cross   5.10
24 Criss   5.11
25 Le Plie   5.7
26 Outer Space   5.8
27 Kansas City   5.12

The Trapps

To avoid damaging the hillsides, use only the main approaches.

28 Belly Roll 5.4 Doug Kerr and Norton Smithe, 1955.

29 Jackie 5.5 Jack Taylor and Lester Germer, 1952.

30 Classic 5.7 Mike Borghoff and Brownell Bergen, 1960.

31 Pink Laurel 5.8 Ted Church and Ann Church, 1955 (5.6 before 1971 rockfall).

32 A-Gape 5.11 – Dave Loeks and Joe Bridges, 1973.

33 Ape Call 5.8 Jim McCarthy, Jim Andress and Ants Leemets, 1962.

34 Matinée 5.10 Yvon Chouinard and Jim Andress, 1961. FFA: Jim McCarthy and John Hudson, 1963.

35 Fetus 5.9 John Lomont and Francis Coffin, 1959. FFA: Dick Williams, 1965.

36 Baby 5.6 Fritz Wiessner, Mary Cecil and Betty Woolsey, 1941.

37 Easy Overhang 5.2 Hans Kraus and Susanne Simon, 1940. Be very careful with the loose rock on the main ledge.

38 Son of Easy O 5.8 Jim McCarthy and Al DeMaria, 1962.

39 Pas De Deux 5.8 Jim McCarthy and Jack Hansen, 1959. FFA: Jim Geiser, 1959.

40 City Lights 5.7 Dick Williams and Art Gran, 1965.

41 Frog's Head 5.5 Fritz Wiessner and Lorens Logan, 1941.

42 Maria 5.6 Maria Millar and Fritz Wiessner, 1946.

43 Modern Times 5.8 Dick Williams, Dave Craft and Brian Carey, 1964.

44 Psychedelic 5.9 Yvon Chouinard and Dick Williams, 1965.

45 High Exposure 5.6 Hans Kraus and Fritz Wiessner, 1941. Absolutely classic.

46 Directissima 5.9 Hans Kraus and Stan Gross, 1956. FFA: Jim McCarthy, 1963.

47 Enduro Man 5.11 John Bragg, 1980.

48 Directississima 5.10 Jim McCarthy, Hans Kraus and John Rupley, 1957. FFA: John Stannard and Howie Davis, 1967.

49 Ant's Line 5.9 Ants Leemets and partner. FFA: Dave and Jim Erickson, 1968.

50 Condemned Man 5.12 – Hugh Herr and Jack Melesky, 1981. Poor pro.

51 The Throne 5.11 + Art Gran and Ants Leemets, 1963. FFA: John Stannard and Steve Wunsch, 1973.

52 Bonnie's Roof 5.9 Bonnie Prudden and Hans Kraus, 1952. FFA: Dick Williams and Jim McCarthy, 1961.

53 No Man's Land 5.11 Dick Williams and Art Gran, 1964. FFA: John Stannard and Ajax Greene, 1973. Difficult pro.

54 Tiers of Fear 5.12 – Russ Raffa and Russ Clune, 1983.

55 The Yellow Wall 5.11 Dick Williams and Ants Leemets, 1966. FFA: John Bragg and Russ Raffa, 1977.

56 Scary-Area 5.11 John Bragg and Mark Robinson, 1979. Only the first pitch is recommended. Poor pro.

Mike Law on Tiers of Fear photo: Russ Clune

57 Airy Aria 5.8 Hans Kraus and Ken Prestrud, 1956. FFA: Jim McCarthy, 1960.

58 Carbs and Caffeine 5.10 Mark Robinson, Kevin Bein, 1979.

59 Wasp Stop 5.11 Dave Ingalls and Roy Kligfield, 1968. FFA: John Stannard, 1975.

60 The Sting 5.11+ Russ Clune, Dan McMillan and Russ Raffa, 1983.

61 Lisa 5.9 Ants Leemets and Jim Andress, 1963. FFA: Ants Leemets, 1964.

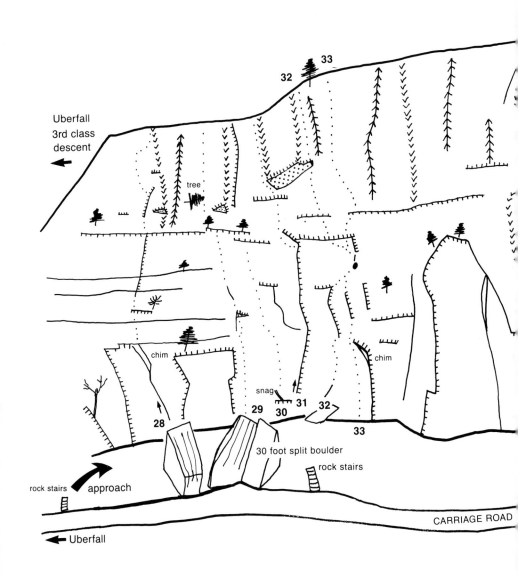

The Trapps

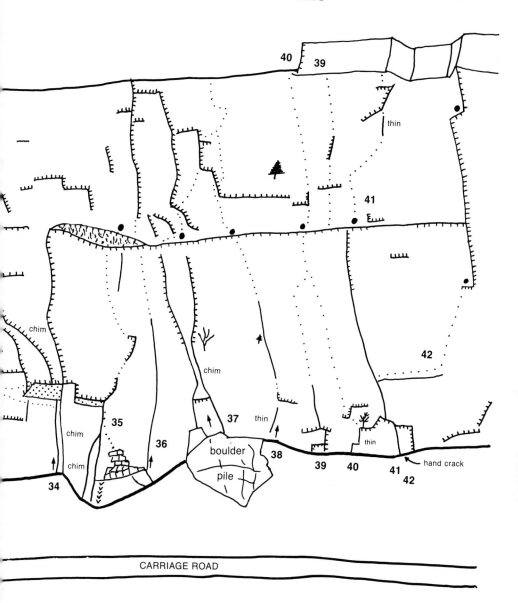

40 39

thin

41

chim

42

chim

35

chim

36 37 thin

boulder
pile 38

chim

34 39 40 41 42

thin

hand crack

CARRIAGE ROAD

The Trapps

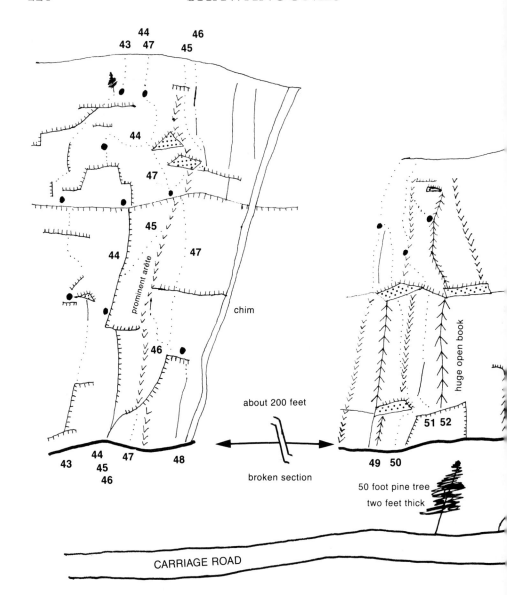

prominent arête

chim

about 200 feet

broken section

huge open book

51 52

49 50

50 foot pine tree
two feet thick

44
43 47 46
45

44

47

45

44 47

46

43 44 47 48
45
46

CARRIAGE ROAD

The Trapps

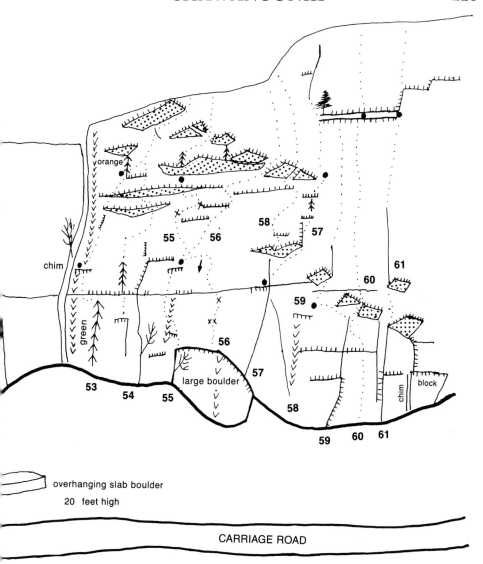

The **High Exposure** prow (route 45), the large open book of **Bonnie's Roof** (route 52) and the huge roofs of the **Yellow Wall** (route 55) area are prominently visible from here.

The Trapps

Sky Top

62 Ringding 5.10

63 Ringwraith 5.10 Roman Laba and Joe Kelsey, 1966.

64 Reign of Terror 5.10 Henry Barber, Rick Hatch and Ajax Greene, 1974.

65 Mechanical Boy 5.11 − Hugh Herr, 1982.

66 Strawberry Yogurt 5.8 Roman Laba and Wally Shamest, 1967.

Sky Top

67 The "V" **5.10** Chuck Calef and Richard Ross, 1978.

68 Lakeview **5.4** Fritz Wiessner and Lorens Logan, 1943.

69 The Mohonk Flake **5.7**

70 Krapp's Last Tape **5.10** Henry Barber and Rick Hatch, 1974.

71 Hans' Yellow Face **5.6** Hans Kraus and Ken Prestrud, 1948.

72 Open Cockpit **5.11+** Dave Loeks and Karl Beard, 1971. FFA: Steve Wunsch, 1973.

73 Sound and Fury **5.8** Dick Williams and Jim McCarthy, 1963.

74 Scare-City 5.10 Dave Loeks and Dick Williams, 1974. Difficult pro.

75 Foops 5.11 Jim McCarthy and John Rupley, 1955. FFA: John Stannard, 1970.

76 Little Face 5.2 Fritz Wiessner and Ed Gross, 1944.

77 No Exit 5.10 John Stannard, 1969.

78 Overhanging Overhang 5.5 Fritz Wiessner, Hans Kraus and Beckett Howorth, 1940.

79 Crack of Bizarre Delights 5.11 Dave Loeks and John Monten, 1971. FFA: Henry Barber and John Stannard, 1973.

Lynn Hill on Vandals photo: Russ Clune

Sky Top

80 Vandals   5.13- Jeff Gruenberg, Hugh Herr, Lynn Hill and Russ Clune, 1983.

81 Supercrack   5.12+ FFA: Steve Wunsch, 1974.   Located on a slightly detached buttress.

Rich Romano on Supercrack photo: Russ Clune

Ken Nichols on Great Expectations, Pinnacle Rock

Merimere Face

CONNECTICUT TRAPROCK

HIGHLIGHTS

Connecticut's cliffs overlook a wooded suburban environment, with forest-flanked reservoirs in the foreground and houses, quickly followed by towns, in the not-so-distant background. On Sunday, churchbells might be heard ringing, while car horns blast more frequently. Though the immediate vicinity of the cliffs is very attractive at times, travelling climbers would not come here in search of the wild environment one traditionally associates with climbing. Nor would anyone touring Eastern crags be impressed with the height of Connecticut's cliffs, which average less than 100 feet and reach 120 feet at their limit. But everyone will be impressed by the climbing within that short span. The term "traprock" refers to the peculiar basalt mixture that once flowed as lava over the region; climbers will appreciate its fine-grained sandpaper-like texture and the plethora of face holds on its usually vertical cliffs.

CLIMBING

Traprock was once known mostly for its crack climbing, and indeed many routes do follow superb cracks that are very condusive to jamming. Advancing techniques and equipment, however, have opened people's eyes to the thin edges that seem to crop up everywhere – so much so, that even crack routes are frequently done mostly by face climbing.

These face holds may be dense, but figuring out how best to use them is not always simple, as the edges may face any direction and be of any shape; the climbing is notorious for forcing the climber to pause to carefully analyze the moves – even when finger strength is rapidly waning. Climbers might also want to note that the black-edged rock tends to be brittle; the good rock is usually brown to yellow.

Ragged Mountain has the best known of Connecticut's crags. Between 50 and 100 feet high, the Main Cliff has a tremendous concentration of routes on its 200 yard long face. Ragged is the principal congregating point for climbers. In fact, the climbing here is so popular, and has become so synonymous with the sport in Connecticut, that the most recent local guidebook was written partially to lure people away and spread them out onto other crags. Climbers should pay special attention to staying on the trail and to minimizing damage to the rapidly eroding ground at the base of the cliff.

East Peak offers perhaps the best combination of excellent climbing and aesthetic environment in Connecticut. The multiple cliffs are on the crest of a high hill that overlooks the broad valley below (populated, of course) and the Merimere Reservoir, in an unpopulated side-valley. One of the prime attractions of this cluster of crags is that during the winter their dark rock is quickly warmed by the morning sun – while somehow the high cliffs seem to stay sheltered from the wind. This means that even when the air temperature is well below freezing, rock climbing can be perfectly comfortable. In summer these cliffs are best left for late afternoon, while Ragged's west-facing cliffs can be explored in the morning. (Climber's interested in an aesthetic experience at East Peak are well advised to avoid Castle Crag – beneath the rock tower – where partying teenagers toss their beer bottles.)

Pinnacle Rock has the tallest cliff of the region, at 120 feet, and actually features a two-pitch climb.

Routes on most cliffs are crammed one next to another. Even entirely crackless faces are thoroughly filled with routes because the ubiquitous face holds provide the means. A very strong local ethic concerning bolts has arisen, however, so one won't usually find bolt protection on these crackless faces. The local ethic is that bolts may only be placed free and on the lead – which on many hard faces results in no bolts at all. This is designed to preserve the aesthetics of the cliff and the diversity of climbing experiences on a limited amount of rock (poorly protected routes being considered part of that diversity). But whatever one's philosophy on bolting, the ability to move almost anywhere over the face (albeit with great difficulty in places) means that if placing bolts on rappel were tolerated, the cliffs would become simply littered with them. The principal activists have adopted the philosophy that if one is not willing to accept what the rock offers in protection options, then one should just toprope the climbs instead of leading them. Bolts placed on rappel are promptly removed.

While the local bolting philosophy is similar to that espoused at many areas in America, the peculiarities of the rock and the style of some local activists have both contributed to the adoption of a new and highly innovative system of protection on the lead: tied-off hooks. Originating with simple weighted hooks – which led to hooks being tied off to other protection just below and culminated with an elaborate system of tying off the hook with a rope running to the ground – the system has a small but devoted following. In its contemporary extreme, up to nine hooks have been placed on the lead. Each is tied-off to the ground with a separate rope, using a pulley system (this prevents the hook from lifting off its sometimes dubious perch during a fall). To further reduce strains on the hooks, up to four separate lead ropes have also been used. The climber downclimbs or lowers off during the securing and testing process for each hook. This protection system has sustained falls of up to ten feet and its success with contemporary aid climbing hooks has stimulated the quest for stronger hooks specifically designed for free climbing. Using this system, locals have managed to lead, with some degree of safety, routes they had only dared toprope beforehand. Over 80 routes have been led using one or more hooks for protection, providing locals with a new approach to climbing on crags which have become a virtual maze of routes. However, it should be noted that hooks are used only on the most esoteric climbs and the vast majority of routes are easily protected with conventional means.

Of more direct importance to most visiting climbers is a somewhat notorious local grading system that is politely called "stiff." The system, which frequently pegs climbs at least half a grade lower on the decimal system from what one might expect, is actually reasonably close to the ratings that once predominated throughout the Northeast. Elsewhere, they were brought to more cosmopolitan standards in the late 1970's, while in Connecticut parochialism prevailed. Locals feel that a visitor's impression of their gradings may also be influenced by the particularly perplexing nature of the face climbing. When combined with strenuousness on the steep walls, the mental difficulty of figuring out the sequences of holds means that on-sight leads are often stopped cold. The local guidebook ratings have been kept in this book, so visitors are urged to initiate their climbing here conservatively.

ENVIRONMENT

Connecticut is the very epitome of southern New England, with its urban and suburban sprawl blending from one community into the next, boundaries blurred beyond recognition. Old churches and buildings dating back over 200 years stand side by side with modern shopping malls and ranch homes. And yet to a Westerner, the woodsy impression given by the foliated trees masks much of the human density. Indeed, even this heavily populated region supports numerous inholdings of forest, either privately owned or part of public water reservoir systems. Horse riding and hiking trails have been cut through the woods wherever a few acres are found in a parcel, and some of these trails can be extraordinarily lovely as they reach the top of a hill, with views across the broad valleys of Connecticut's Central Lowlands. When the pale green buds of April resurrect the gray trees of winter, when the leaves shade the forest floor and the laurel, apple trees and rhododendron bloom in June, when the rich green of summer metamorphoses into the many and brilliant hues of October, these are times when even the backstreets of suburbia are touched by the powers of nature and the scattered parcels of forest become miniature wilderness areas.

These woodlands, then, are the small but alluring settings for the fittingly small but gemlike stones on which climbers come to play.

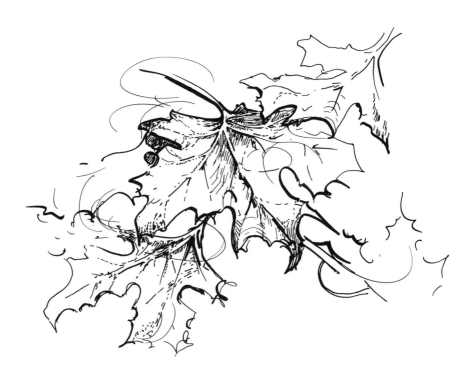

CLIMBING HISTORY

An article dating to 1895 has been found in a local newspaper that referred to "mountain climbing" in Connecticut. While little is known about the true intent of those words, there is no doubt that the history of rock climbing in this area dates to the mid-1920's, when students at Yale who had been to Europe started climbing at Sleeping Giant State Park, a dozen miles south of the cliffs featured in this book.

During the 1930's, exploration of cliffs and development of climbing routes became intense as a small group of climbers, mostly Appalachian Mountain Club members, regularly visited Connecticut's crags. Several of the group's climbers played an active role in high standard mountaineering throughout North America and even in the Himalaya; at home they pressed the standards to 5.8, establishing routes that may have been technically the hardest in the country and were not repeated until the 1960's.

The war years had their usual negative influence on climbing, and in Connecticut a whole generation of climbers left the local scene. When new climbers reappeared in the 1950's, they had virtually no knowledge of past events and assumed, quite wrongly, that anything which did not sprout a fixed piton was a new route. This group, however, did not approach in intensity the dedication of the climbers of the 1930's. The new group was more casual in their approach, and were as interested in exploring as in climbing. In a twist of black humor, Sleeping Giant was closed to climbing due to a fatal accident that occured during a "safety" conference of northeastern climbing clubs at the cliff. Yale Mountain Club climbers felt themselves suddenly banished to the "Siberia" of Ragged Mountain, where climbs were either too short or too hard.

The 1960's marked a major turning point in local climbing, inspired in large part by a local who went to England and returned excited by what he had seen on her gritstone. Not only did he bring back a desire to do difficult routes, he also brought with him the notion of using slung machine nuts for protection. For a few years Connecticut became the one place in America where nuts were regularly used, until by the late 60's the wide distribution of chrome-moly pitons wrought their damage on traprock as on the rest of the nation. 1963 saw the return of 5.8 climbing, and in 1964 several 5.9's were established. That fall also found extremely high forest-fire danger closing most northeastern climbing areas, forcing climbers from all over to descend on Connecticut.

By the early 1970's, 5.10 had arrived and most local climbers had departed. During this period most of the active climbers visited from out of state. New cliffs were explored to some extent, but Ragged continued to dominate attention. By the mid 70's a new group banded together and systematically climbed new route after new route, including the poorly protected faces between crack systems. In 1976 they added 5.11 to the spectrum.

From the mid-70's to the mid-80's, local activists continued to come to the foreground, then move away. One person, however, never left and, in fact, dominated the climbing to such an extent that eventually many climbers felt there was no need to bother doing a new route – whatever they had in mind had inevitably been climbed the week before. The story of local guidebooks illustrates the new route explosion.

When the first guidebook appeared in 1964, there were only a few dozen climbs. The next guide was written in 1973 to cover approximately 100 routes. By 1977, the current guidebook author intended to publish a book with several hundred routes, but his interest dissipated for several years. During the period from 1976 to 1979 only about forty new routes were climbed, yielding a total of 550. Then his interest was rekindled, and in early 1980 he began cataloguing climbs and route possibilities in order to make the book complete. By July, the number of climbed routes had doubled, and by the end of 1980 over 650 new routes had been climbed. When the guidebook was published in 1982, 1,318 climbs were included, eclipsing the size of any other American guidebook – for what many would have considered one of the continent's smaller areas. By the end of 1985, an additional 390 routes had been ferreted out the established cliffs. The guidebook author climbed the vast majority of the routes in his book, making a point of climbing every single day of the year.

CAMPING

Unfortunately, the suburban nature of the region yields extremely limited camping opportunities. Climbers on a tour of the northeast might consider using their days in Connecticut as an opportunity to shower at a hotel. About a dozen miles south of the crags, there is camping for a moderate fee at Sleeping Giant State Park (¼ mile east on a town road from Route 10; Mount Carmel Avenue, Hamden). Overnight parking is not permitted in the parking lots used by climbers. Violations of this ban could involve serious repercussions for local climbing access.

SEASONS AND WEATHER

Approximate Months	Typical Temperatures		Likelihood of Precipitation	Frequency of Climbable Days
	High	Low		
Dec-Mar	30's	20's	medium	medium
Apr-May	60's+	40's+	medium	high-med
Jun-Aug	80's+	70's	medium	med-high
Sep-Nov	70's−	40's−	medium	high

Comments: Summer heat and humidity are limiting factors, as are its mosquitoes, poison ivy, and a few blackflies. Climbing in the winter is best at East Peak.

RESTRICTIONS AND WARNINGS

Parking within easy access of Ragged is very limited, but climbers should avoid private property as cars are frequently towed or ticketed and ill-will towards climbing is thereby generated. Usually easiest is to park where clusters of cars are parked. Swimming is not allowed in the reservoir; violations likewise lead to ill-will towards climbing. Positive feelings are necessary because the cliffs are owned by various groups, including private citizens, and closures are entirely possible.

One should beware, especially at the top of the East Peak cliffs, that cars have been broken into by thieves and vandals.

The impressive cliffs one drives by in New Haven are East and West Rocks. They have been closed by the city since the 1920's and gaining access has been an ongoing battle. Respect the ban in deeds if not in words until the legal fight has been won.

GUIDEBOOKS

Traprock (1982) by Ken Nichols. Published by the American Alpine Club, 113 East 90th Street, New York, NY 10028. A new route supplement is planned by the same author, and will be available from 142 Hartland Road, West Granby, CT 06090.

GUIDE SERVICES AND EQUIPMENT STORES

Nearby equipment stores include: Clapp and Treat, 674 Farmington Avenue, West Hartford, and Eastern Mountain Sports (EMS), One Civic Center Plaza, Hartford.

Local guiding can be obtained from Connecticut Mountain Recreation (CMR), 151 Farmington Avenue, West Hartford, CT 06107, telephone: 203-236-1593.

EMERGENCY SERVICES

In an emergency, call 911 for help. The nearest hospital to East Peak is the Meriden-Wallingford Hospital on Cook Avenue in Meriden, telephone: 238-8200; to Ragged it is the Bradley Memorial Hospital on Meriden Avenue in Southington, telephone: 621-3661; and to Pinnacle Rock it is the University of Connecticut Medical Center on Farmington Avenue in Farmington: telephone: 674-2000.

GETTING THERE

No public transportation reaches the cliffs.

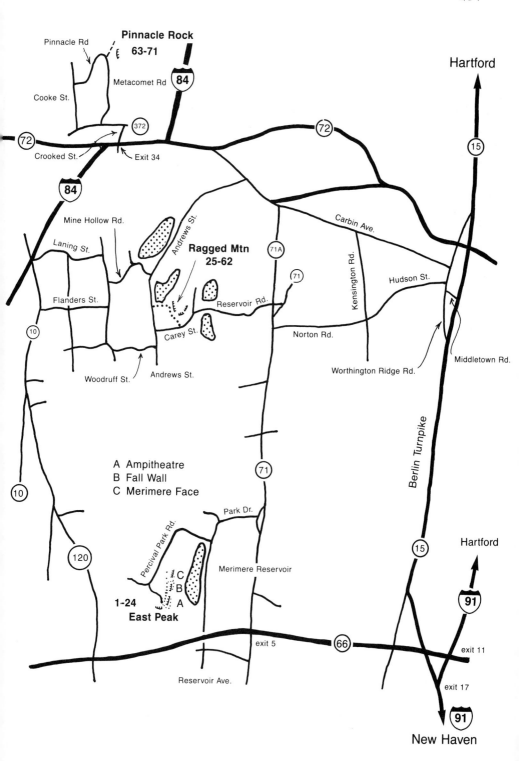

East Peak Ampitheater

1 **Say It Ain't So** **5.9** Jim Adair and Ken Nichols, 1977. The thin rib. Poor pro.

2 **The Window** **5.7** Sam Streibert and John Dowd, 1964. Pass through the window. Poor pro.

3 **Rolling Thunder** **5.10** on both pitches. Ken Nichols and Mike Heintz, 1982. Poor pro 5.8 on first pitch.

4 **Grey Corner** **5.9+** John Reppy and Alan Wegewood, 1964. FFA: Bob Anderson, Sam Streibert and Al Rubin, 1973.

5 **Rat Crack** **5.7** Fritz Wiessner and Percy Olton, about 1933.

6 **Cat Crack** **5.10−** Sam Streibert and Larry Winship, 1966. FFA: Sam Streibert and Steve Arsenault, 1972.

7 **Dol Guldur** **5.11** John Dowd and Ken Nichols, 1975. FFA: Tony Trocchi and Mike Heintz, 1976.

8 **Squirrel Cage** **5.9** Fritz Wiessner, William Burling and Percy Olton, about 1933. FA current line: Sam Streibert and John Reppy, 1964; FFA: Sam Streibert and Al Rubin, 1972. **Sickle (var.)** **5.10+** Mike Heintz and Chip Tuthill, 1975; FFA: Greg Newth, 1976.

9 **Superstructure** **5.10+** Ken Nichols, 1981. Top rope.

10 **Black Corner** **5.8−** Sam Streibert, John Reppy and Sam Black, 1964.

East Peak – Fall Wall

11 Trial and Triumph **5.11** Bruce Dicks and Ken Nichols, 1976. FFA original line: Ken Nichols, 1984.

12 Falling Star **5.11+** Ken Nichols, 1984. Toprope.

13 Reflections of Fall **5.9** Sam Streibert and Bob Anderson, 1973.

14 Stallion **5.11** Toprope: Mike Heintz, 1981. First lead: Ken Nichols and Marko Fedrizzi, 1984; used two cliffhangers tied off to horizontal.

15 Malmedy Massacre/Battle of the Bulge **5.10+** Bruce Dicks, Ken Nichols and Jim Adair, 1977/Ken Nichols, Bruce Dicks and Sam Streibert, 1976.

16 Going Begging **5.9+** Jim Adair and Mick Avery, 1976. Long, thin piton for hand insertion is useful.

17 Superpower **5.11+** Ken Nichols and Sam Streibert, 1984. Poor pro.

18 Hercules Unchained **5.11** Ken Nichols and Marko Fedrizzi, 1984. Need #½ Friend and Crack-N-Up.

East Peak – Merimere Face

19 Spring Cleaning 5.8 – Ken Nichols, Bill Sullivan, Mike Lapierre and Chad Hussey, 1981. Poor pro, loose start.

20 Thunderbolt 5.11 Ken Nichols and Bruce Dicks, 1976. Two pitches, loose start.

21 Mother Earth 5.11 Original line: Sam Slater, 1982; current line: Ken Nichols, 1984. Toprope.

22 Thor's Hammer 5.9 Sam Streibert and John Dowd, 1964. FFA: Mike Heintz, Tony Trocchi and Ken Nichols, 1975. Considered one of the finest routes in Connecticut.

23 Mission Impossible 5.9 Ken Nichols and Bruce Dicks, 1980. A scary lead.

24 Silmarillion 5.10 Ken Nichols, 1977. Best as two pitches.

Bob Clark on Knight's Gambit   photo: S. Peter Lewis

Ragged Mountain – Main Face

25 North End   5.8 John Reppy and Sam Streibert, 1963. Start up left-facing corners; traverse left.

26 Jam Corner   5.4

27 Frostbite   5.9 Larry Winship, 1968. FFA: Henry Barber and Ajax Greene, 1973.

28 Owl Perch   5.7 Bert Arsego and John Reppy, 1955. Left side of huge overhang. Scramble up ledges; move right.

29 Easy Rider   5.10/5.11 Toprope: Tony Trocchi, 1976. First lead: Sam Slater, Ken Nichols and Mick Avery, 1984; Logan hook used just over lip. Left-facing corner to block beneath roof; over roof.

30 Cemetary Vault   5.7 John Reppy and Bert Arsego, 1955. Double cracks to right edge roof.

31 Duck Soup   5.10/5.11 Jim Adair, 1977. Toprope. Face six feet right of left-facing corner.

32 Marlinspike   5.8 Sam Streibert and Marlin Scully, 1963. Crack above broken slabs.

33 Double Crux   5.8− Sam Streibert and Pete Trafton, 1963. Crack above broken slabs.

Ragged Mountain – Main Face

34 Modern Times 5.10 Toprope: Mark Delaney, 1973. First lead: Ken Nichols and Chad Hussey, 1984; used four lead ropes, one cliffhanger, four Logan hooks, two small Tricams. Start up short right-facing corner.

35 Ancient Way 5.4 Betty Woolsey, Roger Whitney and Donald Brown, 1935. Right-facing corner.

36 Leftover 5.8 Sam Streibert and John Dowd, 1964. The crack starting twelve feet above broken slabs.

37 Deception 5.7 Sam Streibert and John Reppy, 1963.

38 Land-o'-Lakes 5.9+ Mike Heintz and Ken Nichols, 1981. The face seven feet right of crack.

39 Visions 5.10+ Harry Brielman and Bill Lutkus, 1979. "First ethical lead": Ken Nichols and Peter Jenkins, 1983. Start up thin crack to block.

Ragged Mountain – Main Face

40 Unconquerable Crack 5.9 Sam Streibert and John Reppy, 1963. FFA: John Reppy and Sam Streibert, 1964. Prominent crack slanting left.

41 Subline 5.10 Sam Streibert and John Reppy, 1963. FFA: Henry Barber and Bob Anderson, 1972. Crack above hanging flake; start on right.

42 Bombay 5.8+ Original line: Layton Kor and John Reppy, 1964. Current line: John Reppy and Bob Durham, 1965. Subline start, followed by two right-facing corners. **Direct 5.10−** John Shelton, 1972. Crack through overhangs leading to upper corner.

43 Main Street 5.4 Fritz Wiessner, Roger Whitney and Charles Houston, 1935.

44 Continuous Creation 5.10+ Top rope: Ken Nichols, 1979. First lead: Ken Nichols and Sam Slater, 1983; used three cliffhangers in one spot. Poor pro. Start sixteen feet right of Main Street.

45 Wishbone 5.7 Original line: Sam Bailey and John Reppy, 1949. Current line: Sam Streibert, 1965.

46 Kor Crack 5.9− Layton Kor and John Reppy, 1964.

47 Bushy Groove 5.8 John Reppy, 1955.

48 Juniper Wall 5.7 Fritz Wiessner, Betty Woolsey and William House, 1934. The Prince 5.9− (var.) John Reppy and Sam Streibert, 1965; FFA: Sam Streibert and John Reppy, 1965.

49 Vector 5.8 Fritz Wiessner and Roger Whitney, 1935.

50 Vajolet Corner 5.9 + Sam Streibert and Dennis Merritt, 1971. Poor pro. The old rusty ¼ inch bolt at the crux can be backed up with a #4 RP in slot to left. The arête.

51 Tower Crack 5.7 Fritz Wiessner, William Burling and Percy Olton, 1933.

52 Wiessner Slab 5.3 Fritz Wiessner and William Burling, 1933. The most popular route at Ragged.

53 Wiessner Crack 5.8 – Fritz Wiessner and Roger and Hassler Whitney, 1934.

54 Knight's Move 5.4

55 Lavaredo Corner 5.7 Sam Streibert, Al Rubin and Tony Julianelle, 1972. Poor pro. Start with small corners right of slab.

56 Knight's Gambit 5.7 Sam Streibert and Ed Arens, 1964.

57 Wet Wall 5.6 Fritz Wiessner and Donald Brown, about 1934. Start with small overhang, followed by right-facing corner above.

58 YMC (Yale Mountaineering Club) Route 5.9 – John Reppy and Will McMahon, 1963. FFA: Dick Williams and John Reppy, 1964.

59 Broadway 5.7 + John Reppy, Gil Young and Frank Carey, 1958.

60 Carey Corner 5.7 Fritz Wiessner, William Burling and Henry Beers, 1935.

61 Ragged Edge 5.10 + Jim Adair, Sam Slater and Bruce Dicks, 1977. Poor pro. Start at memorial plaque.

62 Vanishing Point 5.10 Bruce Dicks, Mike Heintz and Mick Avery, 1976. "First ethical lead:" Bruce Dicks and Jim Adair, 1976.

Ken Nichols on Great Expectations

Pinnacle Rock

63 Brave New World 5.10+ Ken Nichols and Marko Fedrizzi, 1984. Start up the A-frame-shaped arch just left of giant overhang close to ground. Continue straight-up the overhanging face and arete above.

64 Wild Kingdom 5.11− Mike Heintz and Ken Nichols, 1981. After fifteen feet of the A-frame, move right to bolt belay.

65 Dream Weaver 5.9− Tom Egan, early 1970's. FFA: Mike Heintz and Ken Nichols, 1980. Climb through break in the lower roof to underside of second overhang forty feet up; traverse right.

66 Psycho Path 5.9 Ken Nichols and Mike Heintz, 1981. Climb past bolt; over roof; move left and over second roof at small notch; back right and up small corner to third roof; continue as in photo.

67 Great Expectations 5.8+ Rocky Keeler and Al Rubin, 1973. Start up large corner.

68 Lost World 5.9− Ken Nichols, Chad Hussey and Mike Heintz, 1981. Poor pro.

69 Right Wing 5.5 Poor pro.

70 Yucca Flats 5.6 Ken Nichols and Mike Heintz, 1981. Very bad pro.

71 Zambesi Hatchet Head 5.7 Mike Heintz and John Sahi, 1974. Start up seam to small roof. Poor pro.

The Spider's Web and Chapel Pond

ADIRONDACKS

HIGHLIGHTS

Upstate New York's Adirondack Park has been called the "Forgotten East." That such a vast collection of wooded mountains and sheer granitic cliffs could be located in the densely populated Northeast and still host so few climbers is truly remarkable. The Park covers an incredible 5,927,000 acres and, naturally, many cliffs are deep in the wilderness. Also to be expected, the more popular crags – included in this book – lie just a few minutes' walk from a paved road. Here one will find cliffs like the Spider's Web, which remains vertical to slightly overhanging for its entire 160 feet, and Moss Cliff, with an overhanging 400 foot face. Pitchoff and Chapel Pond Slabs are within a stone's throw of the road and located next to the rich blue waters of pristine mountain lakes. The best known and most prized crag in the Adirondacks is Pok-O-Moonshine, with up to 500 feet of steep granite and split by a great number of clean cracks. It extends for nearly a mile.

CLIMBING

Most of the popular Adirondack crags lie in a region about thirty miles in diameter. Within this region the rock type varies considerably, ranging from the granitic gneiss of Pok-O-Moonshine to the coarser anorthosite of most of the other cliffs. Though a geologist views them differently, most climbers see this whole spectrum as granite. One can recognize anorthosite by its roughness; it provides more friction than one usually finds on smooth granite.

Pok-O-Moonshine's Main Face is split by sweeping dihedrals and straight-in, straight-up cracks. Two to five pitches long, the routes can be as demanding as they are beautiful. Nothing less than 5.7 is found here, though nothing above 5.11 has yet been climbed either. The cliff is usually favorably compared to the much more popular Cathedral Ledge in North Conway, but the less intense competitive pressures on climbers at Pok-O have not pushed the standards quite as high. While the Main Face commands most of the attention, The Slabs offers superb face and friction climbing.

Pok-O-Moonshine is isolated from the majority of cliffs in the region. The greatest concentration of crags is in the Keene Valley, with the Spider's Web ranking just behind Pok-O in reputation. Its name refers to the complex of cracks that lace its intensely arm-pumping face, where most routes get a 5.10 or 5.11 rating. The overhanging nature of the face makes it an ideal escape from a light rain.

At the other extreme, all the routes at neighboring Chapel Pond Slabs are 5.7 or below and ascend an exquisite rough friction face for seven low-angled pitches. Though not as famous as Pok-O and Spider's Web, this is the most used piece of rock in New York north of the Shawangunks. Runouts here are long, since there are few cracks and no bolts. Most climbers, however, find the climbing secure because adhesion is excellent.

Pitchoff is a marvelous piece of rock. An exfoliated slab about a dozen feet thick, it stands on its end – separated by a chimney from the hillside. The chimney, in fact, continues a couple hundred feet below ground. The outside face of this 150 foot cliff is covered with sharp-edged face holds and horizontal cracks ideal for protection. The cliff dries quickly after a rain, is but a hundred yards from the road and just ten miles from Lake Placid. Lake Placid residents find it an ideal after work climbing spot, with many excellent routes in the middle difficulty range and a few hard ones as well.

Probably the least visited cliff of those in this book is Moss Cliff, despite the fact that it holds long cracks and corners that are a favorite of some climbers. On its right side is a 400 foot vertical and overhanging face that sports some of the few aid routes in the region.

Numerous cliffs have not been included in this book. Behind the Spider's Web and visible from Chapel Pond Slab are the tremendous Washbowl Cliffs. The High Peaks region holds numerous large cliffs. The most famous of which is Wallface. Roger's Rock is a beautiful slab rising out of Lake George. The Adirondacks are simply full of climbing.

They can also be full of the notorious blackflies that plague the forests of the Northeast. The local guidebook notes that the flies usually hatch to the sound of clanging hardware, just as the cliffs are drying in May. Repellents are quickly sweated off on strenuous climbs and can harm some synthetic fabrics. Climbing during this season is made more tolerable by wearing light-colored clothing, with pants tucked in and turtlenecks rolled high. A headnet and gloves help on the belays.

The other notoriety of the Adirondacks is its weather. Rain is so common here that the region might be nicknamed the "Ducks," instead of its common abbreviation as the "Dacks."

ENVIRONMENT

With almost six million acres, Adirondack Park is nearly three times the size of Yellowstone National Park. It encompasses several dozen "high" mountains – the highest being 5,344 foot Mount Marcy – almost 3,000 lakes and over a thousand miles of streams. Its wilderness is distinctly Eastern, with dense forests of both evergreen coniferous trees and a combination of maple, birch and other deciduous trees that explode in a brilliant fireball of color in the fall (end of August to early October). People come from downstate New York to escape the pressures of the city, to explore the forests and to gaze from high on a mountainside over peaks and valleys that extend as far as the eye can see. For the visitor, the Park is a dream fulfilled with peace and tranquility.

For its administrators, managing the Park can be a nightmare. Forty percent of its acreage is part of the Adirondack Forest Preserve, which celebrated its 100th anniversary in 1985. Entirely State-owned land, the Preserve is classified as "forever wild." This preservation came as a reaction to the region's exploitation in the mid-1800's, when New York had nearly 7,000 sawmills and led the country in lumber production. The other sixty percent of the Park is private land, much of it owned by logging companies. Private and public lands are intermixed in a patch-work quilt, with the boundaries of State land often nebulous, at best.

The quilt-like pattern of ownership and management explains why one finds towns, businesses and homes within Park boundaries. In fact, most of the popular climbing areas are within plain sight – and sound – of a road. Pok-O-Moonshine even borders a freeway. To leave the madding signs of civilization behind, one must spend a bit more time hiking into the unpopulated High Peaks region.

Lake Placid, the major town within the Park, has long been a tourist destination. This climaxed with the 1980 Winter Olympics – the towering ski jumps looming above the road are a testimonial to the Games.

CLIMBING HISTORY

Mount Marcy, New York's highest point, was climbed in 1837 by the surveying team which named the Adirondack Mountains. The word "Adirondack" is steeped in legend; it is said to be the derogatory expression "eaters of bark" which was used against the Algonquin Indians by the Iroquois. The Iroquois felt that their northern neighbors were so incompetent as hunters that by the end of winter they were reduced to eating bark.

Both tribes, however, found the interior of the range too harsh and spent little time in its mountains. Settlers likewise avoided the heart of the Adirondacks and stuck with the more easily accessed lowlands of the Hudson River Valley. Modern climbers enjoy paved roads, but the relative proximity of the Shawangunks and North Conway to the major urban centers of New York City and Boston has helped to keep the Adirondacks in the backwaters of the climbing world. The prestige of the big two Northeastern areas keeps most travelling climbers away from the Adirondacks.

Technical climbing began here in 1916 under the leadership of a resident who learned the sport in Europe. He disdained protection, feeling that it interfered with the flow of the climb. Though he maintained a conservative attitude towards the use of pitons, he went on to become the president of the American Alpine Club in the 1940's. In the Adirondacks, his greatest contribution was to inspire other locals to take up the sport. This small group explored most of the major cliffs, including those of the High Peaks Region, during the period from the 1920's to the 1950's. Occasionally outsiders were persuaded to visit, some of whom put up significant climbs.

It should be obvious that the overhanging face of the Spider's Web was ignored during this period. Interestingly, so was Pok-O-Moonshine. Not until 1957 did Pok-O receive its first route. Then suddenly it became the focus of significant attention to a tightly knit band of Canadians, led by an English climber who kept busy on North American cliffs while avoiding the British army. He was introducing bold crack climbs with minimum protection to North Conway as well.

Canadians continue to visit Pok-O because of its size and proximity to Montreal. Their strong influence on developing the cliff, however, waned during the early '60's. Soon after the Canadians phased out, a gradually increasing number of the Northeast's better climbers began filtering in, exploring various crags, including Moss Cliff. The first guidebook came out in 1967, then a more publicized guidebook was published nine years later. The books further established the Adirondacks as a significant area. While the crowds didn't swarm in after the new publicity, serious climbers attempting to complete their sampling of Northeastern rock did. The Spider's Web suddenly burst open its gravity defying routes in the late 70's.

Despite the influence of a few visitors on other cliffs, the greatest concentration of new routes was put up by a group from nearby Plattsburgh who climbed Pok-O with crusading zeal. While their campaign was based out of a sheer love of climbing, they did their routes with a secrecy born out of fear that the masses would inevitably – and soon – be moving up from the Gunks.

The extra drive from the Gunks and the reputation for rain and bugs have helped to keep the Adirondacks in the background. They have not been completely forgotten, of course, as visitors do keep passing through: a majority of dedicated Northeastern climbers have sampled several Adirondacks crags. Most of the time, however, the locals have the place to themselves. New routes are added and new crags are discovered with steady regularity as the local climbers keep looking over their shoulders, wondering how they could possibly be all alone on such magnificent rock.

CAMPING

There is a fee-campground at the base of Pok-O-Moonshine and another about a mile north of Moss Cliff. Across the road from the parking space for the Spider's Web is a non-fee area frequently used by climbers. Small motels and pay-campgrounds abound in the area, though motels at the resort town of Lake Placid are likely to be high priced. There is also a Youth Hostel in Lake Placid: Park and Main Streets, telephone: 518-523-2008. In Keene, the Bark Eater Lodge is recommended for eating and lodging (telephone: 518-576-2221).

The Fillin' Station in Keene makes a good breakfast stop, as does the Normark Diner in Keene Valley.

SEASONS AND WEATHER

Approximate Months	Typical Temperatures		Likelihood of Precipitation	Frequency of Climbable Days
	High	Low		
Nov-Mar	30's –	0's	medium	very low
Apr-May	60's +	50's –	med-high	medium
Jun-Aug	80's –	60's	med-high	med-high
Sep-Oct	60's –	40's –	medium	med-high

Comments: In April, melting snow keeps many cliffs wet and access trails difficult. Pitchoff and Pok-O-Moonshine might offer the easiest access, while the overhanging wall of the Spider's Web may be difficult to get to, but doesn't hold snow. The blackfly season runs May through June. Snow arrives in October.

RESTRICTIONS AND WARNINGS

The middle section of Pok-O-Mooshine is privately owned. Be especially careful not to litter or do anything that might jeopordize access for yourself or others. Park at the campground and approach from there.

In season, Adirondacks blackflies are notorious. Read the *CLIMBING* section for hints on dealing with them.

GUIDEBOOKS

Climbing in the Adirondacks (1983) by Don Mellor. Lake Placid Climbing School, Inc., Sundog Ski and Sports, 90 Main Street, Lake Placid, NY 12946. A new route supplement is available by the same author and publisher (1986).

GUIDE SERVICES AND EQUIPMENT STORES

The Lake Placid Climbing School is located at Sundog Ski and Sports, 90 Main Street, Lake Placid, telephone: 518-523-3984 or 523-2752.

Equipment stores include The Mountaineer, Route 73, Keene (the closest store to most of the climbing); Eastern Mountain Sports, 100 Main Street, Lake Placid; and in downtown Burlington Vermont, Dakin's Mountain Shop (a ferry can be taken between Pok-O and Burlington).

EMERGENCY SERVICES

For rescues, call or visit the Mountaineer in Keene Valley, telephone: 576-2281, or call the wilderness ranger at 576-4796. The night dispatcher can be reached at 891-0235. The ranger at the Pok-O-Moonshine campground should be contacted for accidents there. The Lake Placid police can be reached at 891-4422, and the ambulance service at 523-9511.

The nearest hospitals to Keene Valley are Lake Placid Memorial Hospital, telephone: 523-3311, or the Elizabethtown Community Hospital, telephone: 873-6377. The closest to Pok-O-Moonshine is the Champlain Valley Medical Center at 561-2000.

GETTING THERE

Both Trailways and Greyhound buses serve Lake Placid and Plattsburgh. Trailways stops in Keene.

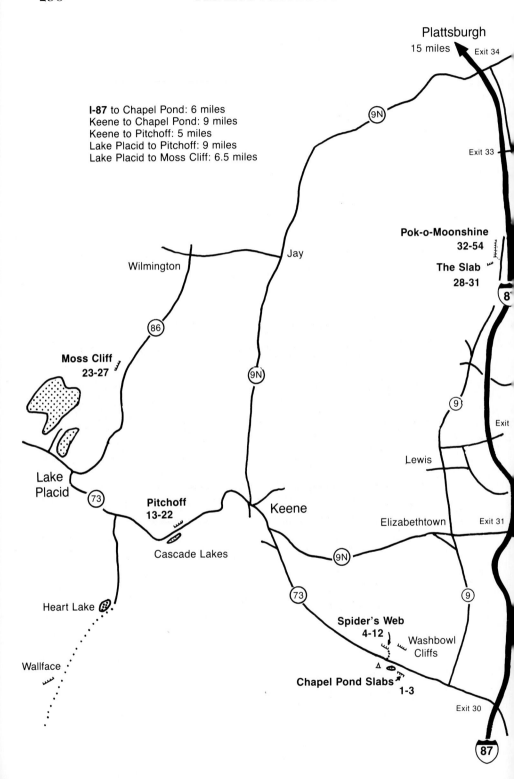

Plattsburgh
15 miles Exit 34

I-87 to Chapel Pond: 6 miles
Keene to Chapel Pond: 9 miles
Keene to Pitchoff: 5 miles
Lake Placid to Pitchoff: 9 miles
Lake Placid to Moss Cliff: 6.5 miles

9N

Exit 33

Pok-o-Moonshine
32-54
The Slab
28-31

Jay

Wilmington

8

86

Moss Cliff
23-27

9N

9

Exit

Lewis

Lake
Placid

73

Pitchoff
13-22

Keene

Elizabethtown Exit 31

Cascade Lakes

9N

Heart Lake

73

9

Spider's Web
4-12
Washbowl
Cliffs

Wallface

Chapel Pond Slabs
1-3

Exit 30

87

Don Mellor and Bill Dodd on the Spider's Web

Chapel Pond Slab photo: Don Mellor

Chapel Pond Slab

All routes are about seven pitches and very runout. No bolts.

Descent The steep, dirty and intricate south gully can be followed without rappels. Bypass overhanging cave on its left.

  1 **The Empress** **5.5+** Fritz Wiessner and Douglas Kerr.
  2 **Thanksgiving** **5.6+** Alpine Club of Canada.
  3 **The Regular Route** **5.5** variations to route by John Case and Bob Notman.

The Spider's Web

  4 **Esthesia** **5.9+** Grant Calder, John Wald and Dave Cilley, 1976. FFA: Todd Eastman and Dave Cilley, 1977.
  5 **Slim Pickins** **5.9** Henry Barber and Dave Cilley, 1977.
  6 **T.R.** **5.10-** Tom Rosecrans. FFA: Steve Hendrick and Jay Philbrick, 1980.
  7 **Mr. Rogers Neighborhood** **5.8** Don Mellor, Chuck Turner and Rich Leswing, 1982. Loose start.
  8 **Drop, Fly, or Die** **5.11-** Henry Barber and Dave Cilley, 1977. Upper route loose.
  9 **Romano's Route** **5.11** (5.11+ bouldering start) FFA: Rich Romano, about 1977.
10 **White Knight** **5.11+** Bob Boushart and Bill Simes, about 1979. FFA: Ken Nichols and Mike Heintz, 1984.
11 **On the Loose** **5.9+** Henry Barber and Dave Cilley, 1977.
12 **Yvonne** **5.9-** Rob Wood, Dave Thomas and Bob Rice, 1968. FFA: Grant Calder and Todd Eastman, 1976.

Pitchoff Chimney Cliff

Descend around north end.

13 Roaches on the Wall **5.10** Jerry Hoover and Bob Bushart, 1979. FFA: Rick Fleming, 1980

14 Run Higher, Jump Faster **5.10+** Chuck Turner, 1982. Two bolts.

15 Dynamo Hum **5.8** Don Mellor and Bob Bushart, 1981.

16 The El **5.7** Grant Calder and John Wald, 1976.

17 Pete's Farewell **5.7** Pete Gibb and Dave Gilyeat, 1968.

18 P.F. Flyers **5.10-** Don Mellor and Bob Bushart, 1981.

19 Hidden Constellation **5.11** Don Mellor, 1985.

20 Star Sailor **5.10+** Don Mellor and Bill Simes, 1980. FFA: Don Mellor, 1981.

21 The Great Chimney **5.3-5.6** Jim Goodwin and Fritz Wiessner, 1949.

22 Brrright Star **5.9+** Chuck Turner and Alen Jolley, 1982. FFA: Chuck Turner and Alen Jolley, 1983.

Moss Cliff

Approach Wade the stream and battle the brush.

23 Falconer **5.10+** Don Mellor and Andy Zimmerman, 1984.

24 Hard Times **5.9+** Al Long and Al Rubin, 1975. FFA: Henry Barber and Dave Cilley, 1977. Start up a giant flake.

25 A Touch of Class **5.9** Al Long, Dave Hoffman and Al Rubin, 1974. Start at chimney/crack.

26 Fear of Flying **5.10** (using **Class** or **Hard Times** start) Al Long, Andy Embick and Al Rubin, 1976. Lots of offwidth.

27 Coronary Country **5.10** Al Long and Al Rubin, 1977. FFA: Don Mellor and Bill Dodd, 1984. Start at huge birch.

Pok-o-Moonshine – The Slab
Approach Directly up through the trees. **Descent** North to gully. Trail leads to campground.
28 Catharsis 5.6 John Turner, Frank Garneau and Ben Poisson, 1957.
29 The Arch Route 5.9 Dick Wilmott and Brian Rothery, 1958. Poor pro on 2nd pitch.
30 New Star 5.10 Geoff Smith and Dave Hough, 1976. Intimidating.
31 Space Walk 5.9 Dave Hough, Geoff Smith and Pat Munn, 1976. No pro on 3rd pitch.

Pok-O-Moonshine
32 The Snake 5.4 John Turner and John Brett, 1957. Poor pro; caution to protect the second.
33 Slime Line 5.9 Geoff Smith and Drew Allan, 1978.
34 Firing Line 5.11 Jim Dunn, Geoff Smith and Gary Allan, 1977. The spectacular left-facing dihedral.
35 Psychosis 5.9+ Claude Lavallée and John Turner, 1958. FFA: Jim McCarthy and Richard Goldstone, 1967.
36 Freedom Flight 5.10 Geoff Smith and Dave Hough, 1976.

escend via
:himney/gully

32-36

37-41

42-47

48-54

'oach
:ampground

descent gully

33

35

32

5.7

5.10

34

35

5.10

36

3 bolts

5.10

5.4 crack

32-36

Pok-o-Moonshine – Nose Area

37 Summer Solstice 5.11‒ Geoff Smith and Jim Dunn, 1977. The left-facing corner/roof.

38 Wild Blue 5.11‒ Dave Hough and Mark Meschinelli, 1978. FFA as described: Steve Larson and Don Mellor, 1983. Bring large nut. The last pitch climbs crack on edge of Nose.

39 FM 5.7 John Turner and Hugh Tanton, 1957. FFA: Claude Lavallée and Michael Ward. First belay on large flake, then up ten feet and crux traverse left.

40 The Snatch 5.10 Gary Allan, Geoff Smith and Pat Munn, 1977. Start with hand-crack.

41 The Great Dihedral 5.9+ Geoff Smith and Dave Hough, 1975. FFA: Richard Goldstone and Ivan Rezucha, 1976.

42 Positive Thinking 5.9 John Turner and Dick Wilmott, 1959. Crack climbing; also the spectacular frozen waterfall in winter.

43 Cooney-Norton Face 5.10 Mark Meschinelli, Dave Hough and Todd Eastman, 1982. Two bolts on 1st pitch.

44 Gamesmanship 5.8 John Turner, Brian Rothery and Wilfied Twelker, 1959. The right of two parallel cracks.

45 Bloody Mary 5.9 John Turner, Dick Strachan and Dick Wilmott, 1959.

46 Fastest Gun 5.10 Lower two pitches (most popular): Geoff Smith and Dick Bushey, 1977; Upper: Jim Dunn. Start at beautiful crack near large tree; move right at roof. 2nd pitch follows double cracks.

47 Sailors Dive 5.8 A3 Dave Hough, Mark Meschinelli and Geoff Smith, 1976.

Pok-o-Moonshine

48 Scallion   5.9 Drew Allan, Pat Munn and Mark Meschinelli, 1980.

49 Green Onion   5.8+ Geoff Smith and Pat Munn, 1977. Start in right-facing corner.

50 Thunderhead   5.10+ Gary Allan and Dave Hough, 1978. Climb roof-crack on second pitch.

51 Cirrhosis   5.9 Dick Williams and Dave Loeks.

52 Paralysis   5.8 John Turner, Brian Rothery and Dick Strachan, 1959. The last pitch appears improbable.

53 Moonshine   5.10+ Don Mellor, Mike Heintz and Mark Meschinelli, 1985.

54 Sunburst Arete   5.8 Geoff Smith and Pat Munn, 1978.

Todd Eastman on Drop, Fly or Die

Cathedral Ledge

Cannon Cliff

NORTH CONWAY CANNON

HIGHLIGHTS

Even the state's tourist machine has officially nicknamed New Hampshire the "Granite State." That should give climbers a hint of what they can find there. The major outcrops are located in the 11,000 square mile White Mountain National Forest, where lie some of the best known crags in North America. Cathedral and Whitehorse Ledges lift 500 vertical feet of gray granite out of the half pastoral, half tourist-industrialized Mount Washington Valley. Cathedral is famous for its unrelenting steepness, while Whitehorse is better known for its slabs – though its South Buttress has plenty of the steep stuff as well. The convenience of North Conway's amenities (five minutes from the cliffs) and approach walks as short as a hundred yards, assure the popularity of these two crags. Cannon Cliff, an hour's drive from North Conway, is one of the largest cliffs on the East Coast, with 1,000 feet of steep exfoliated slabs. It also has a relatively alpine setting, with views that extend across the forested valley to 5,000 foot peaks that reach well above timberline.

CLIMBING

As the Pleistocene glaciers poured into the Mount Washington Valley from the northwest, they passed over a couple of rounded hills and plucked the granite from their lee slopes, thus leaving climbers with their most popular vertical playgrounds in New England. This also partially explains why, though glacially carved, Cathedral and White-horse are not polished. Instead, their rock is coarse enough to allow diverse styles of climbing. Certainly, many routes follow the widely spaced cracks, but many others connect cracks or avoid them with relatively moderate climbing on good edges. Sometimes, of course, the edges are less distinct, and the climbing is distinctly less moderate.

Thin face climbing, steep and overhanging cracks, and a resident community of some of the nation's better climbers have combined to produce a great number of extremely difficult climbs. The myriad of small edges found on New Hampshire granite add more diversity to the climbing than is sometimes found on its Western equivalent.

Each cliff has its unique properties. Cathedral, at 450 feet tall and half-mile long, is the smallest of the big three, but also the most universally steep. It is the centerpiece of New Hampshire climbing, where most of the historical jumps in free climbing standards took place. Despite its intimidating initial appearance, even the blanker appearing sections of the cliff have a number of easier routes (down to 5.6). Most of the cliff, however, is dominated by hard crack and face climbs to eight pitches in length (pitches here are usually less than a rope length). Short routes can also be found. Approach walks will take ten minutes, at most.

Whitehorse, up to 800 feet high, is best known for its tremendous friction slabs. The entire right side is a smooth expanse of almost featureless rock until one reaches the overlaps above, where the stumps of exfoliated slabs provide an obstacle to more slabs above. The routes through this section are popular and exciting, even at their easiest: 5.4. As one moves left, the mile long cliff becomes much steeper and is known as the South Buttress. It has become too steep for friction climbing and routes follow flakes, cracks and, in the outstanding case of **The Children's Crusade,** a faint dike. Further left still is the **Wonder Wall,** where the rock's character changes yet again, becoming increasingly steep and rougher in texture. A number of difficult and committing face climbs can be found here. Approaching the **Wonder Wall** area might take twenty minutes or so, while reaching the slabs is a ten minute stroll.

Cannon Cliff, a thousand feet high and a mile and a half in breadth, is a massive hunk of rock. As might be expected, a great diversity of climbing can be found in that great expanse. Just left of the main section of cliff is a jutting prow of rock. This beautiful fin is the **Whitney-Gilman Ridge,** an all time classic. It is almost unique on the East Coast, because rarely is the opportunity presented to follow such a prominent arête. Many of Cannon's ascents take place on this route – expect company. Recent rockfall, unfortunately, has made the route looser and less desirable than it once was.

The central, and highest, part of Cannon Cliff is known as the Big Wall Section. Though steep, the rock is slabby, with clean sheets of massive granite rarely found this side of the West Coast. Beautiful crack systems, flakes, and thin face climbing dominate. Though several Grade V aid routes tackled the middle of the Big Wall Section, most have gone free. Easier routes follow the edges of this massive piece of rock, while some short climbs explore the lower reaches. Far to the right are The Cannon Slabs, which holds some of the most difficult friction routes in the Northeast. The rock here is steeper than that at Whitehorse, but also rougher. The exfoliation overlaps also provide a greater challenge.

The approach takes up to an hour on the talus slope. All the routes on Cannon are subject to an alpine seriousness. Several deaths have occured on Cannon, most due to exposure. Be sure to read the *RESTRICTIONS AND WARNINGS* section concerning Cannon Cliff.

Though Cathedral, Whitehorse and Cannon comprise the triad of New Hampshire crags, numerous smaller cliffs lie scattered throughout the region, often offering a much quieter and more peaceful climbing experience. Some crags are obvious, many are buried deep in the woods, and others lie high on the flanks of Mount Washington and other mountains. The sample smaller cliff chosen for this book is Sundown Ledge. Accessible yet hidden from roadside view, its one pitch routes offer an enjoyable diversion from the longer commitment needed for most routes on the big three.

ENVIRONMENT

By percentage of people so employed, New Hampshire is the second most industrialized state in the country. Manufacturing is the state's principal industry, but providing vacations is its second. Of all the vacation sites, the White Mountains are the most popular, and North Conway is right at the heart of it. So the commercial strip that one encounters on the drive into town should not be unexpected, nor the crowds of people that pour through during the height of the tourist season. Still, it is the mountains that provide the backdrop for this influx of humanity, and the mountains and most of the surrounding country have retained their serene beauty despite the pressure put upon them.

Mount Washington, 6,288 feet high, is the tallest and most massive of the peaks, but the Presidential Range holds many others that reach above timberline. Timberline is low here because winter weather is notoriously harsh: the world's strongest winds were recorded on the summit of Mt. Washington – 231 miles per hour. Despite their awesome winter climate, the rounded peaks are gentle of slope. Exquisite mountain streams flow down these hillsides, turning into rivers in the valley floors. Pools have been carved into granite, providing delightful swimming holes.

In the timbered zone, one finds mixed forests of deciduous and coniferous trees. During the fall, maples play the lead role in a spectacular display of colors that draws "leaf peepers" from around the world. There is truly no place that surpasses the beauty of this region during the peak foliage season of mid-September to mid-October. By superb coincidence, this is also when the climbing weather is at its finest.

By contrast, the other seasons are much less predictable. Some say that early spring is wet, followed quickly by the black flies and mosquitoes of late spring, leading straight into the heat and humidity of summer. This view is somewhat too negative, however, as fine climbing weather magically appears at any time.

In bad weather, hiking and driving can be wonderful alternatives to climbing. The region abounds in trails and scenic roads. The Kancamagus highway, which will take one to Cannon Cliff from North Conway, is one of the showpieces of the Northeast. This beautiful drive with expansive views is not to be missed. During the peak leaf season (mid-September to mid-October) expect considerable and very slow traffic on weekends. (Route 302 to Route 3 can be faster than the Kancamagus, especially during this period.)

CLIMBING HISTORY

New Hampshire's climbing history is certainly the longest in North America, dating to 1642 when Mount Washington was ascended (a hundred years after having been first sighted from shipboard in the Atlantic). The Appalachian Mountain Club was formed in 1878 – the oldest currently active such group in the country. Though rock climbing came more recently, it, too, dates back nearly to the origins of the sport in North America. During the early 1900's, wealthy New Englanders made a habit of visiting Europe. Many tried climbing in the Alps and some of these young men and women became enamored of the sport and recognized that even if New England didn't have rugged peaks, it did have excellent crags. Thus, serious exploration of the White Mountain region took place during the 1920's, quickly launching onto the largest cliff of them all, the face of Cannon.

Though earlier less difficult routes were climbed in the Mount Washington region, Cannon was climbed in 1928 and the route was declared to be the only one possible on the face. But only one year later, the **Whitney-Gilman Ridge** was also climbed. An incredibly bold first ascent, this 5.7 route not only climbed an intimidating arête, it was also done with no protection between belays. The protection pipe below the crux was installed the following year.

During the next five years, the pace of New Hampshire climbing was rapid. The Shawangunks had yet to be discovered by climbers, and the North Conway area was the hot spot for Eastern climbing. Not just the big three cliffs were explored – many outlying crags were searched out as well. It is interesting to note that some of the earliest ethical "tainting" took place here. Rappelling to inspect the climbing from above and fixing pitons on rappel ("to lasso" from below) were practiced and contemplated respectively.

As the Great Depression ground deeper into the psyches and pocket-books of climbers, activity tapered off radically, and even before World War II, new route activity had virtually come to a halt.

After the war, leading New England climbers seemed principally interested in international expeditions, reserving their home activities for winter climbs and repeating old standard rock routes. Virtually no new route activity occured until the mid-1950's, when eyes started to open again towards climbing new routes.

It took a shock from outside to show New Hampshire climbers how far they had fallen out of the forefront of rock climbing standards. A British climber who was living in Canada to avoid the draft paid a visit in 1958 and climbed **Repentence** – at a stiff 5.9 standard, it was not repeated for twelve years. Other routes, not quite as difficult, fell to him as well.

During the 1960's, college hiking and mountaineering clubs banded together into the Intercollegiate Outing Club Association. Where members of the Appalachian Mountain Club had been responsible for virtually all activity during the 1920's and 30's, now the college students took the fore and established most of the new routes while hunting out more remote crags as well. Developments in Yosemite, of course, had their effect here as everywhere else. With steep, blank walls available, locals began searching out routes where they could maximize the use of aid while training for trips to "The Valley."

New Hampshire climbing during this period was not only considered training for Yosemite, it had also been relegated to "second best" status to what had become by now the principal hot spot of Eastern climbing: the Shawangunks. Not until the end of the 1960's did North Conway get its own guiding service and climbing store. When they came, so did the resident climbers (as staff), who quickly recognized the potential in their backyard and launched a new chapter of activity on the local crags. Standards rapidly came up to par, with 5.10's being established in 1970 and 5.11 a few years later.

The local community of guides and their visiting friends continued to be the principal leaders in New Hampshire climbing, keeping busy with new routes and aid elimination. A new push into the highest standards began during the mid-1980's. Interestingly, it was at least partially spearheaded by a local high school student. After nearly 60 years, climbing on the crags that literally overlook North Conway had finally developed true local roots.

CAMPING

There are unlimited opportunities for bed-and-breakfast inns as well as numerous commercial campgrounds and camping areas in the National Forest. Convenient inns include the Nereledge Inn (River Road, North Conway, NH 03860, tel: 603-356-2831), and the Scottish Lion Inn (Route 16, North Conway, NH 03860, tel: 603-356-6381). Reservations for all Mount Washington Valley inns and hotels can be made by writing or calling North Country Reservations, P.O. Box 747, North Conway NH 03860, tel: 1-800-334-7378 or 603-356-3212.

One can bivouac just about anywhere, except Echo Lake State Park, in which Cathedral and Whitehorse Ledges are located. Popular with climbers is the moderately priced North Conway Pines Campground just east of the Echo Lake State Park; it has showers (West Side Road, North Conway, NH 03860 tel: 603-356-3305). There are several less expensive National Forest campgrounds without showers off the Kancamagus Highway, including one just below Sundown Ledge (the Covered Bridge Campground, 603-447-5448). Next to Cannon is the moderately priced Lafayette Campground, which is extremely convenient and has showers (Franconia, NH 03580, tel: 603-823-5563).

For exciting refreshment when the weather gets a bit hot for climbing, some climbers cliff dive into the river at the Flume, between North Woodstock and Cannon.

SEASONS AND WEATHER

Approximate Months	Typical Temperatures High	Low	Likelihood of Precipitation	Frequency of Climbable Days
Nov-Mar	20's+	0's	medium	low
Apr-Jun	70's+	40's	med-high	med-high
Jul-Aug	80's+	70's −	medium	med-high
Sep-Oct	70's	40's −	low-med	high

Comments: Mosquitoes and black flies are sometimes a severe nuisance in May and June. Humidity can be high in summer. Cannon is usually cooler and windier than North Conway.

RESTRICTIONS AND WARNINGS

CATHEDRAL: The gate at the bottom of the road is shut at 6 pm and is often not open until Memorial Day. *DON'T DRIVE AROUND IT.* Beware of objects thrown by tourists from the overlook above.
CANNON: Be sure to sign in at the little red box on the tree at the trailhead, both before *and after* climbing. Due to freeway construction, the location of this box may change, but one can always sign in at the Cannon Mountain Tramway office ½ mile north of the cliff. Also, the

cliff demands special caution because the routes are long and the mountain is subject to sometimes quick and severe changes in weather. Clouds come in from the northwest – behind the cliff – and a storm might not be visible until it hits. Be sure to be prepared for cold and rainy conditions to come unexpectedly. Several people have died of exposure. A second rope can be crucial for multiple escape rappels in bad weather. A flashlight should be carried. The rock is subject to extensive weathering because of severe winter weather. Watch for loose rocks, large loose blocks, and extremely unsafe fixed protection, including many bad pitons. Route finding can be difficult and many climbers go astray. Isn't climbing fun?

GUIDEBOOKS

Rock Climbs in the White Mountains of New Hampshire (1986) by Ed Webster. Mountain Imagery, P.O. Box 210, Eldorado Springs, CO 80025.

Cannon, Cathedral, Humphrey's and Whitehorse   A Rock Climber's Guide (1982 with 1984 addition) by Paul Ross and Chris Ellms. International Mountain Climbing School, Box 239, Conway, NH 03818.

GUIDE SERVICES AND EQUIPMENT STORES

GUIDE SERVICES:

Mountain Guides Alliance, Box 266, North Conway, NH 03860, telephone: 207-935-3843 (Alain Comeau), 603-447-3086 (George Hurley), 603-466-3949 (Ian Turnbull), 603-447-5776 (Kurt Winkler).

International Mountain Climbing School, Box 239, Conway, NH 03818, telephone (IME Retail Store): 603-356-6316; if no answer: 603-447-6700 or 447-2328.

Eastern Mountain Sports Climbing School, Main Street, North Conway, NH 03860, telephone: 603-356-5433.

EQUIPMENT STORES:

International Mountain Equipment (IME), Main Street (next to the Cinema), North Conway.

Eastern Mountain Sports (EMS), Main Street, North Conway.

EMERGENCY SERVICES

All rescues are conducted by the Mountain Rescue Service. They are staffed by local volunteer climbers. Call IME (356-6316), EMS (356-5433) or North Conway Rescue at 356-2424. The hospital in North Conway is the Memorial Hospital, Mountain Medical Center, Route 16, North Conway, telephone: 356-5461, and nearest to to Cannon is the Littleton Hospital at 444-7731.

GETTING THERE

North Conway is an excellent place for climbers without a car because Trailways buses go there daily from Boston. The cliffs can be reached on foot.

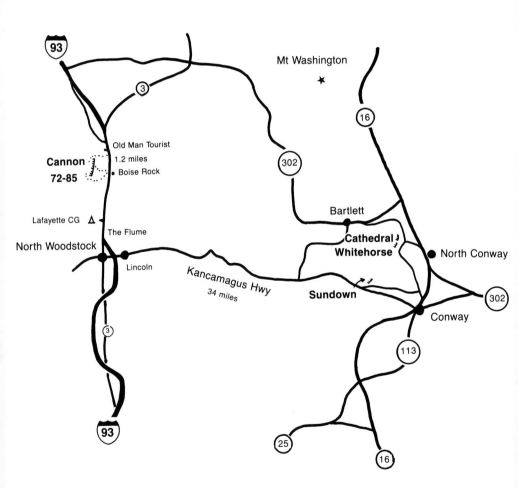

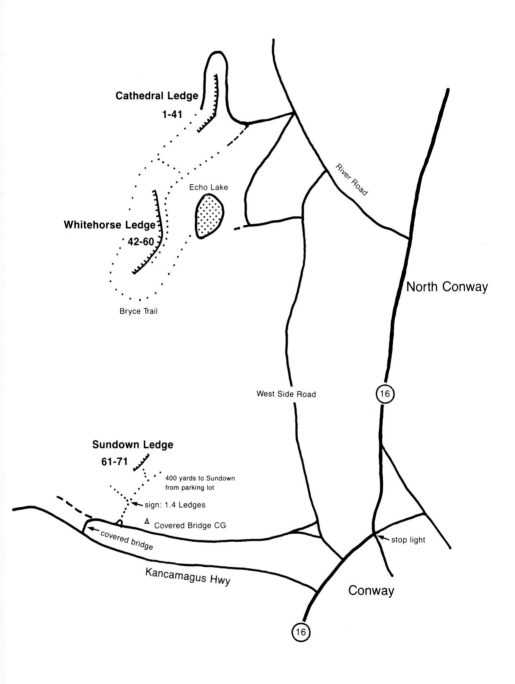

Cathedral Ledge

1-41

River Road

Echo Lake

Whitehorse Ledge

42-60

Bryce Trail

North Conway

West Side Road

(16)

Sundown Ledge

61-71

400 yards to Sundown
from parking lot

← sign: 1.4 Ledges

△ Covered Bridge CG

covered bridge

← stop light

Kancamagus Hwy

Conway

(16)

Cathedral Ledge

Descent from top: Follow road down.

1 **Bombardment** **5.8** Dave Cilley (rope-solo), 1972. Begin on small ledge just uphill from long, low ceiling. Up right to oak tree belay ledge. Stay right of arch to reach left-slanting crack.

2 **Ventilator** **5.10** Joe Cote and A.J. LaFleur, 1972. Three bolts lead to left-diagonalling crack. Many bolts in area; easily confusing.

3 **Yo-Yo (Starfire)** **5.11** Mike Hartrich and Joe Cote, 1975. First pitch climbs left of arch to large pine tree.

4 **Three Birches** **5.8+** Sam Streibert, John Reppy and Harold May, 1963. Climb twenty foot arch to crack. Nasty in wet weather.

5 **Fun House** **5.7** Joe Cote and Larry Poorman, 1969. Start at pine tree above V corner. Climb right-hand of twin corners and continue up to next ledge.

6 **Nutcracker** **5.9+** Joe Cote, Dick Arey and Ward Freeman, 1969. FFA: Henry Barber and Bob Anderson, 1972. The striking vertical crack left of two flaring corners stacked on top of each other.

7 **Lichen Delight** **5.11−** Dave Cilley and Sibylle Hechtel, 1971. FFA: Henry Barber, 1972. Begin in left-facing corner.

8 **Retaliation** **5.9** Dave and Dean Cilley, 1970. FFA: Joe Cote and Eric Radack, 1971.

9 **The Arête** **5.11** Ed Webster and Paul Ross, 1978. 165 foot rope; bring tiny nuts.

10 **Upper Refuse** **5.5** John Turner and Richard Willmott, 1960. The ramp.

11 **Black Lung** **5.7+** Henry Barber, Dave Cilley and Frank Dean, 1972.

12 **Book of Solemnity** **5.10−** Joe Cote and Steve Arsenault, 1971. The beautiful open book. Move left at its top under a roof.

13 **Refuse** **5.6** John Turner and Richard Willmott, 1960. Start at small corner twenty feet right of main corner on small ledge. Pine tree growing at its base. The tree on 2nd pitch is dangerously decayed. The wide crack behind the tree is 5.7.

14 **Wild Women** **5.11+** Ed Webster, et. al. 1976-1979. Above Tree Ledge, the route is **Woman in Love.** Joe Cote and John Porter, 1971. FFA: Henry Barber and Ed Webster, 1978. Start in finger crack.

15 **Recompense** **5.9** John Turner and Richard Willmott, 1959 (except final pitch). The 5.9+ Beast Flake variation on 3rd pitch is highly recommended.

16 **The Prow** **5.11+ (5.6 C2)** Paul Ross and Hugh Thompson, 1972. First free ascent complete route: Jim Dunn and Jay Wilson, 1977.

Chris Plant on Women in Love photo: S. Peter Lewis

Cathedral Ledge – Left

Cathedral – Prow Area

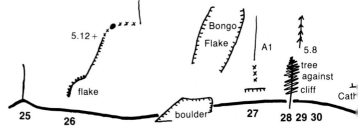

Cathedral Ledge

17 Tourist Treat **5.12** Jeff Pheasant (solo), 1975. FFA: Lynn Hill and Russ Raffa, 1984.

18 Camber **5.11** Jim Dunn, Jeff Pheasant and Ed Sklar, 1978.

19 Stage Fright **5.12+** Sam Sargent and Todd Eastman, 1975. FFA: Hugh Herr, 1985. Thin crack. Considered one of the most dangerous hard leads in the country.

20 Airation **5.11** Sam Streibert and Joe Cote, 1969. FFA: Henry Barber, John Bragg and Bob Anderson, 1973. The prominent central crack.

21 Heather **5.12** Ed Webster and Sam Sargent, 1976. FFA: Rick Fleming, 1980. Thin crack.

22 Pine Tree Eliminate **5.8** Mike Hartich and Rick Ruppel, 1973. The crack above tree stump.

23 Play Misty **5.11+** Ed Webster and Bill Kane, 1976. Nigel Shepherd, Bill Waymand, Kim Smith and Doug Madara, 1978. Thin crack.

24 Thin Air **5.6** Ray D'Arcy and Fran Coffin, 1955.

25 Standard Route **5.6** Robert Underhill, Leland Pollock and P.T. Newton, 1931 (with aid). The 5.7 Toe Crack variation is highly recommended.

26 Mordor Wall **5.7-5.12+ A4** First pitch: Steve Arsenault and Joe Cote, 1970; remainder: Steve Arsenault (solo), 1970. Last two pitches freed by Ed Webster, 1979. First pitch freed to last bolt by Jim Surette, 1985. Bring aid rack including pointed sky hooks. Much is fixed.

27 Mines of Moria **5.6-5.11+ A2** Joe Cote, John Porter and Paul Ross, 1972. Bring pitons and large nuts.

28 Pendulum Route **5.11** Steve Arsenault and Paul Doyle, 1967. FFA complete route: Ed Webster and Ajax Greene, 1976. Start by chimneying against tree.

29 The Bridge of Khazad-Dum **5.11+** FFA complete route: Jim Dunn and Bryan Becker, 1976. Bring large nuts (preferably camming) for the crux.

30 Lights in the Forest **5.11+ (5.10 A3)** Ed Webster and Paul Ross, 1976. FFA: Jim Surette, Neil Cannon and Alison Osius, 1984. Very little aid on aid version; bring a few pitons and a small copperhead.

31 White Eye **5.12** (first pitch) Steve Arsenault and Sam Streibert, 1968. FFA: Mark Hudon and Max Jones, 1978.

32 Intimidation **5.10** Steve Arsenault and Bruce Beck, 1968. FFA: Sam Streibert and Dennis Merritt, 1971.

33 Repentence **5.9+** John Turner and Art Gran, 1958 (using one point of aid below crux and no pro on crux). Follow the chimney-crack.

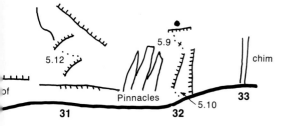

Cathedral Ledge – Right

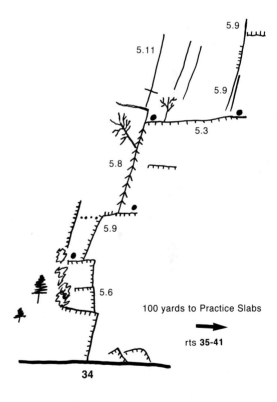

5.11

5.9

5.9

5.3

5.8

5.9

5.6

100 yards to Practice Slabs

rts **35-41**

34

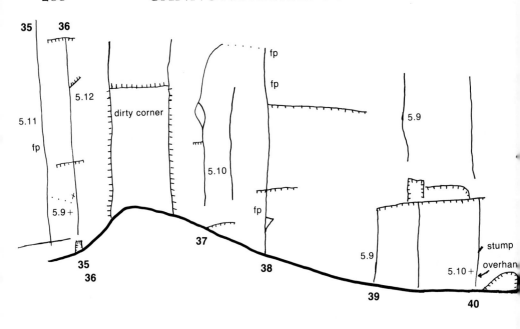

Cathedral Ledge

34 Diedre 5.9 Budapest 5.11 Joe Cote and Dick Arey, 1968. FFA continuous original line: Joe Cote and Ben Read, 1971. **Budapest:** Ed Webster and Jim Dunn, 1979.

35 Jack the Ripper 5.11 Joe Cote and John Merrill, 1970. FFA: Ed Webster et.al., 1976.

36 The Possessed 5.12 Ed Webster and Ken Nichols, 1974. FFA: Jim Dunn, 1975.

37 The Slot 5.10 FFA: Bob Anderson and Henry Barber, 1973.

38 They Died Laughing 5.9 Kevin Bein et. al. FFA: Henry Barber and Joe Cote, 1972.

39 Bird's Nest 5.9 FFA: Henry Barber, 1972.

40 Recluse 5.10+ FFA: Henry Barber, 1971.

41 Child's Play 5.5 The vertical crack with ledge halfway up.

Hugh Herr on Stage Fright photo: S. Peter Lewis

60-53

52-47

slabs

46-42

Whitehorse Ledge – The Slabs

42 Wavelength **5.8** Alain and Janot Comeau, 1981.

43 Standard Route **5.6** First complete ascent: Leland W. Pollock et.al., 1932.

44 Sliding Board **5.7** Bill Crowther and Bob Gilmore, before 1970. Runout.

45 Interloper **5.10** First complete ascent: Mike Heintz and Alain Comeau, 1977.

46 Wedge **5.6** Bill Crowther et. al., before 1970.

Whitehorse Ledge

47 Future Shock 5.11 A0 Alain and Janot Comeau, 1981. Up and right of **Seventh Seal**. First pitch only. friction up a thin, left angling dike; tension left to bolt belay.

48 Seventh Seal 5.10 Alain Comeau et. al., 1976. The right thin crack on a slab below a small roof on the face of a buttress.

49 Ethereal Crack 5.10+ Ed Webster and Bryan Becker, 1975. The left thin crack.

50 Loose Lips 5.10− Jim Dunn, et. al. 1979.

51 Revolt of the Dike Brigade 5.11 Ed Webster and Susan Patenaude, 1980. Bring small camming nuts. Start twenty feet left of left-facing corner. Follow a series of flakes, then a dike.

52 Children's Crusade 5.9 Direct Finish 5.11− Alain Comeau and Mike Heintz, 1978; Direct: Ed Webster and Susan Patenaude, 1980. Follow a faint dike up the smooth wall. Start up prominent dike, then traverse right from small overhang (with piton in hole) to faint dike which is followed up. The **Direct** starts up left facing corner below right facing corner.

53 The Last Unicorn 5.10 Ed Webster and Jeff Pheasant, 1978. Start just left of large spruce. One bolt on 1st pitch; 5 on 2nd. Approach: Follow ledges to the right from the start of **Inferno**; complex and 5th class.

54 Wonder Wall 5.12− Jeff Pheasant and Paul Ross, 1976. FFA complete route: Ed Webster and Russ Clune, 1981. Poor pro on sixth (5.9) pitch. Start with the poorly protected 5.7 slab left of **Hallowed Eve.**

55 Hallowed Eve 5.9+ Ed Webster and Bill Aughton, 1976. At the base of the buttress, climb part way up a twenty foot right-facing corner, then pass a bolt to the tree ledge. Poor pro on first and third, and very poor pro on fourth (5.9+), pitches.

56 Science Friction Wall 5.11 First complete ascent: Ed Webster and Susan Patenaude, 1980. Runout and serious. Follow bolts on upper wall.

57 Ladyslipper 5.9 Susan Patenaude and Ed Webster, 1979. Several bolts. Approach: as for **Last Unicorn.**

58 Inferno 5.8 Bob Anderson and Wayne Christian, 1972. Start at large oak tree. Upper wall: the spectacular hand crack.

59 Atlantis 5.10− (5.9 with escape) Ed Webster and Doug Madara, 1976.

60 Hotter Than Hell 5.9 Matt Peer and Craig Stemley, 1980. Start around the corner from **Inferno**. Up to 1st bolt, right past another to crack, up face above, passing bolts.

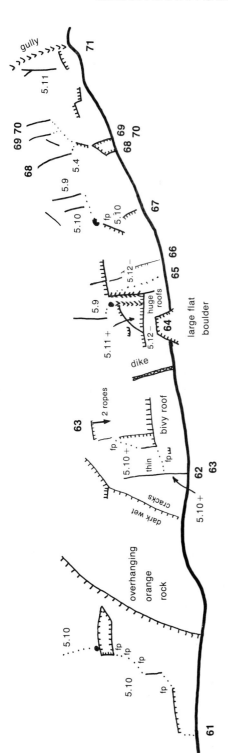

Sundown Ledge

61 Davy Jone's Locker **5.10** Ed Webster and Michael Hartrich, 1981.

62 Vultures **5.10+** Joe Cote, Dick Arey and Jean-Claude Dehmel, 1972. FFA: Henry Barber and John Bragg, 1973.

63 Flight of the Falcon **5.10+** Ed Webster and Susan Patenaude, 1980.

64 End of the Tether **5.12−** (or 5.11+ A0 with shoulderstand) Todd Swain and Curt Robinson, 1979. FFA: Russ Clune, 1985. Rainy day climb.

65 Toothless Grin **5.12−** Jim Damion et.al., 1984. Rainy day climb.

66 Razor Crack **A1** Joe Cote and Dick Arey, 1972. Rainy day climb. Knifeblades and baby angles.

67 Rough Boys **5.10−** Doug Madara and Choe Brooks, 1981. Better pro in right crack.

68 Stiletto **5.4** Dick Arey and Joe Cote, 1972.

69 Todd Foolery **5.8** Todd Swain and Brad White, 1981.

70 The British Are Here **5.7** Todd Swain and Nick Donnelly, 1981.

71 Shadowline **5.11** Michael Hartrich and Albert Dow, 1980. Difficult pro.

Cannon Cliff

Access may change when construction of I-93 is complete. Currently: park at Boise Rock, directly below the **Whitney-Gilman Ridge**, for most of Cannon Cliff, and at Profile Lake for the Slabs.

Descents: Follow trails left from **Whitney-Gilman** (don't attempt to shortcut to base of cliff) or right from other routes. Some people prefer to rappel routes in the Big Wall Section.

72 Whitney-Gilman Ridge 5.7/5.8 (or 5.8 variation) Bradley Gilman and Hassler Whitney, 1929. No protection was used on the first ascent. A classic route, almost unique for the east. Before the recent rockfall, it was the most popular route on Cannon, thus often crowded. The rockfall in upper sections has left loose rock and possibly 5.8 climbing.

slabs

5.10+

very bad belay

5.10

5.10

Walk on the Wild Side

5.10

5.11

Bivy

A4

5.8

5.10+

A2

5.11

5.11

5.9

5.11

5.9+

5.10

5.10+

5.10

5.8

5.10+

5.10

5.7

4th

73   74   75

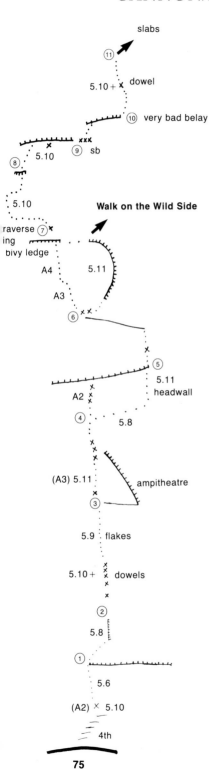

slabs

⑪

5.10+ ✗ dowel

⑩ very bad belay

✗
5.10   ⑨ sb

⑧
5.10

5.10

raverse ⑦✗
ing
bivy ledge

A4   5.11

A3

⑥ ✗✗

✗

⑤
5.11
headwall

A2

④   5.8

✗
✗
✗

(A3) 5.11   ampitheatre
✗
③

5.9 flakes

5.10+ ✗✗✗ dowels
✗

②

5.8

①

5.6

(A2) ✗ 5.10

4th

75

Walk on the Wild Side

Cannon Cliff – Big Wall Section

73 VMC Direct   V 5.11 Dick Williams, Art Gran and Yvon Chouinard, 1965. FFA: Bob Anderson and Sam Streibert, 1974. The first big wall aid climb in New Hampshire.

74 VMC Direct Direct   IV 5.10+ Steve Arsenault and Sam Streibert, 1969. FFA: Jeff Burns and Hans Larsen, 1978. Perhaps the best route on Cannon.

75 Labyrinth Wall Direct   V 5.11 or 5.7 A4 Paul Ross and Michael Peloquin, 1971 through pitch seven; completed by Peter Cole, Rainsford Rouner and Mark Hudon, 1974. The 1st 7 pitches done free with variations and escaping right from Bivy Ledge is **Walk on the Wild Side**, FA: Bob Rotert and Mark Richey, 1981. Extremely tricky route finding on upper route.

The last pitch of the Whitney-Gilman Ridge

Cannon Cliff

76 Moby Grape III 5.8 Variations on a route done by Jan and Herb Conn, 1945. First linked together: Joe Cote and Roger Martin, 1972.

77 Reppy's Crack 5.8 Phil Nelson and Alan Wedgewood, 1965.

78 Union Jack III 5.9 Paul Ross, Ben and Marion Wintringham, 1973.

79 Vertigo III 5.9 A0 (pendulum) John Bragg, Michael Peloquin and Paul Ross, 1971. FFA complete route except pendulum: Doug White and Tad Pheffer, 1975.

Craig Sabina on Whitney-Gilman Ridge

Cannon Slabs

Beware of falling rocks from parties on **Lakeview.** All routes finish up the classic dihedral on the left side of the "Old Man of the Mountains" feature. This is the **Wiessner Corner** 5.5+ Fritz Wiessner and Robert Underhill, 1933.

80 Odyssey 5.10 Chris Ellms, Chris Rowins and Steve Schneider, 1974. FFA: Jeff Burns, Stoney Middleton and Steve Schneider, 1975.

81 Consolation Prize 5.8 FA complete route: John Waterman and Al Rubin, 1970.

82 Vendetta 5.9 Howard Peterson and Peter Chadwick, 1974. Start up small corner.

83 Stairway to Heaven 5.10 Jeff Burns, Chris Ellms and Howard Peterson, 1976. Runout. Start right of 1st bolt 15 feet up.

84 Lakeview 5.5 Dan Brodien, Roger Damon and Andy Fisher, 1962. A very popular route; the line should be obvious. Be sure to include the **Wiessner Corner.** Be careful not to drop loose rocks on parties on other routes.

Butch Consendine near Sand Beach

MOUNT DESERT ISLAND

HIGHLIGHTS

Mount Desert Island, Maine, is a long ways from the rest of the world and its climbing is limited. But that's good in a way, because it means you won't come here for the wrong reasons. Watching lobster boats and a churning Atlantic ocean are as important to the island experience as are its superb granite crags. The seacliffs include Otter Cliff, which is about 500 feet long and 50 to 60 feet high, Hunter's Beach, whose cliffs have only recently been frequented by climbers, and Great Head, whose true potential is just beginning to be explored. About a mile from the sea is the Island's largest crag: the South Wall of Mt. Champlain. The water is clearly visible from Champlain's 200 to 300 foot cliffs and the climbing still has a sea-side character. But perhaps the essence of local climbing is the coastal bouldering between Sand Beach and Otter Cliff. A quiet afternoon spent wandering the coast here is what separates Mount Desert Island from other climbing areas.

CLIMBING

Most of the crags on Mount Desert Island lie within the boundaries of Acadia National Park, and in fact, Acadia is the name frequently used by the climbers who refer to the area. Overcrowded cliffs are rarely a problem on the island, whose out-of-the-way location keeps it off-the-beaten-path for most visitors to New England. Many of the climbers who do frequent Acadia come from North Conway during its hot and crowded summer season. Everyone who comes revels in the unique character of climbing on the many small granite crags that lie scattered over the island.

The cliffs are diverse in character, both in their setting and in the nature of their granite: on inland cliffs it's often cleaved into perfect cracks and dihedrals, on the coast it's usually more blocky and with sharply cut face holds. Though inland cliffs were frequently lichen-covered before climbing routes were established, along the lines of ascent they have usually been well cleaned. In most cases, the granite is superbly sound. Since early climbing was often done on a toprope and high standard climbing did not arrive until nuts were already taking hold in America, the cliffs have virtually no pin scars. In addition, most island activists have been strongly opposed to the use of bolts. This means that most climbs will be found wonderfully pristine.

Otter Cliff has dominated the seacliff climbing scene so heavily that the Park Service is encouraging climbers to spread out onto other cliffs as well. Good alternatives include the rocks at Hunter's Beach and Great Head. Still, most climbers will not be able to resist a visit to Otter. Along the base of this 50 foot tall cliff runs a rock shelf which is partially covered at high tide. When the ocean is rough, spray drenches the lower part of the cliff, sometimes threatening climbers. More commonly, the water churns quietly in the background. An exciting feature of Otter are two horizontal crack systems that traverse the entire face, one at ⅓ height, the other at ⅔ height. These make excellent girdle traverses and are called **Low Tide** and **High Tide.**

Hunter's Beach is on land owned by the Rockefeller Foundation. The setting is magnificent and is rarely visited by tourists – which can make it much more pleasant to visit than tourist-frequented Otter Cliff. There is a great variety of climbing at Hunter's; easy routes are common, yet routes harder than anything found at Otter are also located here. In fact, some feel that Hunter's has the best seacliff routes on Mount Desert Island.

Great Head in Acadia National Park has had very little activity to date; however, locals expect to focus their energies there in the near future. The peninsula seems to have tremendous potential for climbing and exploration.

The 200 to 300 foot Precipice (the south-facing wall of Mt. Champlain) is not just the tallest cliff, but also has some of the finest rock on the island. The cliff's mid-section is broken by a set of large tree-covered ledges whch separate the two or three pitches into individual climbs. This section is the most popular and holds many excellent routes of mid-fifth class difficulty. On the far right side, the wall turns smooth and offers two pitch climbs that include the most difficult on the island. Left of the mid-section is a wall that stretches unbroken for difficult two and three pitch routes. Climbs on Champlain involve face, friction and cracks, all of superb quality.

Many other cliffs are found inland, including the Bubbles and the Beehive, while a few other islands that must be reached by boat hold crags as well. Still, the ones mentioned above have plenty of climbing for an extended visit.

The real joy of Acadian climbing can be found in the bouldering between Sand Beach and Otter Cliff. In places the granite flows in a smooth sheet into the water; elsewhere, ocean waves echo in deep clefts cut into 50 foot cliffs – but along most of the distance, small rock faces lie scattered over the barren shore. Here one can find an experience unlike any other in America.

ENVIRONMENT

Mount Desert Island was already settled by fishermen and lumberers when, in 1844, a painter began extolling its aesthetic attractions. Soon, his visions were disseminated, quickly drawing more artists – and then their patrons and nature lovers – to come experience the wild beauty of Mount Desert. Within a few years, the island became a tourist center, then a summer home for many of the richest families in America. It was these rich families, including the Rockefellers, who donated the land that eventually became Acadia National Park – in 1919, the first National Park east of the Mississippi.

The Park's current popularity stems from the same environment that attracted visitors in the 1800's. The interface of the sea and the granite shore is the essence of Mount Desert Island. Cadillac Mountain, 1,530 feet high, is the highest point on the Atlantic coast and its summit is the first place in the United States to be hit by the sun's morning rays. A few minutes later, the sun strikes the sea at Cadillac's feet, warming the fishermen in their lobster boats as they check traps on the rocky coastline. As the sun heats the mid-day atmosphere, a ship's mirage might loom tall on the blue horizon – probably the ferry from Nova Scotia on its way to Mount Desert Island's Bar Harbor.

Thunder Hole takes its name from the sound and power of waves as they are channeled into a chasm on the granite shore. Because it is a magnet for tourists, guard rails have been installed to keep viewers from being pulverized like the flotsam that is sometimes swept into this cleft. Elsewhere on the coast, an explorer can find other wonderous holes, without names or guard rails. On a rainy dawn, fresh streams are everywhere – cascading down the rocks, meeting surf that smashes on the shore. Surf sprays in the air and seems to be lost in clouds, only to return as rain. Everything is gray: the rain, the streams, the clouds, the surf, the rock, the dawn.

With the coming of the crisp days of fall, thoughts of grayness are banished by the exuberance of the foliage that transforms the island just as it transforms most of the East Coast. Looking down from the warm, sun-drenched cliffs of Mount Champlain, the first hints of fall look like orange paint specks on a green canvas that stretches a mile to the blue sea.

Despite the extensiveness of the National Park (35,000 acres), half of the island is privately owned and is dotted with villages and criss-crossed with paved roads. These communities provide samples of the Yankee towns found up and down the coast of Maine, though here one finds the inevitable influence of millions of visitors each year. Bar Harbor, in particular, caters to the not-always-noble wants of the American tourist.

Fifty-seven miles of carriage roads provide another unique feature of Acadia National Park. These roads wander everywhere and straddle streams on ornate stone bridges, no two of which are alike. The carriage roads can only be travelled on foot, by horse, or by bicycle. Indeed, a bicycle can be the ideal instrument for touring the island, sometimes even allowing one to short-cut the long one-way loop roads that shuttle tourist-filled cars from viewpoint to viewpoint.

Lest one come to think that all the coastline is barricaded by rock, Sand·Beach provides a sample of its namesake – some climbers may enjoy this as much as their beloved crags. Often crowded, but still sweet, this cove can offer a relaxing horizontal break from the adrenalin of the vertical world.

CLIMBING HISTORY

If the island's environment inspires long-windedness, its climbing history allows an economy of breath. True, rock climbing on the island is older

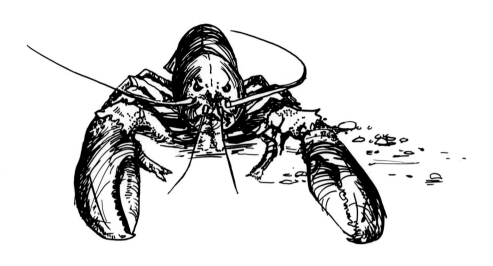

than the birth of the sport as a recognized practice in America: in the late 1800's, a few of the wealthy land owners devised rough scrambling routes up the more rugged aspects of the hills they owned. One owner's bride-to-be fell to her death on such a climb. When roped rock climbing came to the country, Mount Desert Island was immediately so explored – as early as the late 1920's by members of the Appalachian Mountain Club. Climbers visited Otter Cliff and Mount Champlain during this period, as well as many of the other, smaller crags.

Under the combined influences of increasing interest in the Shawangunks and North Conway, along with limitations on travel imposed by the Depression and World War II, climbing passed into a long doldrum phase on the island. Shortly after the War, a major forest fire defoliated most of the island, revealing new sections of cliff to the few climbers who happened to visit. Climbers trickled by on occasion and more came from a nearby campus of the University of Maine, but not until the introduction of a guiding sevice in 1975 did new route activity return in earnest. Suddenly, difficult routes, fully in step with the times, appeared on the island, including a 5.11 in 1977. The climbers were mostly the guides, their friends and fellow guides from North Conway. Some climbers would regularly make the six hour drive from North Conway for a more tranquil weekend than could be found on the crags of home.

A mountain shop was established in the late 70's, but closed after less than a decade of operation. Likewise, the guide service and its attendant mini-boom in route development slipped away. In the mid-80's another guide service became established on the island as a few climbers took residence and initiated a new research and development phase on the crags. The potential of Hunter's Beach was discovered during this period, in the happy coincidence of finding new rock at the same time as the Park Service was trying to reduce the impact of tourist and climber traffic at Otter Cliff.

Several editions of a local guidebook have appeared since the renewed interest in Island climbing that started in 1975, and an entirely new guide is planned for 1987. Local guidebooks have taken the approach of not mentioning first ascent parties, partly because of the difficulty of knowing which transient climber first climbed a route. Many routes have been given different names by any of several separate "first" ascentioners. It was also felt that Mount Desert Island is a place in which to leave behind the ego involvement of credits. In the spirit of local tradition, this book's Acadian chapter does not list first ascent parties and dates. Those who put up a route they think is new are also wise to consider the local anti-bolt ethics. Several bolts placed by insensitive or ignorant visitors have been chopped by outraged locals.

CAMPING

The campground favored by climbers is in the National Park: the moderately priced Black Woods Campground. Reservations may be necessary; write: Acadia National Park at RFD 1, Box 1, Bar Harbor, ME 04609, or call: 207-244-3600. Numerous private campgrounds and lodges are also available on the island. Reservations are strongly suggested for July and August. Write the Chamber of Commerce, Bar Harbor, ME 04609, or call them at 207-288-3393 (winter: 233-5103).

Restaurants and vendors feature lobster as the most famous and delicious of Maine foods. Lobster eaters may enjoy a story recounted in *The Joy of Cooking*. A young cannibal, at his mother's side, saw a strange object flying overhead. "Ma, what's that?" he asked. "It's an airplane. Airplanes are pretty much like lobsters. There's an awful lot you have to throw away, but the insides are delicious."

SEASONS AND WEATHER

Approximate Months	Typical Temperatures High	Low	Likelihood of Precipitation	Frequency of Climbable Days
Nov-Mar	20's+	0's+	medium	low
Apr-Jun	60's+	40's	med-high	med-high
Jul-Aug	80's	60's	medium	high-med
Sep-Oct	60's+	30's+	med-low	high

Comments: The sea's influence helps keep Mount Desert an island of sanity during the summer heat that envelopes most of the East Coast. Bugs will be found here, but not as intensely as in most of the Northeast.

RESTRICTIONS AND WARNINGS

To date, the National Park Service imposes no restrictions. However, if the pressure continues on Otter Cliff, some restrictions may be imposed.

GUIDEBOOKS

A Climber's Guide to Mount Desert Island (1983) by Geoffrey Childs. This third edition is out of print and almost impossible to find. It does not include Hunter's Beach or Great Head.

A more comprehensive guide is expected for 1987, by Jeffery Butterfield, P.O. Box 344, Bar Harbor, ME 04609.

GUIDE SERVICES AND EQUIPMENT STORES

Gale Force Climbing offers guiding and instruction. They can be reached at P.O. Box 344, Bar Harbor, ME 04609, telephone: 207-288-9711.

No climbing equipment shops currently exist on Mount Desert Island. While other equipment stores can be found in Portland and other southern cities, a quintessential Maine experience is visiting the L.L. Bean store in Freemont. It is open 24 hours a day, 365 days a year; customers will be found browsing the racks at 3 am.

EMERGENCY SERVICES
In case of emergency, a park ranger should be contacted at 288-3338. The Mount Desert Island Search and Rescue can be reached at the Fire Department, telephone: 288-5533. The Ambulance Service can be reached at 288-5554; the police at 288-3391. The Mount Desert Island Hospital is in Bar Harbor on Wayman Street, telephone: 288-5081.

GETTING THERE
In the summer, Downeast Transportation serves Bar Harbor from Ellsworth.

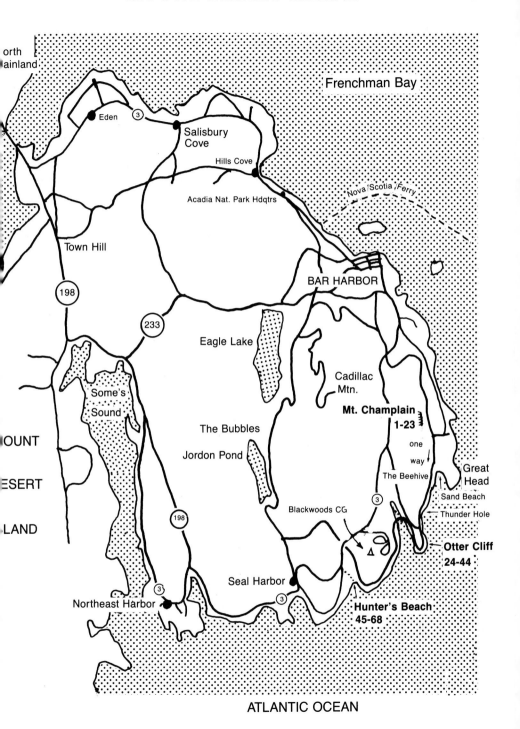

ATLANTIC OCEAN

Tim Forsell on Chitlin Corner

Tim Forsell near Thunder Hole

Precipice Wall of Mt. Champlain

1 **Small Crack Warning**
   5.11+ Thin crack through roof.
2 **Maniacal Depression 5.11**
3 **The Standard (Three Birches)**
   5.6
4 **Fear of Flying 5.9+**
5 **The Story of O 5.6**
6 **Dynamo Hum 5.10**

7 **Gunklandia 5.7** Start in finger
   cracks above old steps.
8 **Gunkland/Direct 5.9**
9 **Grendal 5.7**
10 **Wagger 5.9** Face climb
   following the thin crack behind
   birch tree left of gully near base
   of Gunklandia.
11 **Old Town 5.7** The classic corne

photo: Jeffery
Butterfield

12 **London Bridges or Bitch 5.8**
The offwidth.

13 **Connecticut Cracks 5.11**

14 **Precipice Ledges 5.3**

15 **Selfless Bastard 5.11** Directly
above **Connecticut Cracks,** climb
a shallow, left-facing corner,
move left past a bulge then right
to a different shallow corner and
continue up ledges.

16 **Scaramouche 5.10+**

17 **Return to Forever 5.9**

18 **Birch Ade 5.6**

19 **Emmigrant Crack 5.10**

20 **Chitlin Corner 5.9+** The
incredible corner.

21 **Pressure Drop 5.8**

22 **High Plains Drifter 5.9+**

23 **Sea Gypsy 5.9+**

John Harlin on Rock Lobster photo: Tim Forsell

Otter Cliff

Ed Webster on High Tide

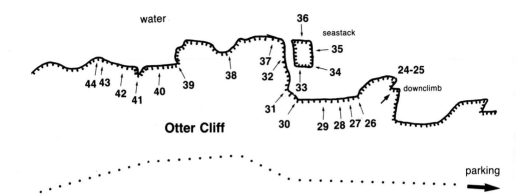

Otter Cliff

24 & 25 High Tide 5.10; Low Tide 5.10 Running the length of Otter Cliff are two horizontal crack systems, one at about ⅓ height, the other at ⅔ height. The upper crack line is a six pitch girdle, the lower is a boulder problem (dangerously high at points). Both lines go around the outside of the Seastack.

26 Overhanging Corner 5.6

27 Razor Crack (Razor Flake) 5.8

28 Riptide 5.11

29 Black Corner 5.7

30 Drunken Sailor 5.10

31 Sober Seaman 5.10 −

32 The Chimney 5.5

33 The Gallery 5.11/5.12

34 Gallery Arête 5.9

35 Rock Lobster 5.9 +

36 Child's Play 5.5

37 Outer Face 5.8 with 5.10 var.

38 Guillotine 5.9/5.10

39 Wonder Corner 5.6

40 Wonderwall 5.5/5.6

41 In the Groove 5.4

42 The Flake 5.7; 5.10 straight up

43 A Dare by the Sea 5.10 +

44 Peak Performance 5.10

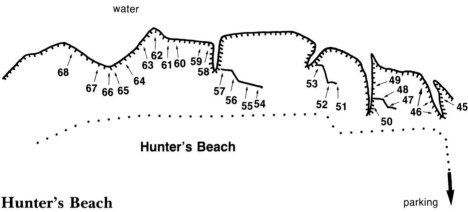

Hunter's Beach

The parking area is about one mile south of Route 3.

45 **Easy Street (The Pinnacle) 5.2**
46 **Chasm View Wall 5.3-5.8**
47 **The Corner 5.6**
48 **Abbrev. Arête 5.8**
49 **Sea Foam 5.8**
50 **Steppin Out 5.4**
51 **Dynamic Retailing in the Midwest 5.10**
52 **Bears in Dumpsters 5.10**
53 **Let's Chat Cracks 5.7 and 5.8**
54 **Waterproof Library 5.9+**
55 **Solid Teak Sneakers 5.11**
56 **Cardiac Arête 5.11**
57 **Complimentary Beverage 5.7**
58 **First Route 5.8**
59 **The Nose 5.8**
60 **Vocabulary Collapse 5.11**
61 **Intermountain Nuclear Medicine 5.10**
62 **Spineless Worm 5.10**
63 **Carniverous Snails 5.8**
64 **Geeks for Translation 5.9+**
65 **Homosexual Armadillo 5.12 −**
66 **Kids Need Sharks Too 5.11**
67 **King of Socks**
68 **Moose on a Leash 5.8**

Tim Forsell on The Flake

Ed Webster on A Dare by the Sea photo: Tim Forsell

Mont King

Mont Weir

LES LAURENTIDES

HIGHLIGHTS

When most climbers think of climbing in western Quebec, Val David comes to mind. In fact, the 50 to nearly 250 foot cliffs of Val David are but a fraction, albeit the most popular fraction, of the Laurentian crags. The other two best cliffs are Weir, the tallest continuously vertical cliff in the region, at 250 feet, and Mont-Nixon, about 200 feet high. Each has unique character and superb climbing of all difficulties on steep granite. All the cliffs lie in a wooded setting, and only Val David gets crowded – and then only on weekends. The French language and the European character of Quebec help to make the visit here more than just a climbing experience. For most people, a climbing trip to this region becomes a tourist outing as well, with much besides granite to explore. The major drawbacks to the area are its legendary biting blackflies and a short, sometimes wet, climbing season.

CLIMBING

Amid the fantastic number of downhill ski resorts that spiderweb their trails over the hills of the Laurentians (Laurentides in the local French) are many granite outcrops. Three localities have been chosen for this book: Val David (including Mont-King and Condor), Weir, and Mont-Nixon. The area is also reknown for its superb bouldering. Val David has the most used boulders, while those at Nixon have excellent potential.

Val David is a village whose neighboring hills contain the most popular crags of the Laurentians. Mont-Cesaire is the focus of beginner outings.

For the eager rock climber, attention is drawn to a group of four cliffs. Mont-Condor is only a hundred yards from the road and dries out relatively quickly after a rain. Its 50 foot cliffs offer thin face climbing and cracks on a steep wall. Mont-King, just under 250 feet high, is the major challenge of the area; here one will find the hard-core climbers. The granite has been compared to Eldorado sandstone because it features a number of small edges. Still, most routes follow cracks. In addition to straight-in cracks, the cliff offers overhanging dihedrals and horizontal roofs to twenty four feet. A number of 5.12's exist already. but if the thin crack, **Zébrée,** goes free, Mont King may hold one of the most awesome short crack climbs on the continent. There are also several excellent routes down to 5.8 in difficulty. Les Fesses and La Bleue are two other cliffs in the immediate area. La Bleue holds a number of excellent cracks and is worth investigation.

Though Mont-Condor overlooks houses, Mont-King is set deeper in the woods, overlooking a pond. The tranquility of the setting partially makes up for the sometimes nerve-wracking climbs. The cliff faces due west, into the setting sun.

The cliff at Weir sits behind a huge telecommunications disk. The area is marked with "No Trespassing" signs, which seem forbidding at first. However, the little fenced-in parking area and pathway were built especially for climbers and the Teleglobe personnel are friendy. A couple of hundred yards behind the disk is an impressive diamond shaped 250 foot cliff. The rock at Weir is not the quality of Val David's; it is blocky and sometimes even large holds will break off. Extra caution should be taken, but on the better routes the rock's quality is fine. The bulk of the climbing takes place on the cliff's left side, where several routes to four pitches in length wind their way up cracks and ramps. The cliff's claim to fame is the prominent corner that runs up the center of the face. **Black and White,** 5.10/5.11, is simply an outstanding, continuously interesting three pitch climb. To the right of that, only a few lines have been climbed on the vertical face; most that have been done involve considerable aid.

Mont-Nixon is currently less frequented than either Val David or Weir, but it has some of the finest climbing. This is the favorite haunt of some locals who compare its cracks with those of Yosemite. The rock, however, is medium grained and occasionally flakey. Continuous cracks, roofs, and occasional face climbing are found here, while the view extends over forested hills that are broken only by the slopes of a ski area.

ENVIRONMENT

The Laurentians are the backyard playground of Montreal residents, while Montreal itself is a vacation playground of tourists from throughout the world. Climbers with even the smallest interest in foreign cultures will enjoy exploring Montreal, the second largest French speaking city in the world. It is reputed to have the best restaurants in Canada – in fine French tradition – and Old Montreal can occupy several days of leisurely exploration.

Val David lies 50 miles north of Montreal, in the heart of the forested hills of "Les Laurentides." Carved out of the wooded hillsides are a seemingly endless number of ski slopes that are filled in the winter by an endless supply of skiers. The slow season for the ski resorts – spring through fall – sees weekend crowds from Montreal visiting Val David. Weir and Nixon are no more difficult to reach, but on weekends they seem far more remote because fewer people go there. For an English speaking visitor interested in cultural diversity, a crowd of Quebec-ers may prove more entertaining than climbing in solitude.

The Laurentians, like Montreal, are filled with good restaurants and hotels. The region has long been known for its "joie de vivre."

CLIMBING HISTORY
Though Quebec has the oldest settlements in Canada, climbing here began much later than climbing in British Columbia and Alberta. Quebec's crags simply didn't seem big enough for the sport when

compared with the alpine peaks to the west. From the late 1920's until
World War II, a few climbs were established, mostly by visiting foreigners
and immigrants. A former Swiss was largely responsible for the climbing
during this period and for establishing a Montreal section of the Alpine
Club of Canada in 1942. This club greatly increased the number of
climbers, along with the McGill Outing Club and, in 1949, the Club de
Montagne Canadien. In 1954 a major camping store opened in Montreal
that finally stocked the modern climbing equipment that was coming
increasingly into demand. Routes at Mont-Cesaire and Mont-Condor
bore ever greater traffic. Still, standards languished as difficulty wasn't
the *raison d'etres* for most local climbers.

It wasn't clubs or pitons that finally increased the standards of Quebec
climbing: it was the arrival of a new group of climbers. Spearheaded by
an English draft dodger, the group pressed standards to the 5.9 level
during the late 1950's and discovered Weir. The Englishman brought
with him a dedication to clean climbing, fifteen years before the notion
caught on elsewhere in North America. This small group pushed the
highest standard of climbing on the East Coast. They were active in the
Val David area, and also made many trips to Pok-O-Moonshine in New
York and Cathedral Ledges in New Hampshire. Their period of activity
was brief, however, because when the itinerant Englishman returned
home in 1962, his small following lost momentum.

The power of the clubs redoubled, however, when in 1968 the Federation des Clubs de Montagne du Quebec was formed, which became, in 1974, the Federation Québecoise de la Montagne (FQM). The latter is ongoing, having become a department of the Quebec provincial government with a full-time salaried director and staff. Originally founded to promote exchange with the outside climbing community and to promote safety, it became increasingly bureaucratized and resistant to the evolution of the outside climbing world. A number of Canada's finest climbers began as part of the club, then were ostracized as their skills improved. The ethics, attitudes, and even the clothing of modern free climbers simply didn't jibe with the entrenched ideas of the club leadership. By the 1980's, the split between the FQM leadership and the young hard-cores was so great that they were often antagonistic towards each other.

During the 1970's, Montreal climbers of both persuasions began exploring the wild country to the east in Charlevoix, and by the 1980's a handful of people had taken free climbing to heart. Standards, which had been languishing, suddenly caught up with the rest of North America. Young Quebec-ers had sampled the challenges in the States and realized that their home cliffs offered potentially taxing routes as well. A number of 5.11 climbs and, in 1984 and 1985, a veritable explosion of 5.12 routes occured. While a small number of Americans had always visited Quebec to sample the climbing and culture, with the increasing local standards, undoubtedly the number of visitors will increase as well.

CAMPING

Camping can be done near the cliffs at any of the areas, though some discretion should be observed because of private property. Locals claim that most stream water is drinkable. Apparently, the curse of giardia has yet to arrive. In Val David, a good alternative is the inexpensive Chalet Beaumont. Available are a refuge, dormitory and semi-private rooms. This is also the weekend center of activity for many Montreal climbers. c/o Bernard De Pierre, 1451 Beaumont CP 38, Val David JOT 2NO, telephone: 819-322-1972.

SEASONS AND WEATHER

Approximate Months	Typical Temperatures High	Low	Likelihood of Precipitation	Frequency of Climbable Days
Nov-Mar	10's	0's	medium	very low
Apr-Jun	70's	40's	medium	high
Jul-Aug	90's −	70's	medium	high-med
Sep-Oct	70's −	30's	medium	high

Comments: April and October are transitional months, with less certain climbing. See *RESTRICTIONS AND WARNINGS* for a discussion of the blackfly season. Summer humidity can be oppressive.

RESTRICTIONS AND WARNINGS

Outdoor pursuits in the backwoods of Quebec are notoriously plagued by blackflies. These small bugs have a nasty bite that has been known to drive people and other animals mad. Still, the Val David region is not as bad as the wilderness further north and east. June to early July is the worst period, though some locals insist that even then the flies aren't too bad. Mosquito repellents work to keep flies away; unfortunately, a climber's sweat flushes the repellent off, while the chemical damages the nylon of climbing ropes. White clothes, with pant legs tucked in and turtlenecks high, and perhaps a headnet and gloves for the belayer, are one way to help cope with the pests. Best is to climb on windy days.

GUIDEBOOKS

Parois D'Escalade Au Québec (1978) by Jean Sylvain. This is the encyclopedia of Quebec crags, most of which are rarely visited. Published by the government, the book is found throughout Quebec. Also available from La Federation Québecoise de la Montagne, 4545, Avenue Pierre-De-Coubertin, C-P. 1000, Succursale M, Montreal, Quebec H1V 3R2, telephone: 514-252-3000.

GUIDE SERVICES AND EQUIPMENT STORES

Guiding services include: Passe-Montagne, 2025 A, rue Masson, Suite 217, Montreal, Quebec H2H 2P7, telephone: 514-521-9548. Also offering local guides is Cirrus, 206 Rang Ruisseau des Frênes, Ste-Agnès de Charlevoix, Quebec GOT 1RO, telephone: 418-439-2949.

The major mountaineering equipment store is in Montreal: La Cordee, 2159 East, rue Ste-Catherine, telephone: 514-524-1106. Passe-Montagne also sells equipment.

EMERGENCY SERVICES
In case of emergency, call the Surete Du Québec, 326-2222. The nearest hospital is the Centre Hospitalier Laurentien, 234 St-Vincent, Ste. Agathe-des-Monts, telephone: 326-3551.

GETTING THERE
The Voyageur Bus serves Val David from Montreal, telephone: 514-843-4231.

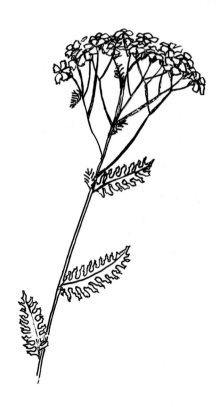

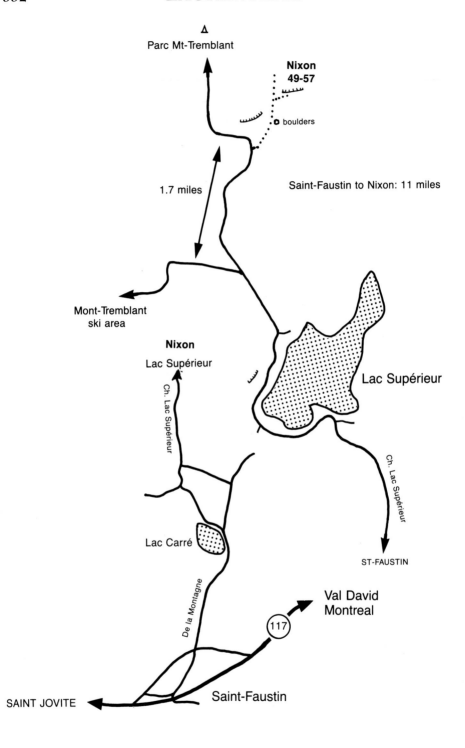

Parc Mt-Tremblant

Nixon 49-57

boulders

1.7 miles

Saint-Faustin to Nixon: 11 miles

Mont-Tremblant ski area

Nixon

Lac Supérieur

Ch. Lac Supérieur

Lac Supérieur

Ch. Lac Supérieur

Lac Carré

ST-FAUSTIN

De la Montagne

Val David
Montreal

117

SAINT JOVITE

Saint-Faustin

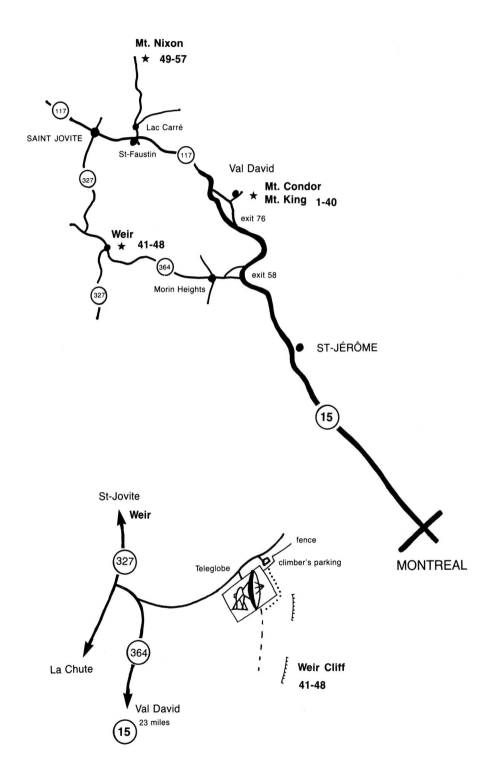

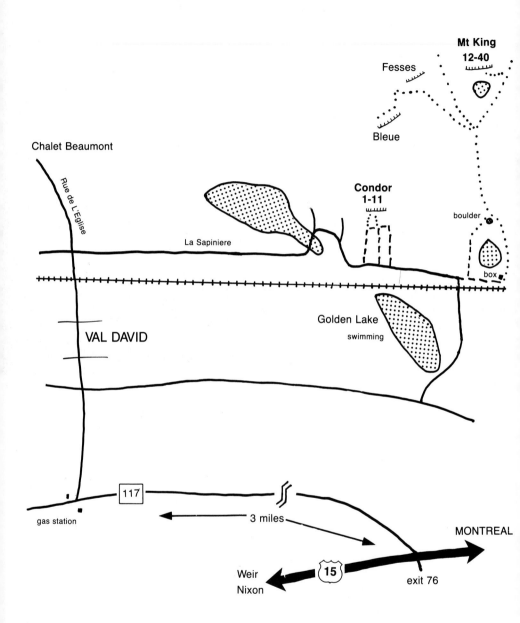

VAL DAVID
Condor

1 **Face Directe** **5.10** Marc Blais, 1980. **Surplomb de Gérard** **5.11** Gérard Bourbonnais, 1982. Overhang variation

2 **Poussez Pas Directe** **5.10** Paul Duval and Marc Blais, 1985.

3 **La Dulfer** **5.4** Georges Hampson and Fritz Wiessner, 1943.

4 **Midnight Express** **5.10** Jeff Powter and Mark Abbott, 1979.

5 **Face Ouest** **5.8** Bernard Poisson and Pierre Garneau, 1959. FFA: Normand Cadieux and Marc Blais 1976.

6 **Orca** **5.10** Paul LaPerriere, 1984 top rope. Right side of face.

7 **Centre de la Face Nord** **5.10** Paul LaPerriere, 1982. Middle of face.

8 **Face Nord (Arête de Gauche)** **5.10** Claude Lavallée, 1956 top roped. One of the region's first 5.10's. FFA lead: Daniel Levesques, 1983. Dangerous lead.

9 **Double Fissure Droite** **5.11−** Jeff Powter and Gérard Bourbonnais, 1982.

10 **Double Fissure** **5.10** Claude Lavallée, 1956. FFA: Normand Cadieux, 1977.

11 **Bloody Hand** **5.7** Claude Lavallée and Françoix Garneau, 1957.

Mt King

12 Faucon Rouge 5.7 Paul and Jean LaPerrière, 1972.

13 Batman 5.11 Guy Laselle and Paul LaPerrière, 1982. Camming nuts useful on traverse.

14 Rateau de Chèvre 5.12 Bernard Poisson, Dick Willmott and Pierre Garneau, 1962. FFA: Thomas Ryan, 1985.

15 L'Ampithéatre 5.7 Claude Lavallée and Bernard Poisson, 1958. Poor pro for second.

16 L'Éclair 5.9+ Jacques Lemay and Daniel Perreault, 1972. FFA: Normand Cadieux. **Variation exit 5.9** Traverse right to edge of dihedral half-way up. Marcel Lehoux, 1983.

17 Toit de Ben A3 Bernard Poisson, Claude Lavallée and Erwin Hodgson, 1958. A 24 foot roof crack that should soon go free.

18 Émergence 5.12 Alain Hénault, 1971. FFA: Thomas Ryan, 1985. Pro difficult.

19 Zébrée A3 Alain Hénault, 1972. Free attempts have yet to get far on this incredible crack. **Exit 5.11+** Gérard Bourbonnais and Richard Auger, 1982; the exit is from the ledge of Émergence.

20 La Mère qui Chie 5.12+ Thomas Ryan 1985. Camming nut useful.

21 Chimère 5.10+ Paul LaPerrière first pitch solo. Second pitch **Cat's Ass 5.10** Jeff Powter and Mark Abbott, 1982. Pitches can be combined.

22 L'Impériale 5.8+ Fritz Wiessner, 1949.

23 L'Impériale Variation 5.8+ Dick Willmott, 1950. Flake/crack exiting dihedral.

24 Abracadabra 5.10+ Benoit Dube, 1983. Need #1½ Friend.

25 Le Sceptre 5.8+ Possibly John Turner, 1960's.

26 Surplomb Du Sceptre 5.9+ Normand Cadieux, 1977.

27 Symbiose 5.10 Julien Dery, 1982.

28 Syndrôme Chinoise 5.11+ Benoit Dubé, 1985.

29 Minha 5.10 Paul LaPerrière, 1980. One bolt of pair is bad, no one knows which.

30 La Lou Variation 5.8 Camille Choquette, 1970; variation: Pierre Edouard Gagnon, 1977.

31 Marie-Lou 5.10 Benoit Dubé, 1981.

32 Le Diedre de Richard 5.11+ Richard Auger, 1982 top-rope. First lead: Thomas Ryan and Louis Babin 1984.

33 Élimination 5.11− Normand Cadieux, 1979. The area's first 5.11.

34 Levitation 5.11 Normand Cadieux and Hubert Morin, 1977.

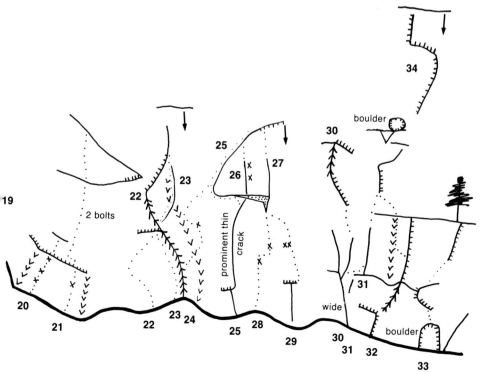

Marcel Lehoux on Chimère   photo: Gérard Bourbonnais

Upper Mt. King

35 The Anchor 5.9 Brian Rothery, early 1960's. FFA: Marc Blais and Pierre Edouard Gagnon, 1978.

36 Diadème 5.10 − Marc Blais and Jean-Pierre Renault, 1978.

37 Les Diamants de la Couronne 5.10 Normand Cadieux and Marc Blais, 1977.

38 Crown 5.8 Richard Willmott and Georges Tait, 1960.

39 Crown Direct 5.9

40 Vol au-Dessus d'un Nid de Coucou 5.11 Thomas Ryan and Benoit Dubé, 1985. Camming nuts useful.

Weir

Descent Walk off right.

41 Adagio   5.8 Brian Rothery and Keith Miller, 1959.

42 Subversion   5.11 Jean-François Denis and Jacques Lambert, 1985.

43 Centenaire   5.11 Claude Lavallée and Jean Pillet, 1967. FFA: Jean-François Denis and Jacques Lambert, 1985. Bad pro for second on traverse.

44 La Raboutée   5.10 Jean-François Denis, Serge Roy and Suzanne Fournier, 1973. Marc Blais and Pierre Edouard Gagnon, 1978.

45 Bi-Centenaire 5.11/5.12 Marc Blais and Pierre Gougoux, 1973. FFA: Georges Manson and Rob Rohn, 1979.

46 Black and White 5.10/5.11 Claude Lavallée, Hugh Tanton and Bernard Poisson, 1958. FFA: Normand Cadieux and Marc Blais, 1978. Considered one of the East Coast's finest routes.

47 Claire de Femme 5.10+ A3 Marc Blais and Jean-Marie Brissette, 1982.

48 Le Cordonnier 5.9 A1 Marc Blais and Gerard Bourbonnais, 1979.

Benoit Dubé on Illusion photo: Gerard Bourbonnais

Phillipe Boursier aiding Zébrée

Mont Nixon

Nixon

49 XYB* 5.11 Louis Babin, Benoit Dubé and Marcel Lehoux, 1985.

50 Flute Enchantée 5.6 A2 (5.11/5.12 freed to lip of overhang; upper part will go free when cleaned.) Alain Hénault and Marc Blais, 1974.

51 2 + 1 5.6 Denis Gravel, Real LaLonde and Claude Lavallée, 1966.

52 L'Illusion 5.10+ Bernard Poisson and Pierre Edouard Gagnon, 1975-1976. FFA: Benoit Dubé, Alain Hénault and Marcel Lehoux, 1982. **Right exit 5.10+** Gérard Bourbonnais and Marcel Lehoux, 1982.

53 Zorba 5.11+ Gérard Bourbonais and Alain Hénault, 1982.
54 Robert Cartier 5.9− Claude Lavallée and Maurice Charbonneau, 1966. FFA: Marc Blais and Pierre Edouard Gagnon.
55 La Ridée 5.7 Regis Richard and Pierre Desautels, 1972.
56 Amitiée 5.9− Paul Duval and Marc Blais, 1984. Start on the boulder.
57 Grand Galop Tire Vite (Quick Draw McGraw) 5.10+ Gérard Bourbonais, Marcel Lehoux and Benoit Dubé, 1981.

Along the St-Lawrence

Mont de l'Ours

CHARLEVOIX

HIGHLIGHTS

The scenic attractions of the Charlevoix Region, on the north shore of the Saint Lawrence River, have been drawing tourists since the mid 1700's. The river – a deep blue fiord which hosts whales and ships alike – the European-style villages on pastoral land hacked out of the dense forests, and the distinctly French-Canadian culture are all facets of this marvelous land. Scattered throughout countryside are numerous granitic cliffs. Many are so vegetated that they can hardly be distinguished from the surrounding forests, but many others offer solid and fairly clean rock with a great diversity of climbing. While innumerable cliffs can be ferreted out of the landscape and some prominent crags are omited, the two most popular groups of cliffs are included herein: Les Palissades of Saint-Siméon, with almost two miles of vertical cliffs averaging about 300 feet in height, and the collection of diverse cliffs near Saint-Urbain, with climbs that range from two pitch friction-face to six pitch vertical walls. Cap Trinité is also included, not for its popularity, but for its historic significance and the unique experience of climbing a thousand foot plumb vertical wall which rises straight out of a fiord.

CLIMBING

In a generally positive commentary on climbing in Quebec published in *Mountain Magazine* (1978), Raymond Jotterand wrote, only semi tongue-in-cheek, the following introduction:

The temperature ... is either too cold or too warm, never just right; and if by chance it was right, the swarms of black flies and mosquitoes would ensure that nobody climbed. And if the wind blew the flies away, you would still be faced with the uninviting prospect of having to bushwack for hours, having to cross large rivers, arriving at the cliff only to find out that the crack system you were planning to climb was hopelessly filled with lichen and mud, and that you lacked the time and patience to clean your way up.

The temperature and bugs were described reasonably accurately, and will be discussed in more depth later, but the access problems and dirty routes are not found for climbs in this book. In fact, the access to all but Cap Trinité is remarkably easy. Paved roads lead to within a few hundred yards (sometimes just 100 feet) of the cliffs, and Quebec climbers, partly through the collective spirit of their myriad clubs, have generally carved excellent trails to the climbs' bases. At the Dome and Mont de l'Ours in St-Urbain, and the Palissades of St-Siméon one will even find huts near the cliffs.

The rock is quite variable within the granitic medium, though it is generally anorthosite and provides excellent frictional qualities. It fractures with long and continuous cracks that form the line of most routes. The climbing potential, at least for difficult routes, has only barely been tapped. This is due both to a sparsity of climbers capable of the hard routes and to the short climbing season. Winters are long, and the window of time between cold weather and the invasion of the blackflies is short and often wet. Occasional climbers can suffer through the bugs, but most would be driven insane. Bug dope can be quickly sweated off and damages some synthetics, and doing strenuous or difficult moves with a headnet and gloves is annoying. The best solution is to wait for August, when the bugs leave, and climb until late September, when the snows come. If early summer is the only available time for a visit, wish for windy weather.

The first area reached by the visitor is Saint-Urbain. The Mont du Gros Bras presents a daunting introduction, with five to six pitch climbs on a formidably steep wall. The routes follow major crack lines and are mostly 5.10, though there is one 5.7. Be sure to avoid this cliff for a couple of days after a rain, as the water drains straight down the cracks. This north-facing cliff can be cold, even in summer.

Much more popular are the moderate routes on the next visible cliffs: Mont de l'Ours and Le Dôme. Most routes here are long and in the 5.5 range, though a slab and a steep crack offer short, hard climbs. From L'Initiation on Le Dôme, one gets good views of the Saint Lawrence in the distance.

Les Palissades near Saint-Siméon offers a 1,000 foot slab, with delightful moderate climbing that is considered a must even by some hardcore climbers. However, most of the convoluted cliffband consists of steep 300 foot faces split by cracks. Though the faces were carved by glaciers, never is the ancient rock polished smooth. Crack climbing is often supplemented with face moves and always aided by good friction on the rough rock. The area is part of a "forest education" nature reserve.

Cap Trinité, on the Saguenay River, is generally considered purely in the aid climber's realm, though its 1,000 foot face has recently been pushed free by one route and more will surely follow. Part of the problem with establishing a new free route is the plethora of rotten old wooden wedges (left behind by aid ascents) which must be cleaned before the crack reveals its jams. The other problem is simply getting to this spectacular face, which lifts directly and vertically out of the water. The cliff drops an extra 900 feet into the fiord below, while tides of fifteen feet sweep the base of the face. A canoe, usually brought by the climbers (though they can probably be rented in the region) is paddled for a mile across a bay to reach the cliff. Difficult access by scrambling can also be made.

Of the many cliffs not discussed, the most significant are those of the Malbaie Valley. While deservedly reknown – for high quality rock and steep faces that stretch to 1,000 feet in height – they lie at the end of a long dirt road and most involve considerable bushwacking and scrambling to get to.

Though the rock climbing season may be short, the ice climbing season goes on and on. Vertical ice enthusiasts will find much to climb, including the celebrated La Pomme d-Or, which exceeds 1,000 feet in height.

English speakers will find a few key French words useful, words not found in most French-English dictionaries: "du mou" means "slack," "avale" is "up rope," and "relais" is "belay."

ENVIRONMENT

Though a map will show the Charlevoix region to be 400 miles from the Gulf of St. Lawrence and 700 miles from the ocean, the sea's influence is shown by the annual return of at least ten species of whales. Every year, near the end of July, they can be seen in the estuarine waters of the Saint Lawrence and the Saguenay Rivers. The Baie-Sainte-Catherine, near the mouth of the Saguenay, becomes the headquarters for whale-watching boat tours. With luck, a climber high on a route on the Cap Trinité might spot a surfacing whale as well, possibly even a 140 ton, 90 foot blue. All the whales return to the sea by late fall.

Aside from Cap Trinité, where fifteen foot tides lap the base of the cliff, the sea does not directly influence climbers on Charlevoix rock; instead, its effect is seen while driving along the Saint Lawrence from the south. Villages lie scattered along the shore of this massive river, which was once the only path of communication and formed the basis for the entire livelihood for the region. The river's width varies considerably from point to point, being less than a mile across at Quebec City, about fifteen miles across where the Saguenay enters, and considerably wider still as it approaches the Gulf.

The villages along the river's shore, like most in Quebec, are far more European in appearance than North American. This is partially because the province, formerly "New France" before the English took it militarily, has made every effort to keep its French identity. Between the language, the architecture, and the distinctly Catholic French-based culture, the tourist experience seems European. It can be a true delight for the North American traveller (who is used to a great variation in natural environments and a homogeneity of human ones) to find such a distinctly unique and fascinating place on this continent.

The human effect on the natural environment is significant here (as almost everywhere further south, of course). Inland, forests had to be cleared to convert land to pasture, and occasionally, to farm. Lumber also became a big local industry, and the forests that fill the valleys below the cliffs near Saint-Urbain and at Les Palissades are young. Growth rates in this harsh, sub-arctic climate are slow, yielding dense stick-like spruce and mixed hard and softwood forests. Considerable wildlife is found in the region, once supporting a large fur industry. A short distance north from the river, beginning near the cliffs of Saint-Urbain, the great northern forests extend to the arctic. They are only rarely broken by human habitation. A taste of the Far North can be found in the Parc des Grands-Jardins, a large preserve where caribou roam the taiga forest.

Anyone driving to Charlevoix will likely pass through Quebec City, known locally as simply "Québec." (French-Canadians make the distinction as "Québec" meaning the city and "le Québec" meaning the province. To go to either is "a Québec" and "au Québec," respectively.

It can be confusing in conversation.) This historical town is well worth budgeting some time for, especially the old, walled city of Vieux Québec. It goes without saying that the city takes pride in its restaurants. Some good bouldering and small roped-climbing cliffs can be found in and just outside of town. See the Other Areas chapter for access details.

CLIMBING HISTORY

The colony of New France was founded in 1608 at the site the Algonquin Indians refered to as "Kebec," meaning "place where the river narrows." This was twelve years before the Mayflower brought the first Pilgrims to New England. The region's climbing history, however, is among the shortest in North America – certainly very short considering the great number of cliffs and the proximity to urban centers such as Quebec City and, a few hours more distant, Montreal.

Despite the size of Charlevoix's cliffs, this region also suffered from the prevailing Canadian bias towards the mountains of Alberta and British Columbia and away from the crags. A discussion of the early development of Quebec climbing can be found in the Laurentides chapter of this book.

The influence of Quebec's late blooming rock climbers didn't spread to the comparative wilds of the Charlevoix region until the mid 1950's. Only a tiny handful of routes were climbed, however, until the beginning of the 1960's when the Palissades became popular. The newly founded Club d'Escalade Laurentien built a hut on the valley floor in 1962, increasing the ease of climbing at these already very accessible cliffs. Despite other, much more easily reached crags, the next major cliff to feel a piton was the massive face of Cap Trinité. A team of French Canadians attempted the first ascent in 1964, but was beaten back by bad weather. A German team finished their route in 1966, creating feelings of bitter frustration among the nationalistic Quebec team. To set things straight, they then made a much more direct ascent in 1967, tackling the longest section of the 1,000 foot face in a route that took them twelve days to complete, the **Direttissime.** Further expressing his feelings, the leader of the Quebec team wouldn't publish the date of the German ascent in his 1978 guidebook to Quebec climbing.

In 1970 the cliffs of the Malbaie valley and those of Saint-Urbain were investigated. During the 1960's, Charlevoix climbers had been involved with exploration and adventure in the outdoors, but were generally uninterested in the challenge of difficult climbing. During the early 1970's a new breed started visiting the region. They liked hard climbing, having tasted it in the Montreal region and in the States, and began establishing difficult new routes, including some on the intimidating face of the Gros Bras. Though most of these climbers learned to climb within the Federation Québecoise de la Montagne, their modern attitudes soon set them at odds with the establishment. The first of several breakaway clubs (deliberatly unaffiliated with the Federation) was launched in Quebec City. Focusing on the active aspects of climbing, they named themselves "Ecole de Grimpeur" rather than some variation of Montagne. Among the obstacles they faced from the old guard was resentment when old wooden aid-blocks were cleaned from routes that were being freed (such as on the magnificent **Pilier**).

The first 5.10's were put up around 1973, becoming routine among a small group of climbers within a few years. 5.11 arrived in 1981, while the 5.11/5.12 **Toit des Anges** was freed in 1984. Still, the group of climbers who could climb difficult routes consisted of a handful of close friends, only a couple of which actually lived in the region. Most commuted from Quebec City or Montreal, sometimes bringing friends from the States. Activity on Cap Trinité continued, though mostly as aid. This was, after all, Quebec's big wall and was thought of in those terms. Free climbing was not brought here until the mid 1980's, in part because of the work involved in first aiding the route to clean out the wooden blocks. That effort, combined with the hassle of boating to the base, made the cliff unattractive to almost everyone capable of hard free climbing.

Climbing activity, in terms of numbers of climbers on the easier routes, can sometimes be heavy. But activity on new or difficult routes is light, with only a couple of dozen harder new routes established between 1977 and 1985.

The guidebook to the region was published in 1978 by the FQM, under the authority of the Official Editor of Quebec, a department of the government. It is an encyclopedic documentation of the cliffs of Quebec, though it leaves access to those cliffs to the imagination. Users need to beware of the fact that virtually all cliffs with routes have been included, with little regard to their quality. Also, the freeing of aid routes has often been ignored. Reportedly, its publication was held up for several years due to the author's fear of an American invasion once the word was out on Quebec's climbing. His worries were unfounded, however, as few Americans make the drive so far north. Most of the serious local climbers are eager for visits from their southern friends, if just to find climbing partners.

CAMPING

Camping is free and unregulated on most of the government land surrounding the roads and cliffs. The locals generally consider the water to be safe to drink. Moderately priced campgrounds with showers can also be found in the Parc des Grands-Jardins (near the cliffs of Saint-Urbain) and at Saint-Simeon (near Les Palissades). Saint-Siméon has a wide sandy beach which is popular with tourists. Two huts ("refuges") exist next to the cliffs of Saint-Urbain. Both are operated by the Federation Québecoise de la Montagne and reservations are needed. FQM, 4545 Avenue Pierre-de-Coubertin, C-P 1000, Succursale M, Montreal, Quebec H1V 3R2, telephone: 514-252-3000. The hut at the base of Les Palissades is operated by the Club d'Escalade Laurentien, c/o Yolande Sylvain, C-P 96, Lac Beauport, Quebec G0A 2CO, telephone: 418-849-8532. There is a spring behind the hut.

Perhaps the best alternative to camping out is the new refuge operated by Cirrus. It is moderatly priced and features a sauna, a fireplace, a climber's workout area, and good comaraderie. Meals are also sometimes available. The proprietor, Alain Hénault, is the only local climber active at the higher standards. The refuge is seven miles northeast of Saint-Hilarion. Take the paved road leading uphill on the southern side of Highway 138; the refuge is the second house on the right. For reservations: Cirrus, 206 Rang Ruisseau des Frênes, Sainte-Agnès de Charlevoix, Quebec G0T 1R0, telephone: 418-439-2949. Alain and his wife Jean speak excellent English.

SEASONS AND WEATHER

Approximate Months	Typical Temperatures High	Low	Likelihood of Precipitation	Frequency of Climbable Days
Nov-Apr	0's −	20's −	medium	very low
May-Jun	50's +	30's +	med-high	medium
Jul-Aug	80's +	60's	medium	med-high
Sep-Oct	60's	30's	med-low	med-high

Comments: The blackfly season is perhaps more important than the weather. Late June through July is usually worst. August and September provide the best combination of temperature and lack of bugs.

RESTRICTIONS AND WARNINGS

Clearly, the greatest impediment to an enjoyable climbing trip is the insect problem: blackflies especially, but also mosquitoes. For notes on dealing with them, see the section in the Laurentides chapter. The flies are usually worst on cloudy days with low pressure, and are least bad on sunny days during high pressure − and, of course, when it is windy.

GUIDEBOOKS

Parois d'Escalade Au Québec (1978) by Jean Sylvain. Published by the government, the book is found throughout Quebec. Also available from FQM, 4545 Avenue Pierre-de-Coubertin, C-P 1000, Succursale M, Montreal, Quebec H1V 3R2.

For more current information, visit Alain Hénault; directions given under CAMPING. A new organization may write an updated guidebook: Association des Guides de Charlevoix, Sainte-Agnès de Charlevoix, Quebec G0T 1R0.

GUIDE SERVICES AND EQUIPMENT STORES

The nearest major outlet for equipment is in Quebec City: Bivouac Import-Export, 1328 Maguire, Sillery.

Guiding is available through Cirrus, 206 Rang Ruisseau des Frênes, Sainte-Agnès de Charlevoix, Quebec G0T 1R0, telephone: 418-439-2949. Excellent English is spoken.

EMERGENCY SERVICES

The police can be reached at telephone: 435-2012 from the Saint-Urbain area, and at 665-6473 from the Palissades area. Ambulance services can be reached anywhere from 1-800-463-4742. The nearest hospital to the Saint-Urbain area is Centre Hospitalier de Charlevoix, 74 boulevard Fafard, Baie-Saint-Paul, telephone: 435-5150. The nearest to Les Palissades is Clinique Medicale, 347 rue Saint-Laurent, Saint-Siméon, telephone: 638-2404. A bigger hospital can be found in La Malbaie: Centre Hospitalier Saint-Joseph, 303 rue Saint-Etienne, telephone: 665-3711.

GETTING THERE

Voyageur serves all villages along Highway 138. Air flights serve Charlevoix from Quebec City two to three times weekly.

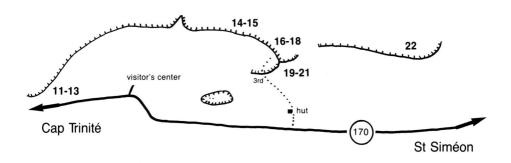

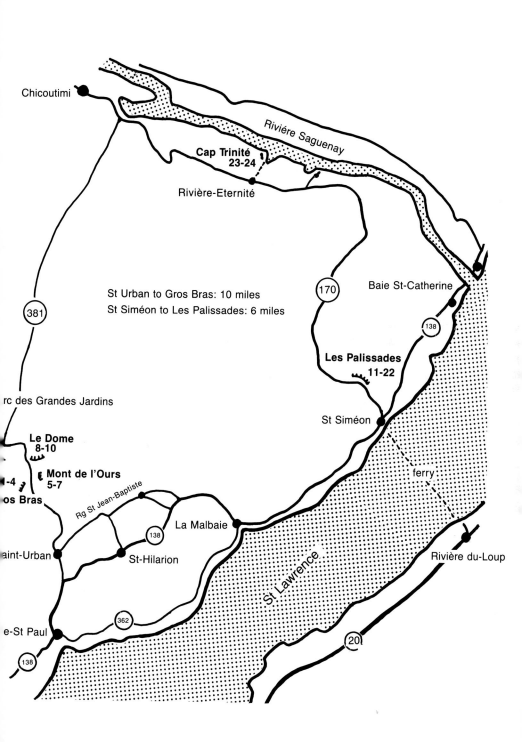

Chicoutimi

Rivière Saguenay

Cap Trinité
23-24

Rivière-Eternité

St Urban to Gros Bras: 10 miles

St Siméon to Les Palissades: 6 miles

170

Baie St-Catherine

381

138

Les Palissades
11-22

rc des Grandes Jardins

St Siméon

Le Dome
8-10

ferry

Mont de l'Ours
5-7

-4

os Bras

Rg St Jean-Baptiste

La Malbaie

138

aint-Urban

St-Hilarion

St Lawrence

Rivière du-Loup

362

e-St Paul

20

138

SAINT-URBAIN
Mont du Gros Bras

Descents: Rappel route or close to it. Anchors usually fixed.
Routes are about seven pitches long.

1 Campanule 5.7 Stephan Frick and Leopold Nadeau, 1973.

2 No. 2 5.10+ Louis Babin and Tom.

3 Li-Do 5.10+ Louis Babin and Claude Bérubé, 1973. FFA: Louis Babin and Claude Berube, 1974.

4 Harmonie Intérieure 5.9/5.10 Louis Babin and Hubert Morin, 1981.

Mont de l'Ours

Descents: Rappel and scramble.

   Routes are about four pitches long.

5 La Directe   5.6 Alain Hénault and Daniel Hénault, 1974.

6 L'Arête Sud   5.5 Jacques Lemay and Claude Lavallée, 1971.

7 Chodreur   5.5 Jean-Pierre Cadot and Pierre Desautels, 1971.

Les Palissades   photo: Alain Hénault collection

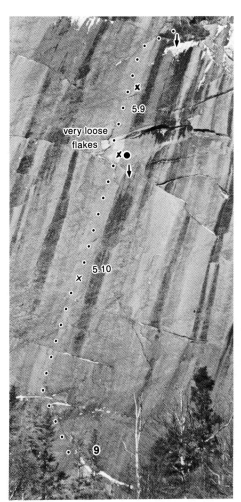

Le Dome

8 L'Initiation **5.4** François Xaxier Garneau, 1970. About six pitches, with good views to Saint Lawrence River.

9 Tache Blanche **5.10** Regis Richard, François Xaxier Garneau, 1972. FFA: Louis Babin and Claude Bérubé, 1976.

10 Two Slings Route **5.10/5.11** Alain Hénault and Francois Roy, 1985.

SAINT-SIMÉON
Les Palissades
11 Les Araignées Pedestres **5.10 +** Paul Duval and Alain Hénault, 1985.
12 **5.9** Michel Hayes and Alain Hénault, about 1981.
13 L'Arête **5.6** Dick Wilmoth and Brian Rothary, 1960.

Les Palissades

14 Rimouski 5.9 Pierre Edouard Gagnon and Alain Hénault, 1981.

15 Le Pilier 5.11− Jean Sylvain and André Robert, 1967. FFA: Louis Babin and Hubert Morin, 1981. The area classic.

Gérard Bourbonnais on Le Pilier photo: Alain Hénault

Les Palissades

16 Detaché 5.10+ Alain Hénault and Michel Hayes, 1976. FFA: Gérard Bourbonnais, Alain Hénault and Marcel Lehoux, 1982.

17 L'Enver de Detaché 5.10 Gérard Bourbonais and Alain Hénault, 1982. Exit finished in 1984. The big corner.

18 Cirque Volant 5.9 Beverley Bowens and Gerard Bourbonnais, 1985. The big crack on the face.

19 Wags Up North 5.9 Felix Modugno and Alain Hénault. The big crack finishing in an overhanging chimney.

20 Reflection 5.10+ Guy Laselle and Pedro Tessier, 1982.

21 Toit des Anges 5.11/5.12 Gilles Chabot, 1967. FFA: Louis Babin, 1984. Ten foot roof. Can be approached by climbing 5.9 and 5.10 pitches below, or directly from the descent gully on the left.

Palissades

22 La Granuleuse   5.5 Jacques Demers and Jean Sylvain 1961. Wander anywhere up the slabs.

Mark Richey on Vire du Curé Dallaire photo: Louis Babin

Cap Trinité photo: Louis Babin

23 Vire du Curé Dallaire 5.11 or 5.7 A3 Marc Blais, Pierre Gaugaux and Bernard Lefèbre, 1973. FFA: Louis Babin and Paul Duval, 1982.

24 Les Grands Galais 5.8 A3 Leopold Nadeau and Claude Bérubé, 1973. Free attempts are being made.

aid   free

24

23

photo: Louis Babin

Le Champlain at Québec City

OTHER AREAS

ADDITIONAL EAST COAST CRAGS AND BOULDERING AREAS

Small crags sprout from the eastern forests like mushrooms from an autumn lawn. Keeping track of them all would be a monumental task, and deciding which were the most significant and deserving of treatment as full chapters in this book was both subjective and sometimes arbitrary. Even drawing geographical boundaries on this East Coast volume was difficult; the final verdict forced the exclusion of many fine Ontario and Kentucky crags. This chapter briefly describes some additional East Coast crags and bouldering areas – only a fraction of the many which provide excellent climbing, albeit most of the best known cliffs are probably described.

OLD RAG MOUNTAIN, Virginia

Offering the only granite between New England and North Carolina, this complex of giant boulders and cliffs (to 150 feet high) holds many crack and face climbs. The rough-textured rocks are found near a wooded ridgetop at the end of a 3½ mile hike, located in the eastern edge of Shennandoah National Park. Most of the climbing on Old Rag is at least 5.9 in difficulty. From Route 231 in Etland, (eleven miles south of Sperryville), turn west on Route 643 and continue five miles. Turn right on Route 600 and follow it to its end. Walk up the dirt road (Berry Hollow Road) to a saddle with intersecting dirt roads. Turn right to Old

Rag Shelter and continue up Saddle Trail to Ridge Trail, then turn left for the summit of Old Rag Mountain. Continue down Ridge Trail for several hundred yards and the rocks will be found on the right. An article by Greg Collins in *Rock and Ice #8* (May, 1985) is the current route guide.

Dave Sipple at Chestnut Ridge   photo: Rick Thompson

CHESTNUT RIDGE, *West Virginia*
This 75 mile-long ridge is the western boundary of the Allegheny Mountains and spans both southern Pennsylvania and northern West Virginia. Scattered along its flanks are thirty or so climbing areas that many people feel offer the premier gritstone climbing in the Eastern United States. Cooper's Rock is the best known and most developed of these areas. The maze of boulders here is staggering, and there are in excess of 250 routes on cliffs to 90 feet high. Most faces are in the thirty to fifty foot range and are composed of an extremely coarse-grained

sedimentary rock with sharp crystals. Toproping is popular as protection is often lacking otherwise. Unfortunately, Cooper's Rock was closed to climbing in 1984, however it is expected to reopen soon. Check with the park authorities on the way in. Even when the area becomes available for climbing, the impressive Overlook Block will remain closed due to the lookout platform on its summit. The view from the platform is spectacular, extending out over the broad expanse of the 1,200 foot deep Cheat River valley. The gate to the access road is usually closed November through April, although an enjoyable walk or ski keeps the climbing accessible. Located on the crest of Chestnut Ridge, about ten miles east of Morgantown, West Virginia, this area is reached by taking the Cooper's Rock exit from Interstate 48. Fee camping is available.

A currently legal alternative to Cooper's Rock is Decker's Creek. A number of cliffs up to 50 feet in height are found there, and they offer over 50 routes of all grades – though the best climbs tend to be 5.9 or harder. East of Morgantown, take Route 7 south from Interstate 48 (this is the second exit east from Interstate 79). After about four miles one reaches the small town of Dellslow; a mile past this a left-hand fork will appear with a sign: "Pioneer Rocks." Continue ¼ mile down Route 7 and park in one of the good pulloffs on the right. The cliffs lie above and left, running parallel to the road for a mile.

A guidebook to over fifteen areas along Chestnut Ridge, including in excess of 550 routes, will be published in 1987. *True Grit* by Richard V. Thompson II, available from P.O. Box 387, Sewickly, PA 15143.

RALPH STOVER STATE PARK, Pennsylvania

The main cliff presents 60 to 150 foot high faces and buttresses of slick shale. About a quarter mile long in the early 1970's, its length keeps growing as more faces and buttresses are exhumed from layers of vegetation. Lead-climbing is the normal style of ascent here, as the upper sections of cliff are often too loose for a safe toprope anchor. The lower rock, however, is remarkably solid for shale and offers numerous thin incut holds as well as cracks. Because protection would otherwise be very poor, bolts are the normal protection on face climbs. The escarpment is shaded in summer by the dense trees and poison ivy. The cliff has a long climbing history, dating to the mid 1930's. It is located just west of the Delaware River, halfway between Trenton and Easton, off Route 32. Just north of Point Pleasant, the road forks around a church. Bear north on Cafferty Road for several miles, then take a left on Tory Road and soon another left on a dirt road leading into Ralph Stover State Park. The parking lot is on the right, while the cliffs are to the left, facing away from the road. The guidebook, *Red Rock: A Climber's History and Guide to High Rocks* (1985) by Thomas N. Stryker and Warren B. Musselman (Wu Li Publications, Boulder, CO) is available in nearby Doylestown from Appalachian Trail Outfitters, Main Street and Oakland.

STONEYRIDGE, *Pennsylvania*

This cliff may only reach 70 feet in height, yet its arm-blowing angle will test the strength of any climber. The quartzite crag has an average tilt of 110 degrees, with many small roofs thrown in for good measure. Most climbs are at least a strenuous 5.9 in difficulty. Thin cracks and face climbs are well protected, hence locals rarely toprope. Facing north, the crag is shady and relatively comfortable even in the summer. It is located 20 miles north of Allentown. Approach 1) from the south, turning off Interstate 78 at the McArthur Road/Route 145 exit and driving north almost twenty miles to Route 248, which is followed to the Bowmanstown exit, or 2) from the north, reaching Route 248 via Route 209. Turn left at the first intersection on the north side of the highway. Pass a gas station and follow signs to Stone Ridge Manor Apartments. Park past the apartments at an open area on the right, with a brick pumphouse on the left (*do not* park at the apartments). The guidebook, *Stoneyridge: A Crag Climber's Guide* (1983) by Richard Pleiss is available at Wilderness Travel Outfitters, 2530 McArthur Road in Whitehall, located north of the Route 145 exit from Interstate 78.

BELLEFONTE QUARRY, *Pennsylvania*

This old limestone quarry is reknowned for spectacular thin cracks that shoot up a 75 degree wall for nearly a full pitch. Faces between the cracks tend to be flaky, and some poorly protected routes ascend these shaky edges as well. In addition to the superb climbing, the quarry's proximity to Interstate 80 places Bellefonte on the travelling climber's map. From I-80, take exit 23 and travel south on Route 220 for one mile (four-lane road). Exit right to Route 150 South and continue for about two miles, then turn left on a rough road just *before* the obvious Brass Wire Mill complex. Parallel the factory for a couple hundred yards to good parking at some pulloffs. Continue walking down the road to a high-angle wall, seen on the left, which is the lower quarry. The best cracks are at the back end of the upper quarry, which is reached by walking left around the lower quarry.

Rick Thompson at Bellefonte Quarry   photo: Thompson collection

Cat Rock, Manhatten

MANHATTEN, New York

The city that considers itself the center of the world somehow manages to provide excellent inner-city bouldering. Central Park holds two fine metamorphic boulders. Rat Rock is the most extensive, with the north face offering a long, hard traverse and the east face holding many vertical problems on a ten to fifteen foot wall. Cat Rock faces south, is about fifteen feet tall and has a collection of superb problems. Cats are reputed to live in the carpeted hole at the rock's base. Climbing is forbidden at some other areas in the park. Both Rat and Cat Rocks are located at the level of 63rd Street. Rat is on the west side of the park, at the southern edge of a field with several baseball diamonds. Cat is on the east side, near the bridge and overlooking (though set back from) The Pond.

The retaining walls to Riverside Drive (in Riverside Park) offer superb traversing on edges. The 72nd Street Wall is vertical, while the Boat Basin at 79th Street is just shy of vertical and therefore easier. The walls are about 30 feet high. To reach the former, go west on 72nd Street to enter the park, then take the tunnel to the lower level. Immediately out of the tunnel, the wall is on the right. The Boat Basin is easily found at the end of 79th Street.

Fort Wetherill, RI   photo: Adele Hammond

FORT WETHERILL STATE PARK, Rhode Island

Memorable bouldering and toprope cliffs (to about 40 feet high) rise sometimes straight out of the water, though more typically they sit on a bed of wave-splashed rocks. One narrow cove offers superb cliff-diving. The granite is coarse and weathered, but generally solid. Nasty landings make use of a toprope highly desirable. Located 1½ miles south-east of downtown Jamestown, on Jamestown Island, historic Newport is visible across the bridge.

LINCOLN WOODS STATE PARK, Rhode Island

Some fine granite bouldering is found in the woods next to a beautiful pond. The Park is located a few miles north of Providence on Route 146. Go east from Route 146 to the fork in the road, which signals the beginning of a one-way loop. Park, and walk up the one-way road for about a hundred yards, or follow the loop around the lake.

Marilyn Harlin at Lincoln Woods, RI

BOSTON, Massachussetts

A wealth of small cliffs, boulders, quarries and bridges keep climbers well entertained in Boston's suburbs. The best known, most extensive and most crowded climbing is found at Quincy Quarries. The Quarries are the location of the first railroad in New England (one walks up the old tracks to reach the cliffs). The 50 to 100 foot high granite cliffs feature many very thin slab routes, as well as crack and face climbs on steep walls. South of Boston, they are located in Quincy, just off of Interstate 93. Take exit 9, then either: 1) from the north, turn left onto Adams Street, or 2) from the south, cross the freeway, then turn left on Adams Street. Parallel the freeway south for about a half-mile, then turn left on Bates at the dead-end sign. Take the 1st right (O'Connell), turn left on Mullin and continue to the parking lot at its end. The Quarries are on the right, up the hill. Past the first cliffs to be seen, another set of walls can be found on the right. A new method of access that avoids the residential streets will be available soon.

Located just south of Quincy Quarries, Rattlesnake offers shorter cliffs (about 30 feet tall) that are in the woods of the Blue Hills Reservation and are less frequented than the Quarries. A variety of climbs can be found, though most are nearly vertical or overhanging. Located just south of the Quarries. From the Quarries, cross Interstate 93 on Upton, then turn right on Willard. In a half-mile one passes under the freeway; nearly a half-mile further, bear right at the fork (Interstate 93 exit 8 is here) toward "Milton Canton." Past the gate to the Reservation 0.8 miles is a parking lot on the right. Walk down the valley on the right; the cliffs will be found in a few hundred yards, also on the right.

Hammond Pond's many small cliffs are composed of a peculiar conglomerate known as "puddingstone." Approximately a dozen mini-cliffs can be found. From route 9 in Brookline pull into the Chestnut Hill Shopping Center. The back end of the parking lot abuts the pond.

A guidebook, *Boston Rocks* (1987), by Larry LaForge will be available from the MIT Outing Club, MIT, Cambridge, MA 02139.

Ad Carter and Jim Chase at Quincy Quarries

Crow Hill   photo: Marilyn Harlin

CROW HILL, *Massachussetts*

This 100 foot high cliff has been very popular among Boston area climbers for several decades, despite its extremely steep, often overhanging angle. In fact, several of the earliest Eastern 5.11's were established here. Both face and crack climbs abound on smooth gritstone, including a few easy routes. The wooded setting and nearby swimming add to Crow Hill's charm; the slow speed of drying after a rain and the frequent crowds detract. It is located in Leominster State Forest, just west of

Leominster (north of Worcester). From Route 2, proceed exactly two miles south on Route 31, towards East Princeton. On the east side of the road is a paved parking lot at a lake; Crow Hill lies up the steep hill west of the road (follow trail). One can also park at a turnoff just north of the main parking area. Coming from the south, proceed up Route 140 two miles past East Princeton, turn right on Route 31 and drive 1.3 miles to the parking area. Sam Streibert's guide to Crow Hill, appearing in *Climbing in Eastern Massachussets* (1975) by Stephen D. Hendrick, is out of print. When a new guidebook appears, it will be available through the Appalachian Mountain Club, 5 Joy Street, Boston, MA 02108 and at Boston area stores.

PAWTUCKAWAY STATE PARK, New Hampshire

Steep granite slabs nearly 50 feet tall, with friction, thin edges and long, vertical flakes provide excellent, if little-known climbing in southern New Hampshire. There are also piles of tall boulders with superb cracks. Deep in the woods next to a small pond, the area has a comfortable, backcountry atmosphere despite its short approach walk. Few climbers other than students from the nearby University of New Hampshire are found here. Located just north of Raymond, turn north from Route 102 onto Route 156. Stay on Route 156 past the Pawtuckaway State Park sign for several miles to an intersection on a hillcrest with a statue on the right (statue engraved "Cilley") and farm buildings on the left. Turn left and proceed 3.3 miles. Here is the first expansive view (to the right) and a dirt road that cuts sharply back left. Take the dirt road a half-mile and park above the steep descent. Hike down the road several hundred yards, past a small pond to broken, large rocks on the right (do not continue to the pond just beyond). To reach the slabs, follow a trail right past the rocks to another small pond. There is a fee campground at the main State Park entrance. Todd Swain's *Climber's Guide to Pawtuckaway and Southeast New Hampshire* (1980) is out of print. When future route guides are published, they will be obtainable from Wilderness Trails, Mill Road Plaza, in Durham.

PORTLAND, Maine

Enjoyable bouldering on coastal cliffs can be found just south of Portland, between Cape Elizabeth and South Portland. The mostly metamorphic rock is sometimes high enough for toproping. The greatest quantity of rock is in Fort Williams Park at the Portland Headlight – the first lighthouse commissioned by the United States. More limited offerings can be found near Two Lights (the cliffs are *not* in the State Park itself). Any published information available will be obtainable from International Mountain Equipment, 18 Exchange Street, Portland. Twenty miles north of Portland is the landmark L.L. Bean store, open 24 hours a day and offering literature as well as climbing gear.

Portland, Maine   photo: Marilyn Harlin

PAYNE LEDGE, Maine

This 150 foot cliff overlooks Twitchel Pond and is a lovely stop for a swim and climb while on the way to Mount Desert Island from North Conway. The climbing is good, well-developed, and one can drive to the base of the cliff. A fee-campground is nearby. Payne Ledge is located at Locke Mills, about five miles east of Bethel on Route 26.

MOUNT KATAHDIN, Maine

The access trail for Mt. Katahdin spans nearly the entirety of this volume of the *Climber's Guide to North America,* beginning over 2,000 miles away in the state of Georgia: the 5,268 foot summit of Katahdin is the northern terminous to the Appalachian Trail. Most rock climbers will choose to short-cut a few switchbacks on the famous AT, and start their hike four miles from the cliffs, at a subsidiary trailhead in Baxter State Park. There are two "Basins," North and South, which lure rock climbers with rock walls up to 2,000 broken feet in height. The cliffs do not have the massiveness of Cannon, but there is certainly plenty of rock. The most classic route, the **Armadillo (5.7)**, is considered Grade IV. Most

Mt. Katahdin　photo: Olaf Sööt

popular with rock climbers is the South Basin, which has a campground in the floor of the cirque. Both Basins are above timberline, and the experience of hiking into the cirques – let alone climbing their headwalls – is distinctly alpine. Foul weather should be prepared for. Loose and falling rock is also a possibility, especially when hikers roll boulders off the summit. The Park Service requires climbers to wear helmets and requests that climbers check in with a ranger to indicate their intentions.

The major drawback to climbing here is the need for reservations several months in advance for camping at the Chimney Pond Campground in the South Basin. Lean-tos are found here for $3 per person per night; twelve spaces are available in a bunkhouse (drier) for $4 per person per night (1986 prices; the money must be sent with the reservation application). More spaces are available at Roaring Brook Campground, which involves hiking in 3½ miles to the South Basin daily. Early reservations are required for Roaring Brook as well. Camping outside of campgrounds in the State Park is strictly prohibited. Reservations should be sent to the Reservations Clerk, Baxter State Park, 64 Balsam Drive, Millinocket, ME 04462. A private campground exists about fifteen miles outside the park.

Though Mt. Katahdin is located deep in the wilds of northern Maine, access by car is simple. Take the Medway exit from Interstate 95 and drive west on Route 157 to Millinocket. Park Headquarters is located here, should information be desired. Continue 20 miles on a smaller road to Baxter State Park; enter at the Togue Pond Entrance and drive 8 miles to the Roaring Brook Campground.

SHERBROOKE, *Quebec*

Two superb granite cliffs can be found near the town of Sherbrooke in southern Quebec. While the cliffs are well worth visiting for their excellent climbing alone, for climbers in North Conway, these Quebec crags also provide an excellent excuse for a quick sample of a foreign culture. Two major cliffs are found. Southernmost and largest – with routes to 350 feet – is Mont Pinnacle, on the shores of Lac Lyster. Located just a few miles north of the border, turn south from Route 141 in Barnston (five miles west of Coaticook). The cliff at Lac Larouche is shorter – 75 feet at best – but its climbs are especially outstanding. The crag is located on Route 222 about nine miles west of Interstate 55 (the freeway exit is on the north edge of Sherbrooke). Lac Larouche is the small lake just west of larger Lac Brompton. The guidebook, *Escalades dans les cantons de l'est* (1979) by Bertrand Cote is currently out of print. Route information and any updated guides are obtainable from the store, Escalade Estrie, in Sherbrooke.

QUEBEC CITY, *Quebec*

Excellent bouldering, most of it high enough to demand a toprope, can be found in Quebec City. Vieux Quebec (inside the walls of the old city) is the place to tourist while in town. An enjoyable festival takes place there during the first two weeks of July, which makes this the best time to visit. Unfortunately, this is when the blackflies are at their worst in Charlevoix.

Near the shore of the St. Lawrence in Quebec City are two cliffs about twenty feet tall. Le Champlain is slightly overhanging along its entire length, resulting in highly strenuous face and thin crack climbs. A long traverse offers entertainment to those not wishing to take out the rope. Le Pylone features short roofs, though generally easier climbing. Its height was increased significantly by climbers who dug the ground away from the base. Located adjacent to the twin bridges of Pont Pierre-Laporte and Pont du Quebec (which cross the St. Lawrence to feed into the west side of Quebec City), Le Pylone is visible under power towers on top of the hill. Le Champlain is not visible from the road. For either, gain Boulevard Champlain (first exit north of the bridge) and park nearby.

Larger cliffs can be found ten miles north of the city along Route 175. North of Stoneham 2.8 miles, the road widens briefly and a Petro Canada station is seen on the right. Where the road narrows again, take the dirt road right (Rue Caroline), then turn left on the first road and park. From here (and more clearly from the Petro Canada station) one can make out what appear to be tiny rocks sticking out of the trees high on the hill. In fact, the vertical cliff is about 50 feet tall and offers excellent lead and toprope routes with both crack and face climbing. Like many Quebec crags, the cliff was stripped of its dense vegetation,

Le Champlain at Québec City

and large trees were cut to allow the sun to dry the rock. To reach the cliff from the car, strike into the woods and find a faint trail which is followed for about a half mile.

If one continues driving north from the Petro Canada station for another mile, an RV campground is found on the left. Up the hillside behind this is another cliff that has been literally unearthed. Good lower angle routes in excess of 100 feet are found here. A good campground with a warm pool is located further north on Route 175; follow the brown signs.

Any route information that becomes available will be found at Bivouac Import-Export, 1328 Maguire, Sillery, Quebec City.

INDEX

(Route Information)

JOHN HARLIN:
Although born in California, John Harlin's early years were spent in the Alps – where his father climbed and his mother taught science. After his father's death on the Eiger in 1966, the family returned to America. During his teenage years, John spent as much time as possible in the wilderness, including several month long hiking and kayaking trips to the North Slope of Alaska. But climbing did not become a serious passion for him until his enrollment at the University of California, Santa Barbara, for a degree in Environmental Biology. Since then, he has climbed in numerous rock and mountain centers throughout North America and Europe. Besides writing, John shares his love of the mountain environment through guiding and lecturing.

ADELE HAMMOND:
A native of Colorado, Adele Hammond received her undergraduate art training at the College of Creative Studies, University of California, and her MFA from the School of Visual Arts in New York. She is a professional fine artist who makes colorful, interpretive paintings and pastels. Her art has little in common with the illustrations in this book, except that it shows a similar love of nature.

LUPINE HAMMOND-HARLIN:
Lupine has played an important role in the research of nearly every area in each volume of the *Climber's Guide to North America*. She continually pressed for more in-depth field research and urged the inclusion of areas with long approach walks and short climbs. Born in the mountains of Colorado, Lupine has travelled through much of North America.